The Cambridge Introduction to
Byron

Author of the most influential long poem of its era (*Childe Harold's Pilgrimage*) and the funniest long poem in European literature (*Don Juan*), Lord Byron was also the literary superstar of Romanticism, whose effect on nineteenth-century writers, artists, musicians and politicians – but also everyday readers – was second to none. His poems seduced and scandalized readers, and his life and legend were correspondingly magnetic, given added force by his early death in the Greek War of Independence. This introduction compresses his extraordinary life to manageable proportions, and gives readers a firm set of contexts in the politics, warfare and Romantic ideology of Byron's era. It offers a guide to the main themes in his wide-ranging oeuvre, from the early poems that made him famous (and infamous) overnight, to his narrative tales, dramas and the comic epic left incomplete at his death.

RICHARD LANSDOWN is Associate Professor of English at James Cook University, Cairns, Australia.

The Cambridge Introduction to
Byron

RICHARD LANSDOWN

CAMBRIDGE
UNIVERSITY PRESS

CAMBRIDGE UNIVERSITY PRESS
Cambridge, New York, Melbourne, Madrid, Cape Town,
Singapore, São Paulo, Delhi, Mexico City

Cambridge University Press
The Edinburgh Building, Cambridge CB2 8RU, UK

Published in the United States of America by Cambridge University Press, New York

www.cambridge.org
Information on this title: www.cambridge.org/9780521128735

First published 2012

Printed in the United Kingdom at the University Press, Cambridge

A catalogue record for this publication is available from the British Library

Library of Congress Cataloguing in Publication data
Lansdown, Richard, 1961–
   The Cambridge introduction to Byron / Richard Lansdown.
      pages   cm
   Includes bibliographical references and index.
   ISBN 978-0-521-11133-1 (hardback) – ISBN 978-0-521-12873-5 (paperback)
   1. Byron, George Gordon Byron, Baron, 1788–1824–Criticism and
   interpretation.   I. Title.
   PR4388.L36   2012
   821'.7–dc23
   2011052554

ISBN 978-0-521-11133-1 Hardback
ISBN 978-0-521-12873-5 Paperback

In memory of Andrew Nicholson

Contents

Figure and tables

Figure

Tables

ix

Preface

Ever since his first appearance in print, Byron has made an impression on his readers as a personality as well as a source of linguistic expression. 'There is … a tone of self-willed independence and originality about the whole composition', the critic Francis Jeffrey wrote of *Childe Harold's Pilgrimage* in 1812, 'a certain plain manliness and strength of manner, which is infinitely refreshing after the sickly affectations of so many modern writers.'[1]

As often as not, therefore, his readers and acquaintances have assessed Byron in morally as well as aesthetically evaluative terms. A British resident in Constantinople wrote of meeting Byron in 1810, long before his years of fame, that 'there was that irresistible attraction in his manner, of which those who have had the good luck to be admitted into his intimacy, can alone have felt the power.'[2] An Armenian priest in Venice, with whom Byron briefly worked on a grammar of that language in 1816, recalled him as 'a young man quick, sociable, with burning eyes.'[3] A few months before the poet died, another priest – this time a Scottish evangelical one – testified to the indivisibility of life and art in his case. 'In the course of the day', James Kennedy wrote,

> He might become the most morose, and the most gay; the most melancholy, and the most frolicsome; the most generous, and the most penurious; the most benevolent, and the most misanthropic; the most rational, and the most childish; the most sublime and elevated in thought, and the most frivolous or trivial; the most gentle being in existence, and the most irascible. His works bear the stamp of his character, and Childe Harold is no less faithful a picture of him at one part of the day, than Don Juan is at another.[4]

We can assume that Kennedy was not thinking simply of the heroes of those two poems as emanations of Byron's nature, but of the two poems themselves as different projections of the same, complex individual.

'No man ever lived who had such devoted friends,' his best friend John Cam Hobhouse recalled of Byron. 'His power of attaching those about him was such as no one I ever knew possessed. No human being could approach him without being sensible of this magical influence.' 'The affection felt for him', Hobhouse concluded – in a most unusual turn of phrase for one nineteenth-century Englishman to use of another – 'was as that for a favourite and somewhat froward sister.'[5] But the critic Matthew Arnold (who did not know Byron at first hand) came to a quite different conclusion regarding his personal qualities. 'We talk of Byron's *personality*,' he wrote; 'but can we not be a little more circumstantial, and name that in which the wonderful power of this personality consisted?' Arnold then famously borrowed the poet Algernon Swinburne's assessment (itself reminiscent of Jeffrey's) of 'the splendid and imperishable excellence which covers all his offences and outweighs all his defects: *the excellence of sincerity and strength*'.[6] Like a favourite but naughty sister, or like an epitome of manly sincerity? Only an unusual individual could leave two such contrasting impressions.

Byron's influence is a matter of the force of his example and personality as much as his writings, therefore. The two were difficult for nineteenth-century people to separate – nor did they try. It is small wonder, then, that Byron's stock fell sharply between the 1920s and the 1970s, when various schools of Anglophone literary criticism operated under T. S. Eliot's dictum (from his essay 'Tradition and the Individual Talent') that 'the more perfect the artist, the more completely separate in him will be the man who suffers and the mind which creates.'[7] As Byron had apparently failed to make that separation, he fell from favour as poet and personality alike.

Modernists like Eliot did not hold the Romantic group of writers in particularly high esteem anyway; but even as a Romantic Byron seemed to some twentieth-century readers like an interloper or an anomaly. He did not possess Blake's elaborate private symbology, for example, or Coleridge's theoretical sophistication, or Wordsworth's moral sublimity, or Shelley's political radicalism, or Keats's pronounced degree of aesthetic self-consciousness. But gradually and steadily since the Second World War – and largely due to the biographical and editorial efforts of American scholars Leslie Marchand and Jerome McGann – Byron's reputation has risen, and his place among his poetic peers is now assured. Indeed, nowadays his writings can and frequently do serve as a standard by which to measure those of other poets – a reverse of the situation as it stood for much of the twentieth century, when Byron was castigated for being insufficiently Wordsworthian or Keatsian in some respect or other. It was a brave but also a prescient critic who wrote in 1923 that 'What is important is that Byron's poetry is alive; so full of life indeed that it threatens other more dignified sorts of poetry.'[8] So it does. The life his poetry manifests is something with which we are still only beginning to come to terms, 200 years after it was first published.

Byron has often been seen as a more lucid and less complex poet than his five great peers. But coming to an understanding of him – as his nineteenth-century readers often understood better than his twentieth-century ones – is not just a matter of understanding what he has said. 'You cannot find out what a man means', the English philosopher R. G. Collingwood argued, 'by simply studying his spoken or written statements, even though he has spoken or written with perfect command of language and perfectly truthful intention. In order to find out his meaning you must also know what the question was (a question in his own mind, and presumed by him to be in yours) to which the thing he has said or written was meant as an answer.'[9] The more light we shed on the questions Byron carried with him, the more we will shed on the life his writings manifest, and this study seeks to discover at least a few of the questions Byron had in his mind and presumed to be in ours. Still: his creativity is very diverse, even by the standards of his fellow Romantic poets, and in the interest of providing a clear outline of what is central to it, some parts of Byron's work – particularly his lyrical and satirical poems – suffer neglect here, for which I apologise.

Apart from the dedicatee, I would like to acknowledge the support of my family, near and far, and the continued critical excellence of Dan Jacobson and Peter Pierce, who brought their knowledge and experience to bear throughout. A research grant from the School of Arts and Social Sciences at James Cook University was invaluable. Thanks also to Linda Bree and the rest of the team at Cambridge University Press.

Abbreviations

Bride	*The Bride of Abydos*
CHP	*Childe Harold's Pilgrimage*
CMP	Byron, *Complete Miscellaneous Prose*, ed. Andrew Nicholson (Oxford University Press, 1991)
CPW	Byron, *Complete Poetical Works*, ed. Jerome J. McGann, 7 vols. (Oxford University Press, 1980–93)
DJ	*Don Juan*
HE	*Heaven and Earth*
LJ	*Byron's Letters and Journals*, ed. Leslie A. Marchand, 12 vols. (London: John Murray, 1973–82)
Marchand	Leslie A. Marchand, *Byron: A Biography*, 3 vols. (London: John Murray, 1957)
MF	*Marino Faliero*
Sard.	*Sardanapalus*
Siege	*The Siege of Corinth*
TF	*The Two Foscari*

References to short poems are given by volume and page number in *CPW*; references to longer poems (*Childe Harold's Pilgrimage, Don Juan*, the tales, and the plays) are given by canto and line number; line number; or by act, scene, and line number, as appropriate.

Map: Lord Byron's Europe

Map (*Continued*)

Chapter 1

Life

Childhood, boyhood, youth (1788–1809)

On 9 June 1779, a penniless army captain and remote member of an ancient English aristocratic family married his lover, the recently divorced and independently wealthy Amelia, Marchioness of Carmarthen, at Bath, the marital meat market of Georgian England. Their only surviving child, Augusta, was born in January 1783. Amelia died a year later, at which point Captain Byron lost the use of her income. (Augusta was brought up by relations until her own marriage in 1807.) In May 1785, 'Mad Jack' Byron was married again, once more at Bath, to Catherine Gordon, inheritor of a Scottish estate worth £30,000. Within three years he had almost expended his second wife's inheritance, and she was pregnant in London with their only child.

The boy born on 22 January 1788 would become one of the most famous men in Europe, Britain's first authentic literary celebrity, one of its most eminent poets and enduring personalities, the author of the greatest long poem in English since *Paradise Lost* (1667) and the greatest comic poem in any language, and an example to freedom fighters worldwide for decades after his death in 1824. Yet he was born with a club foot in a rented room off Oxford Street, while his father kept away from London to avoid his creditors. Captain Byron soon escaped to France, and would die there in 1791 in the arms of his sister – with whom he had had a sexual affair. His wife had managed to secure a portion of her estate that gave her an income of £150 a year, and in the summer of 1789 she went home with her child to live in Aberdeen. Her son scarcely saw his father again.

1

A life of genteel poverty beckoned until the grandson of the fifth Lord Byron died on an obscure front of the French Revolutionary Wars in 1794. Unexpectedly, the Scottish schoolboy became heir to a title and a substantial estate in Nottinghamshire, and after his grand-uncle's death in 1798 he duly succeeded. Mother and son camped in the uninhabitable family seat of Newstead Abbey before retreating to local lodgings. While Byron was there repeated attempts were made to heal his foot, and a Scottish nurse was dismissed for sexually abusing him while drunk. He was also introduced to the family lawyer, John Hanson, whose ineptitude would be the bane of his adult life, though Byron was too loyal to give him the sack.

As an apprentice aristocrat Byron required a proper education, and after some hurried teaching at a preparatory school in Dulwich he entered Harrow school in April 1801. Newstead having been leased, he spent holidays either with the Hanson family or his mother, depending on the state of their relations. (Mrs Byron – widowed at 26 – was shrewd, tactless, literal-minded, forthright, proud, obstreperous, and stout; but she also used money to curry favour with her son, as she had with his father.) Byron's early years at Harrow were unstable, but his last eighteen months there were happy, marked by a series of intense friendships, often with boys younger than himself.

In his vacations Byron spent time with another surrogate family, the Pigots, neighbours of his mother, who brought him out of his shell and encouraged his early poetry. He also fell in love with a distant cousin, Mary Chaworth, two years his senior. As a 16-year-old he experimented with London life, and perhaps lost what May Gray had left of his virginity – certainly he recollected attending 'Whore's Hops' at London taverns 'when I was a younker in my teens' (*LJ* VII. 224).

On 24 October 1805, Byron arrived at Trinity College, Cambridge to read for a Bachelor of Arts. 'It was one of the deadliest and heaviest feelings of my life', he wrote sixteen years later, 'to feel that I was no longer a boy' (*LJ* IX. 37). Though he resided at college for only three of the nine terms required for his degree, and attended no lectures – 'nobody here seems to look into an author ancient or modern if they can avoid it' (*LJ* I. 80) – aristocratic privilege allowed him to graduate with a Master of Arts degree in July 1808. He had an allowance of £500 a year, which he spent liberally among local tailors and wine merchants, but also on forays into London. His overspending rapidly grew out of control, and to finance it he resorted to loans on the basis of his inheritance. He also prepared his first volume of poems, *Fugitive Pieces*, printed in November 1806 and republished the following year as *Hours of Idleness*. A lifetime's campaign against his plumpness started with a regime of exercise and under-nourishment, and the 19-year-old declared himself an agnostic.

By the end of 1807, Byron was finished with Cambridge, but not with the friendships he had made there: his life-long friend John Cam Hobhouse, the homosexual radical Charles Skinner Matthews, and a Trinity College choirboy, two years his junior, John Edleston. He entertained various plans for poems and travels before starting a satire, 'British Bards'. In February 1808, a withering critique of *Hours of Idleness* appeared in the prestigious *Edinburgh Review*, over which Byron stewed as 'British Bards' gradually became a more all-encompassing broadside, *English Bards and Scotch Reviewers*. Relations with his mother deteriorated as those with his undergraduate cronies matured during country-house entertainments at Newstead – one side effect of which was an illegitimate child by a maid at the house in 1809.

By November 1808, Byron's debts already amounted to the very substantial sum of £12,000 and the only avenue of escape he could conceive of was to follow his father's footsteps to the Continent, where living costs were lower. His depression was deepened by the death of his Newfoundland dog, Boatswain: the first of many beloved dogs and other pets. (There would be another Newfoundland, Lyon, with him when he died.) On 13 March 1809, just after his twenty-first birthday, he took his seat in the House of Lords. On 2 July, Byron and Hobhouse set sail to Lisbon from Falmouth after a long delay during which he wrote suggestively to Matthews about the homosexual possibilities of the ancient naval town.

Grand Tour and years of fame (1809–1816)

Byron's Grand Tour was unusual in that he was driven south by Napoleon's occupation of central Europe (see Table 1). He and Hobhouse arrived at Lisbon on 7 July and within three weeks were at Gibraltar, having visited Seville and Cadiz, cities safely to the south of the Peninsular War. Even as they travelled, the bloody but indecisive battle of Talavera was being fought south of Madrid. From Gibraltar they sailed to Britain's other Mediterranean stronghold, Malta, where they arrived on 31 August and stayed three weeks. There, Byron had his first recorded love affair with a woman of his own class, the glamorous Mrs Constance Spencer Smith.

By the end of September, Byron and Hobhouse were well off the beaten track, at Patras on the Gulf of Corinth, from where they travelled north-west into Albania. At Tepelene, where they arrived on 19 October, Byron introduced himself to the Muslim warlord Ali Pasha, who praised his aristocratic features and sexually propositioned him. Byron also began writing a narrative poem

Table 1. *The itinerary of Byron's Grand Tour (1809–11)*

DATE	PLACE
1809	
19 June	Leaves London
21 June–2 July	Falmouth
7–20 July	Lisbon
12–16 July	Visits Cintra [Sintra], Portugal
25–27 July	Seville [Sevilla], Spain
29 July–3 Aug.	Cadiz, Spain
4–16 Aug.	Gibraltar
27 Aug.	Cagliari, Sardinia
31 Aug.–21 Sept.	Malta
26 Sept.	Patras [Patra], Greece
28 Sept.–1 Oct.	Prevesa [Preveza], Greece
5–11 Oct.	Jannina [Ioannina], Greece
12 Oct.	Zitsa, Greece
19–23 Oct.	Tepelene [Tepelenë], Albania
26 Oct.–3 Nov.	Jannina
8–13 Nov.	Prevesa
20 Nov.	Missolonghi [Mesolongi], Greece
22 Nov.–4 Dec.	Patras
5–14 Dec.	Vostitza [Aigio], Greece
14 Dec.	Salona [Amfissa], Greece
15 Dec.	Delphi, Greece
22 Dec.	Thebes [Thiva], Greece
25 Dec.	Arrives Athens
1810	
23 Jan.	Cape Sunium [Sounio], Greece
28 Feb.	Visits the Parthenon
5 Mar.	Leaves Athens
8 Mar.–11 Apr.	Smyrna [Izmir], Turkey
13 Mar.	Ephesus [Efes], Turkey
15 Apr.	Troy [Trava], Turkey
3 May	Swims the Hellespont [Dardanelles]
13 May–14 July	Constantinople [Istanbul]
10 July	Audience with Sultan Mahmoud II
18–21 July	Athens
25 July	Vostitza
26 July	Patras
Aug.	Tripolitza [Tripolis], Greece
19 Aug.–15 Sept.	Athens
late Sept.–early Oct.	Patras
13 Oct.	Athens
1811	
22 Apr.	Leaves Athens
30 Apr.–2 June	Malta
14 July	Arrives London

about his travels. By November, he and Hobhouse were back at Patras, having stopped at a swampy port in western Greece named Missolonghi. Byron would die there fifteen years later. They spent December travelling East by way of Parnassus, Delphi, and Thebes, and arrived at Athens on Christmas Eve, six months after leaving England.

Local sightseeing having been attended to, the pair sailed for Smyrna on the western coast of Turkey, visited Ephesus and the field of Troy, and arrived in Constantinople on 13 May 1810. During Byron's two-month stay at the capital of the Ottoman Empire he twice attended an audience with the Sultan before sailing for Athens once more in mid-July. Hobhouse now returned home, much to Byron's relief – 'I feel happier, I feel free' (*LJ* XI. 157). He continued to tour in western Greece, once with a boy named Eustathius Georgiou, the second time with another, Niccolo Giraud. The second half of 1810 saw his homosexual life at its zenith. 'Tell Matthews', he wrote to Hobhouse on 4 October 1810, 'that I have obtained above two hundred pl & opt Cs ['*plenum et optabile coitus*': the Latin poet Petronius's coded reference to 'full and perfect' sex] and am almost tired of them' (*LJ* II. 23).

The importance of Byron's homosexuality is hard to gauge. In October 1810, he was boasting of it, but nine months later he wrote to Hobhouse: 'tell Matthews I have bade adieu to every species of affection', before quoting a line from Horace to the effect that neither women nor boys interested him any more (*LJ* II. 49). From that time till his return to Greece in 1823 the only evidence we have of homosexual contact is an ambiguous letter from Percy Shelley about Byron's habits in Venice in 1818 ('He associates with wretches ... who do not scruple to avow practices which are not only not named but I believe seldom even conceived in England')[1] – and in 1823, his affection for the Greek boy Loukas Chalandritsanos would appear to have been unrequited and unconsummated. Perhaps a better explanation for his numerous relationships with younger males lies in his quest for the paternal affection he had never experienced and therefore idealised. ('Can Rank, or ev'n a Guardian's name supply,' he wrote in 'Childish Recollections', 'The Love, which glistens in a Father's eye?'; *CPW* I. 165.) Unable to receive that affection from his own father, he compensated by giving it to others in sentimentally demonstrative terms.

Byron left Athens for home on 22 April 1811 – having written a satire on Lord Elgin's removal of the Parthenon marbles (*The Curse of Minerva*) as a parting shot. He took Niccolo Giraud with him, but left the boy at Malta where he himself was treated for 'a *Gonorrhea* a *Tertian fever*, & the *Hemorrhoides, all* of which I literally had at once' (*LJ* II. 58). On 14 July, he was back in London, and by the end of the month his travel poem had been accepted for publication by the firm of John Murray, which would publish his work until almost the end of his career.

There then followed a series of deaths: his mother on 1 August; Charles Skinner Matthews two days later; and John Edleston, who had in fact died in May, though news reached Byron only in October. His relationship with his mother was a complicated one, but there is no need to doubt the authenticity of his grief-stricken remark to her maid: 'Oh, Mrs. By, I had but one friend in the world, and she is gone!' (Marchand, 285.)

Byron's financial situation was as bad as he had left it two years before. Immersion in London literary life constituted an escape from depression; as did a brief but humiliating affair with a Newstead housemaid, Susan Vaughan; as did his return to the House of Lords, where he delivered his maiden speech (27 February 1812) on the plight of the 'frame-breakers': industrial vandals protesting in Nottinghamshire. But on 2 March, his potential career in Parliament was abruptly terminated by the publication of his travel poem, *Childe Harold's Pilgrimage*, Cantos I and II: 'I awoke one morning and found myself famous.'[2]

Fame brought attention of a kind that a lame, socially insecure, and impecunious aristocrat found difficult, but also gratifying. In April, one particular admirer, Lady Caroline Lamb – wife of George Lamb, later Lord Melbourne, Queen Victoria's favourite prime minister – began to pursue him in definite terms. 'Mad – bad – and dangerous to know', she said of him before they had exchanged a word; but also, 'That beautiful pale face is my fate' – which it proved to be, indeed (Marchand, 328, 331). The affair was short but scandalous, involving a planned elopement and numerous visits to Byron's London rooms by Lady Caroline dressed as a page. Byron wished it over very quickly, but in her head it dragged on for years, until she fictionalized it in *Glenarvon* (1816): '"kiss and tell" bad as it is,' Byron noted as regards that book, 'is surely somewhat less than – – – and *publish*' (*LJ* V. 85). Her exasperated family eventually took Lady Caroline off to Ireland, but not before Byron had dropped hints to her of his sexual activities in Greece.

Between scandal and indebtedness, Byron's depression took on a manic flavour. Newstead was put up for auction in August 1812 and he accepted an offer of £140,000 that failed to materialize over the next two years. In this mood he began *The Giaour*, the first of his 'Eastern Tales', which would be interpreted in autobiographical terms by a public eager to associate the poet with his protagonists, just as he was projecting his paranoia on to a Mediterranean backcloth.

Lady Caroline's importunities drove Byron into the arms of a woman much more to his taste. The political hostess Lady Oxford also flattered what remained of his parliamentary ambitions, and he seriously considered a second escape to

Europe with her and her husband. But late in 1812, he also proposed marriage to the high-minded Annabella Milbanke, whom he had met in the aftermath of *Childe Harold*: the only daughter of a baronet resident in County Durham. She rejected the proposal, but unconventionally sustained a correspondence with him as a fascinating soul it was her mission to save. In June 1813, *The Giaour* was published, and Byron's plans to accompany Lady Oxford collapsed, ending their relationship. The Newstead purchaser continued to haggle, and Byron's financial situation grew worse.

That situation was intensified by Byron's shopping addiction, itself a sign of depression and low self-esteem. Aristocratic gentlemen were expected to dress well, but Byron's lavishness in proportion to his poverty is frightening. Take fine white quilted waistcoats, for example, 'for which he had an enthusiasm which caused him to buy them in surprising quantities', as his biographer Doris Langley Moore puts it, drawing on surviving outfitters' bills: 'six on March 23rd and six again on April 7th, and yet a dozen more on June 20th, 1812 – £31 4s in all':[3] the equivalent of one-fifth of his mother's annual allowance. Byron ran up debts to the value of £900 with one tailor alone between January 1812 and September 1813. Booksellers, furnishers, jewellers, and wine merchants were similarly accommodating.

But Byron's shopping would soon become the least of his problems. He had first met his half-sister Augusta in 1803, when he was 15 and she 20. They continued to correspond, and in July 1813, they began to meet again in London. By August they had begun a sexual relationship. (Six years later he wrote to her that he had 'never ceased nor can cease to feel for a moment that perfect & boundless attachment which bound & binds me to you'; *LJ* VI. 129.) His next plan, accordingly, was that he would escape to Europe with her rather than Lady Oxford.

Incest contravened ecclesiastical law in Britain, and was punishable by six months' imprisonment, whereas homosexuality was a civil offence punishable by death. But incest was hardly less scandalous. In the two years after his return from Greece there is a pattern of social as well as financial self-destructiveness in Byron that verges on the hysterical. Each affair, in combination with his literary fame, personal beauty, and mysterious reputation, seemed designed to both affront and compel public attention. The relationship with Augusta (married with several children by a dim-witted colonel, who was also her cousin) could never be revealed, but Lady Caroline had enough information on him already, and was constantly on the lookout for more. By 1815, his debts stood at £30,000, and the situation over Newstead meant that Byron remained tied to England while increasingly desperate to escape: to Sicily, the Holy Land, Holland, or Russia, as the mood took him.

Almost as soon as his affair with Augusta began, Byron resumed his correspondence with Annabella Milbanke. Then, in October 1813, he veered towards the young wife of a friend of his, Lady Frances Wedderburn Webster, whom he 'spared' only at the eleventh hour of a melodramatic courtship at Newstead. In November, he wrote *The Bride of Abydos*, concerning an apparently incestuous couple coming to a sticky end. *The Corsair* – in which the hero loses a worthy love for a murderous and shameful one – followed in December. 'A wife', he wrote in January 1814, 'would be my salvation' (*LJ* III. 241). His political profile was dramatically radicalized by the republication of 'Lines to a Lady Weeping', which ridiculed the Prince of Wales, alongside *The Corsair* in February.

A codicil to the Eastern Tales, *Lara*, was published in August 1814; it was the first publication for which Byron accepted payment from John Murray. Byron's epistolary courtship of Annabella continued alongside his affair with Augusta until September 1814, when the former unexpectedly accepted him. They had not seen each other for nearly a year, and he delayed visiting his fiancée for six weeks, by which time the Milbanke family was almost prostrate with nerves. Byron and Annabella married at the bride's home on 2 January 1815, and after a 'treaclemoon' (*LJ* IV. 263) they arrived in London at the end of March, settling in an oversized townhouse in Piccadilly belonging to the Duchess of Devonshire. In early April, Augusta arrived for what became a ten-week visit.

Many of the stories told of the Byrons' marriage are, by their nature, unsubstantiated. But they suggest a pattern of mental cruelty and uxoriousness certainly not inconceivable in a man under intolerable pressure who feels he has made a grave mistake by involving someone else in his predicament. It seems Byron made hurtful remarks, paraded his affection for Augusta in ambiguous terms, scandalized his wife with accounts of his previous activities, and demanded anal sex of her. Yet there also exist touching letters between them both when they were apart. By no means everything Byron said was to be taken at face value, as his friends and half-sister had long understood. But Annabella was as literal-minded as she was sanctimonious, and had no sense of humour whatsoever. Their marriage is one of the unhappiest in English history.

In May 1815, Byron joined the management subcommittee of Drury Lane Theatre, which gave him some distractions from a dismal life at home. This was also the summer Napoleon returned to the French throne and was finally defeated at Waterloo. In November, Byron, too, seemed to be facing humiliation. Bailiffs had moved into his house, and only his title prevented him being arrested for debt. His daughter, Ada, was born on 10 December. On 15 January, she and Lady Byron left the Piccadilly house to visit her parents, apparently on good terms with the poet. Neither mother nor child saw Byron again.

On 2 February 1816, Annabella's father wrote to Byron requesting a separation: 'circumstances have come to my knowledge, which convince me, that with your opinions it cannot tend to your happiness to continue to live with Lady Byron' (Marchand, 571). Byron rejected the proposal and wrote to Annabella in disbelief, but she corresponded only in guarded terms, and refused an interview. By mid-March it was apparent the marriage was over. In early April, Byron's library was sold. Rumours spread rapidly through aristocratic circles, and his social popularity evaporated. On 21 April, Byron signed a deed of separation, and two days later his extravagant travelling coach (cost, £500) rolled out of London for Dover, leaving a mountain of debt behind it. Four days later he was in Bruges.

Exile (1816–1823)

On 4 May 1816, Byron visited Waterloo and continued a third canto of *Childe Harold's Pilgrimage*, tracking his journey up the Rhine to Geneva. On 27 May, he met his fellow-poet and fellow-aristocrat Percy Bysshe Shelley there, accompanied by Shelley's lover Mary Godwin and her stepsister Claire Clairmont. The meeting had been arranged by Claire not only to show off her poetic acquaintance with Shelley, but also to resume her affair with Byron, which she had initiated during his final days in London. By 10 June, Byron had rented the Villa Diodati on the shores of Lake Geneva, with the Shelley group in a smaller house down the hill, and one of the most famous house-parties in English literary history began, involving a ghost-story-writing competition which only Mary Godwin took seriously – *Frankenstein* being the result.

Byron toured the region with Shelley for a week before the latter's party returned to England at the end of August, Shelley carrying the new canto of *Childe Harold*, Claire carrying Byron's unborn child. In September, he toured the Alps again, this time with Hobhouse, writing a travel journal for his sister, and an unprecedented drama, *Manfred*, seething with suicidal guilt and defiance. On 5 October, the friends descended into Italy. They mingled with literary and political circles in Milan, and arrived in Venice – '(next to the East) the greenest island of my imagination' (*LJ* V. 129) – in early November, just as *Childe Harold* III was published in London to continued acclaim. Byron would base himself there for three years, until the end of 1819.

In Venice, Byron at last shook off his (prodigiously productive) state of depression. He threw himself into the Venetian carnival with gusto, and began an equally prodigious number of sexual affairs – 'I think at least two hundred of one sort or another' (*LJ* VI. 66) was the total by late 1818 – though there were two mistresses who were much more than one-night stands: Marianna Segati (October 1816–February 1818) and Margarita Cogni (August 1817– April 1819). In mid-April 1817, he set off on another pilgrimage, this time through Bologna and Florence to Rome. 'As a *whole – ancient & modern* – it beats Greece – Constantinople – every thing – at least that I have ever seen' (*LJ* V. 221). He returned to Venice by the end of May, and began the fourth canto of *Childe Harold* at the end of June, just after the publication of *Manfred*. The poem was completed in a month and by the end of October he completed another remarkable transition, this time to the comic, vernacular, and digressive style of *Beppo: A Venetian Story*, published anonymously in February 1818 and a trial for the greatest poem of his career, *Don Juan*, which he started in July of that year.

When a schoolmate from Harrow made a genuine offer of £95,000 for Newstead in December 1817, these sexual and artistic resurgences were accompanied by a financial one. Claire's daughter, Allegra, had been born in England in January, and the 18-month-old child was delivered to Byron in June 1818 at his palazzo on the Grand Canal: 'very pretty – remarkably intelligent – and a great favourite with every body' (*LJ* VI. 62). As 1818 wore on his friends in England expressed concerns about *Don Juan* and its barely concealed references to Lady Byron, but its author was unapologetic. For the first time in his life he was also driving hard bargains with John Murray for his work. Byron's Venetian life came to a climax in the carnival of February 1819, when he suddenly took it upon himself to reform – a decision that was not overdue. The son of the family lawyer reported meeting him in November 1818: 'Lord Byron could not have been more than 30, but he looked 40. His face had become pale, bloated, and sallow. He had grown very fat, his shoulders broad and round, and the knuckles of his hands were lost in fat' (*LJ* VI. 78).

In April 1819, he became acquainted with the 19-year-old Teresa, Countess Guiccioli, up from Ravenna on a visit with her 58-year-old husband. Within days they were lovers. She was already pregnant, and on her trip home she miscarried. On 1 June, Byron followed her, and their affair deepened during his visit. In August, he followed the Guicciolis back to Bologna, then (with the Count's permission) returned to Venice with Teresa, having planned and abandoned an elopement. Byron continued work on *Don Juan* and gave his memoirs to his friend the Irish poet Thomas Moore, while the Count left his wife in Byron's care until November, when he returned to collect her.

Byron now came to a fork in the path of his relationship with Teresa. Her health was re-established, and he could step aside, for her sake as well as his own. He had thought of emigration to Venezuela with Allegra; then England seemed a possibility. But the threat of departure made Teresa ill again, and by the end of 1819 Byron was back at Ravenna. His Venetian life was over, and his longest, most important affair had taken root. 'You shall be my last Passion', he had written to Teresa the month he had met her (*LJ* VI. 112), and he was right.

Living in Count Guiccioli's palazzo while conducting an affair with his wife was not easy. In May 1820, they were caught 'quasi in the fact' (*LJ* VII. 102), and things came to a head. Teresa's father, Count Gamba, requested a marital separation for his daughter from the Church, and Guiccioli was in a difficult position, having sanctioned the affair for as long as he had. None of this put Byron off his writing, and in April he mounted another step on the stairway of surprise, starting work on the first of a series of neoclassical tragedies: *Marino Faliero*, set in medieval Venice, and involving an aristocratic leader who led a rebellion against his own class. In July, life imitated art: an uprising broke out in the Kingdom of Naples, inspired by a nationalist secret society, the *Carbonari* ('charcoal-burners'). Hopes were high elsewhere in the peninsula, but an Austrian army passed by to suppress the revolt, and though Byron had joined, armed, and equipped the Ravenna *Carbonari*, nothing eventuated. Teresa's separation was awarded, however, and she moved in with her father and brother, both of whom became close to the man who had ended her marriage – and who was still living under her ex-husband's roof.

Marino Faliero grew slowly, and it was October 1820 before Byron resumed ⋆ work on *Don Juan*. Having written one of its most triumphant cantos (the fifth), he abruptly abandoned the poem in December – at Teresa's request, he said – and only took it up again fifteen months later, in April 1822. Meanwhile a second neoclassical history play, *Sardanapalus*, followed in early 1821, alongside a quixotic literary-critical defence of his neoclassical poetic hero, Alexander Pope. A third drama, *The Two Foscari*, followed in summer.

Allegra was not entirely lost sight of in these developments. She had been left with the English Consul in Venice, nearly adopted by an English widow, passed on to the Danish Consul, installed at Byron's Venetian summer house on the Brenta river, and finally brought down to Ravenna to be spoiled by Teresa. Claire Clairmont kept asking for increased access to her, but Byron was concerned about the Shelleys' unconventional lifestyle, and asserted his paternal rights. ('A Girl is in all cases better with the mother,' he wrote, 'unless there is some unusual objection'; *LJ* VII. 251.) Allegra's upbringing suffered amidst these uncertainties, and in March 1821, Byron placed her at a convent school at Bagnacavallo, twelve miles outside Ravenna – an institution of the kind at which Teresa herself had been educated.

England had not disappeared from Byron's view either. In April 1821, *Marino Faliero* was staged without his consent at Drury Lane. In the same month, the poet laureate, Robert Southey, published a memorial poem for the recently deceased George III called *A Vision of Judgement*, in the preface to which he took aim at a 'Satanic school' of English poetry, of which Byron was clearly a member. Byron's long-established hatred of the 'Lake school' of poets – onetime radicals turned conservatives, Southey, Coleridge, and Wordsworth – became fused with his neoclassical dramas, with *Don Juan* (Cantos III–V of which were published in August), and with his defence of Pope. In July, he started work on his most provocative piece yet, an adaptation of the book of Genesis called *Cain*, in which the hero was given an extended lesson in scepticism from Satan before killing his twin brother as a result. In the same month, Teresa's father and brother were banished from Romagna by the authorities. Within weeks Teresa followed them to Florence and Byron was left alone – quite happily, as he did not leave Ravenna until the end of October. While alone he finished *Cain* and wrote his own *The Vision of Judgment*, in which Satan and the Archangel Michael haggle over the right of George III to enter the Kingdom of Heaven.

Another biblical drama, *Heaven and Earth*, concerning the legendary loves between angels and women, was composed before Byron finally left Ravenna – not for Florence but for Pisa, where the Shelley group had reconvened itself, including a number of the younger poet's hangers-on. Teresa and her family were in the city also, but as they had no access to Italian society there Byron's life entered a new phase, as a member of an English expatriate circle. Awake most of the night writing, he would get up at lunchtime and ride out in company in the late afternoon, often for some shooting practice while the ladies looked on. His relationship with Shelley deepened, but also became more ambivalent as the younger poet's genius seemed to falter beside Byron's: 'I do not write – I have lived too long near Lord Byron and the sun has extinguished the glow-worm.'[4] On 27 January 1822, Greek Independence was proclaimed. On the next day, Byron's mother-in-law, Lady Noel, died, leaving him substantially better off at the price of attaching her name to his own – as her will dictated, he began to sign himself 'Noel Byron'. On 20 April, Allegra died suddenly at Bagnacavallo of a fever, aged 5. Byron had never visited her there, nor made any plans to bring her nearer to his new base. Still, his expressions of grief were clearly genuine, and he arranged for her body to be interred in the church at Harrow, where he had been a schoolboy.

As Shelley and Byron's relationship began to fracture, the former tried to weld it together with the kind of co-operative scheme writers have often dreamed of but rarely succeeded in sustaining. The plan was to found a literary and political journal, the *Liberal*, using Byron's money to bring its editor, the radical journalist Leigh Hunt – whom Byron had visited in jail in his days as a *cause célèbre*, imprisoned for libelling the Prince Regent in 1813 – over from England.

The *Liberal* was a fascinating venture, but a doomed one. Hunt arrived in July 1822, setting up home with his wife and six children in Byron's palazzo, much to the latter's annoyance. Within days Shelley drowned in a sailing accident. Hunt and Byron attended an informal cremation of the poet's body on the beach at Viareggio on 16 August, but their relationship rapidly disintegrated as Hunt ('a great coxcomb and a very vulgar person in every thing about him'; *LJ* VI. 47) came to resent the sums of money he continued to request from Byron. In the end, the *Liberal* was published only four times. Perhaps it was the presence of the Hunts that encouraged Byron to reconsider emigration. As it was, he moved to Genoa, to a house now shared with Teresa and her family. Hobhouse saw him for the last time before his departure: 'He is much changed – his face fatter and the expression of it injured' (Marchand, 1030). Mary Shelley and the Hunts established themselves nearby, and the first number of the *Liberal* appeared in October, with *The Vision of Judgment* as its lead publication.

Byron's relationship with John Murray, too, now began to collapse. *Don Juan*, though published anonymously, had been bad enough; *Cain* caused outrage in the increasingly pious middle-class readership Murray served; but *The Vision of Judgment* and the relationship with Hunt were the last straws for the conservative publisher. By November 1822, their long partnership was at an end. Byron's politics were increasingly mercurial: too far to the left for Murray and Hobhouse; too aristocratic for what remained of the Shelley circle. The charms of domesticity were beginning to wear thin, also. In January 1823, he mentioned the possibility of a return to Greece – he had met a number of expatriate Greek nationalists among the Pisa expatriates. Work on *Don Juan* and a poem on the *Bounty* mutiny, *The Island*, sustained him during this period. Then a meeting with representatives of the Greek government in exile in April caused him to offer his money and services to that cause, and to be 'of some – at least *temporary* utility' there (*LJ* XI. 102). On 6 May, he finished the last complete canto of *Don Juan*, and a week later he committed himself to the Greek uprising, despite Teresa's dismay. He spent money – lavishly as ever – on all sorts of preparations, and by the end of June had hired a ship for himself and his fellow travellers. July 16 saw him at sea once more, fourteen years after setting sail from Falmouth for Lisbon.

To Missolonghi (1823–1824)

On 3 August 1823, the *Hercules* arrived at Cephalonia, western Greece, and Byron began to draw down the money from his own estate that would bring many interested parties to him. The provisional Greek government was seeking an £80,000 loan from the London Greek Committee and Byron lent £4,000 of his own money as an interim measure. A group of philhellenes began to assemble as events unfolded, and Byron negotiated carefully offshore from the mainland while visiting sites associated with Homer's *Odyssey*. After this cautious approach to the many parties involved with Greek independence he made his choice (the reasonably peaceable prince Alexander Mavrocordatos) and arrived at Missolonghi on 3 January 1824, where he was greeted as a kind of messiah.

The town was chaotic and, unwisely, Byron hired a band of Suliote tribesmen from southern Greece to retain order. Once hired, they became emboldened, and weeks of futile negotiation with unpatriotic thugs ensued. Missolonghi was under a naval blockade, and the first order of business was a land-based attack on Lepanto, to the east, to outflank Turkish naval superiority, but Byron's time and resources were increasingly expended on local disorder. He had also brought with him from Cephalonia the last of his 'pages', the 15-year-old Loukas Chalandritsanos, for whom he wrote a few last poems. The boy was a vain creature, and returned little of Byron's affection.

In early February, a long-awaited English artillery expert, Major William Parry, arrived. He and Byron got on well, but Parry's infectious drinking habits helped undermine Byron's health. So did the weather in a town he called a 'mud basket': 'the Dykes of Holland when broken down are the Desarts of Arabia for dryness in comparison' (*LJ* XI. 107). Byron was invited to a conference of Greek powers at Salona, but poor weather prevented his attendance. His nervous condition worsened, and on 9 April, he was soaked to the skin while out riding. A fever set in, which he fought for a week before retiring to bed. His panic-stricken medical advisers drew blood from him to counteract the fever, but weakened him in doing so. On 18 April, he realized he was dying and refused further treatment. He died at six in the evening of 19 April 1824.

'Let not my body be hacked, or be sent to England', were Byron's last requests (Marchand, 1224–5). Both were disregarded: during an autopsy his lungs were removed and later lost, whereas his other internal organs were packed with his embalmed body and sent back to Britain in a barrel of spirits on 2 May, arriving there at the end of June. The body lay in state in a house on Great George Street, a few hundred yards from the House of Lords, on 9 and 10 July. Those who came to see it were generally humble people, not Byron's fellow-aristocrats, who stayed away from his funeral procession, too, as it left London a few days later. Lady Caroline Lamb happened upon the procession purely by chance outside her country house in the Midlands. The body lay in state once more in Nottingham, and was buried in the family vault at Hucknall Torkard church on 16 July. 'They told me that his coffin stood upon that of the late Lord', Hobhouse recalled, 'and I saw that beside it was the coffin – all mouldered & with the plate barely visible of his mother – I wished to have his coffin placed on this – but was told that it would give way' (Marchand, 1263).

Epilogue

'Byron is dead!', Jane Welsh, the future wife of Thomas Carlyle, wrote in May 1824. 'I was told it all at once in a roomful of people. My God if they had said that the sun or the moon had gone out of the heavens, it could not have struck me with the idea of a more awful and dreary blank in the creation.'[5] The poet's memoirs, which he had given to Thomas Moore in Venice in 1818, were burned in the fireplace at John Murray's Mayfair office on 17 May 1824, ostensibly to protect his reputation against the rising tide of middle-class morality Byron himself had confronted all his life – 'fit only for a brothel', according to one of the publisher's cronies (Marchand, 1246).

One of the incendiarists, John Cam Hobhouse, was himself made a baron for services to the Whig party in 1851; he lived on until 1859. John Murray died in 1843 having made his firm a great British institution – it survives today as an imprint of the French publishing group, Hachette. Caroline Lamb died four years after Byron, and Augusta, on whom Lady Byron battened like a moral vampire after the separation, died in 1851. Annabella dedicated her life not only to her sister-in-law's reform but also to that of prisons and the abolition of slavery. Before her death in 1860 she gave details of her marriage to a fellow abolitionist, Harriet Beecher Stowe (author of *Uncle Tom's Cabin*), who published *Lady Byron Vindicated* in 1870, which brought Byron's personal reputation to an absolute nadir.

Lady Byron had been an amateur mathematician – a 'Princess of Parallellograms' as Byron maliciously called her (*LJ* IV. 48) – and their daughter, Ada (who died in 1852), showed real talent in the field, eventually assisting Charles Babbage with his 'analytical engine' – origin of the modern computer. (The Ada programming language developed in the 1970s is named after her.) Claire Clairmont died aged 81 in 1879, at Florence, having worked as a governess in Russia and Germany after Shelley's death. Teresa Guiccioli also died in 1879, after many years living luxuriously on her memories of the poet, which she committed to paper on numerous occasions.

The poet's death substantially raised the media profile of the Greek War of Independence. The Turks were driven out of Greece by 1828 and the independent nation was recognized in 1832. Many Greek cities have streets, squares, and statues in Byron's honour. 'I should prefer a grey Greek stone over me to Westminster Abbey' (*LJ* X. 157), he wrote a few months before leaving Italy in 1823. But the Abbey refused him burial there, and it was not until 1974, the sesquicentenary of his death, that a plaque was unveiled in Poets' Corner, twenty years after Keats and Shelley had been similarly memorialized.

Context

Byron was born in 1788 and died in 1824: as arbitrary a pair of dates as those relating to any other human life. But in his case they cover, with curious precision, a period of pronounced change in Britain and in Europe.

In 1788, Britain was governed by a monarch (George III) who had been on the throne for twenty-eight years, and by a class (the aristocracy) whose rise to power during the eighteenth century seemed irreversible. By 1824, the monarch's role in the governance of the state was showing clear evidence of decline, and a set of forces were in motion that would lead to the democratic Reform Bill of 1832.

In 1788, Europe was made up of a group of nation states in which representative institutions of the kind established in Britain were almost unknown, and which had passed through a long history of violent rivalry for power and territory. By 1824, a republican revolution had been carried out and temporarily reversed in France, a twenty-two-year-long series of continental wars had been fought to a conclusion, and the European powers had organized themselves into a new set of relations which underwrote peace in central Europe until 1914.

Finally, whereas Germany was already the prosecutor of a vigorous reaction against the Enlightenment in 1788, that reaction had only just begun to emerge in Britain when Byron was born (Blake's *Songs of Innocence* would be published – if that is the word – in 1789). By 1824, the Romantic movement was recognized throughout Europe as a prodigious cultural innovation, and English-speaking writers (and painters) were in its vanguard.

What Byron called these 'gigantic and exaggerated times' (*LJ* IX. 155) are the context for all the great English writers of his time: for Blake (1757–1827), Wordsworth (1770–1850), Scott (1771–1832), Coleridge

(1772–1834), and Austen (1775–1817), among the first generation of English Romantic writers, and for Shelley (1792–1822) and Keats (1795–1821), among the second. But Byron played a unique role in this context. As a peer and a member of the British Parliament he was in a position to witness the political changes of his era; as a traveller and resident in Europe between 1809 and his death in Greece he saw the effects of war and resurgent nationalism at first hand; and as the most famous writer of his time he played a role in directing and embodying the Romantic movement, as opposed to simply being influenced by it.

Politics and aristocracy

An undeniable sign of change in late eighteenth-century Europe was the French Revolution, inaugurated by the fall of the Bastille in the summer of 1789, when Byron was 18 months old. In Britain, the Revolution was seen as a welcome reform of a feudal nation, presumably leading to a constitutional monarchy of the kind in power in England for 100 years. But in 1791, the French king was arrested and in 1792, the monarchy was abolished. In January 1793, Louis XVI was guillotined, in February, France declared war on Britain, and in July, the period known as 'the Terror' began under the Committee of Public Safety chaired by Maximilien Robespierre. A year later, Robespierre himself was executed. By 1795, all pretence of representative government had been abandoned, and France was ruled by the Committee of Public Safety until it, too, was swept aside by a military coup in 1799, led by the young general Napoleon Bonaparte, who installed himself initially as First Consul, and as Emperor of the French in December 1804. He would reign until 1814, return briefly from exile thereafter, and collapse completely after the battle of Waterloo in June 1815.

The English aristocracy

It was a mystery to some why the British monarchy and aristocracy did not share the fate of their French counterparts in this period. French revolutionary principles were eminently exportable, and British intellectuals had certainly contributed to the Enlightenment that sponsored them. More importantly, Britain underwent great changes in the late eighteenth and early nineteenth centuries – both demographic change in terms of growth and movement of population from the country to the city and economic change as increasing numbers of people rose out of poverty. The British government was demonstrably out of touch with these developments: 'Rulers who neither see nor feel nor know', as Shelley described them in his sonnet, 'England in 1819'. The population of Britain grew by 33 per cent between 1801 and 1821, while that of Byron's own county town, Nottingham, increased in size from 11,000 in 1750 to 30,000 in 1801.[1] Yet in 1760, only one English family in seven had a total income of over £50; in 1806, one English family in four had an income of over £100[2] – which is to say that within fifty years the number of Britons living below the poverty line had nearly halved, despite a steep rise in population. The number of English provincial newspapers trebled between 1780 and 1830; the value of British exports in the 1810s was double that of the 1790s.[3]

Yet despite these changes and countless others associated with them, no British government lost power at an election until 1830. Before that date, too, less than 12 per cent of adult males in England and Wales had the vote, and on average only 30 per cent of seats were even contested at 'general' elections[4] – the county seats of Nottinghamshire went uncontested between 1722 and the early nineteenth century.[5] True, the Reform Bill of 1832 increased the male suffrage by 45 per cent – from 3.2 per cent to 4.7 per cent of the general population.[6] But the French aristocracy disappeared in 1789, whereas its British equivalent survived until the First World War. The House of Lords dominated British cabinets until the 1860s, and provided its last prime minister, Lord Salisbury, as late as 1900 (or as late as 1963, if you count the 14th Earl of Home, who descended to the House of Commons as plain Sir Alec Douglas-Home and held office for a little over a year).

For many years the British aristocracy explained its imperviousness to revolution in terms of its openness to change. It claimed to be 'an open elite', in which rank sought money through intermarriage with the rising middle class. It is true that the daughter of Byron's solicitor married Lord Portsmouth in 1814, but her case was far from common (and the lord in question was insane). In fact, the rulers of Britain were a tightly cohesive ruling caste, which tolerated few interlopers.

Why did the British nobility fail to attract social envy and disillusion, then, as the French one did? Part of the reason is that it was industrious, involved in government, administration, land tenure, and the armed services. It was also more involved with rural life than its French counterpart, gathered around the court at Versailles. When strangers did enter its ranks through money or merit they tended to be assimilated comparatively swiftly. By European standards, too, the British aristocracy had few privileges. British peers were not above the law or immune to taxation. Only the head of a British noble family held the title, and only his nearest male heir could inherit it. The younger sons of the gentry either lived on the charity of their families or had to make their way in the world in the professions or the military – and the professions meant contact with everyday people, if only in the law court, the Church, and the barracks.

Furthermore, if the British aristocracy was only lightly penetrated by upward mobility, what Peter Laslett calls 'semi-circular' mobility was a significant influence.[7] In a period of high mortality, and in a system depending on primogeniture, father-to-son inheritance was statistically likely to last only a few generations. Every so often the title was almost certain to pass to a remoter branch of the family. Byron's case is illustrative: at the age of 10 a grammar-school boy from unglamorous Aberdeen unexpectedly became the heir of an English noble house.

The older the house, therefore, the longer it was likely to survive, insuring its future through a far-flung web of male relations. The Byrons had come over from France with William the Conqueror in 1066, and fought for the Tudors at the battle of Bosworth (1485), in reward for which Henry VIII gave Newstead Abbey to 'our beloved servant' Sir John Byron at the dissolution of the monasteries in the 1530s (Marchand, 4). Another Sir John was similarly loyal to the English crown, serving as a general for Charles I in the English Civil War (1640–9), and created a baron for his pains. After that, history passed the Byrons by until the 6th baron published *Childe Harold's Pilgrimage* in 1812: 'substantial landowners, not perhaps in the first rank of the English aristocracy but sufficiently well endowed to have acquired a peerage and to be considered a major county family'.[8]

What was handed on in such a family was a package comprising five elements: the seat (the 'stately home'), the valuables inside it, the land, the name, and the title. The aim was to keep all this together, and again the British aristocracy is unusual by virtue of its lack of interest in titles as such. A peer without land was an anomalous object, and whereas many British houses fizzled out for lack of male heirs, only a tiny number sold out, as Byron did in disposing of Newstead.

Selling out was not normally a matter of choice, in any event. Succession was legislated by the 'letters patent' of the original title and (normally) by deeds of settlement between the sitting peer and his inheritor as the young man approached the age of majority. The holder of the title might live on for several years after that date, of course, so the heir would need an allowance in the mean time. Equally, the occupant might use a settlement to raise some money by selling part of the estate. So the generations arranged the details of succession, and that is what happened between the 5th Lord Byron and his son. When that son died and the inheritance moved to a 4-year-old nephew, a new settlement never took place. Settlement lapsed yet again when the nephew himself died in Corsica in 1794. So the poet could sell his estate and raise debts using it as security because it was entirely his to dispose of. Byron's heir was his cousin, George Anson Byron, who could only sit and watch as Newstead eventually went under the hammer. But George did what he could to advance his own interests in this complicated game. He supported Lady Byron's desire for a legal separation, so making the birth of a direct male heir more unlikely. Byron's entry to the British aristocracy was unexpected, his tenancy irregular, and his departure deplorable.

The legal privileges accorded the British nobility were few but significant. A peer could not be arrested for debt, for example, which no doubt contributed to Byron's shopping addiction. He could claim trial 'before his peers' in the House of Lords – as the 5th Lord did when a neighbour died at his hands in a brawl. (The Lords found him guilty of manslaughter, but did not punish him, deciding he had been provoked.) But the most important privilege was membership of the House of Lords itself.

The Lords is the weaker of the two houses of Parliament, though nominally the upper one. It could not interfere with financial bills, for example, even in Byron's time. But that would be to misunderstand its power. In 1713, 8 per cent of the members of the House of Commons were peers' sons; in 1796, the proportion had risen to 21 per cent. In 1784, 70 per cent of the members of the Lords had a relative in the Commons.[9] 'Between 1782 and 1820, sixty-five individuals held cabinet office. Of these forty-three were peers, and of the remaining twenty-two, fourteen were the sons of peers.' Aristocratic influence over the Commons reached a peak half-way through Byron's life, in 1807, when 236 Commons seats out of 658 were in their gift.[10] The two Nottinghamshire constituencies, for example, were to all intents and purposes the appointments of the Duke of Portland. It would be going too far to say that the Commons were in the Lords' pocket, but the great aristocratic oligarchy had them safely under control. Nor did the parliamentary arrangements of Byron's day resemble the Westminster system developed during the Victorian period. Party discipline, cabinet government, the modern civil service, 'His Majesty's Opposition': none of these was in place during Byron's parliamentary career.

Change (1789–1824)

What the Parliament of Byron's time inherited was a melange left over from the end of the seventeenth century, when the pro-Catholic Stuart monarchy under James II was finally evicted in favour of an imported Protestant one under William of Orange, in the 'Glorious Revolution' of 1688. In that crisis two terms of abuse were adapted from the sectarian wilds of Ireland and Scotland, respectively: a 'Tory' was loyal to the Stuart King, the Court and (perhaps) to Catholicism; a 'Whig' was loyal to the Dutch replacement, Parliament, and (presumably) to Protestantism.

The Glorious Revolution put the Whigs in power for almost the whole of the eighteenth century. To be a Tory was to be (at worst) a treasonous fellow traveller with an evicted monarchy, or (at best) to be a supporter of royal as opposed to parliamentary privilege. The Whigs bickered among themselves, and called each other Tories if some of their number got too close to the king, but there was no party system and no parliamentary discipline – which state of affairs in effect handed power to the Hanoverian kings (the four Georges), who exercised massive amounts of patronage. The reigning monarch chose his prime minister, and the prime minister chose his government, which then transformed itself over time with barely any reference to the public at large – unless they rioted.

Then two developments shattered the great oligarchy: the Hanoverian monarchy became more popular, and the French Revolution forced British politicians to take sides in an ideological debate on republicanism. To be loyal to the Stuarts after the Glorious Revolution had been political death. To be loyal to the Hanoverians after the execution of Louis XVI in France was to be a patriotic subject. On this issue the Whigs firmly split: the loyalists stayed with William Pitt the Younger, the reformers sided with Charles James Fox.

Since the 'Friends of Mr Pitt' were loyal to George III, and benefited from his support, the Foxites called them Tories. As the war went on – and changed from being arguably an ideological conflict to one of national self-defence – 'Tory' became a badge of pride rather than opprobrium, and that is why Pitt is often named as the founder of what would become a new political grouping, the Conservative party (still called Tories to this day).

This is the great political development Byron witnessed even if he did not understand it. The Whig oligarchy had broken into two parties: the Tories based in King and Country, the Whigs wailing for peace and reform during an extended period of national crisis. At such a juncture the Whigs were unlikely to gain sympathy from a reigning monarch; nor could they go to the country in a modern election. So they resorted to a kind of cultural politics, in which Byron played a minor role (before his departure in 1816) as poet and poster-boy.

Benefiting from this new-found conservatism and patriotism, Pitt held office from 1783 to 1801. There then followed seven administrations in rapid succession, including Pitt's return and the Whigs' moment of opportunity in the 'Ministry of All the Talents' formed after his death in 1806. When that collapsed the Tories returned again, leaving the Whigs to dream of the death or final insanity of the acutely ill George III, at which point their royal supporter, the Prince of Wales, would give them what they wanted. 'On the one side', Byron wrote in January 1809, 'we have the later underlings of Pitt, possessing all his ill Fortune, without his Talents … on the other we have the ill assorted fragments of a worn out minority' (*LJ* I. 186).

In 1811, George III descended into outright lunacy and his son became Prince Regent – but things did not go according to Whig plans. When the Tory prime minister, Spencer Perceval, was assassinated in the lobby of the House of Commons by a disgruntled businessman – two months after the publication of *Childe Harold's Pilgrimage* in 1812 – the Prince Regent abandoned the Whigs. Lord Liverpool was appointed prime minister and would serve until 1827. ('Nought's permanent among the human race', Byron joked in *Don Juan* (XI. 655–6), 'Except the Whigs *not* getting into place.') The Liverpool government has been characterized as the last eighteenth-century administration in terms of its structure and duration, and the first nineteenth-century administration in terms of its problems and achievements.[11] By the time of Byron's death it had become the first British government to discover 'that politicians were no longer playing an aristocratic game, but were answerable for social ills. In other words … the beginnings, not only of Cabinet government, but of modern government itself.'[12]

The French Wars also furthered the process of party building. The war budget necessitated cuts in government spending, particularly on patronage. Four hundred sinecures were abolished between 1783 and 1793; two thousand between 1815 and 1822.[13] Without patronage, power drifted away from both the prime minister and the king. If a prime minister cannot rule with sinecures he must rule with policy and discipline; and if the king is weakened the cabinet grows stronger. Thus the British Parliament in Byron's day was in motion between two poles: 'the focal point of politics was no longer the [king's] closet nor yet the ballot box but the division lobby. For a few brief decades … what was said in the Commons actually swayed the outcome of legislation. Appropriately, it was also a golden age of parliamentary oratory'[14] – to which Byron contributed on a tiny number of occasions before turning his back on his political responsibilities.

Protest and repression

'Revolutions require a renegade minority of the élite to give leadership and a discontented mass to provide destructive brute force to be applied against the existing regime.'[15] This particular French recipe was not repeated in Britain in the thirty years after the Revolution, but that is not to say the situation was tranquil. The proletarian sphere was as tumultuous as the patrician one, and the government responded accordingly, with varying degrees of moderation and good sense.

Surveying the period between 1789 and 1824 it is hard not to be reminded of the modern-day War on Terror. The British government felt itself to be in a time of crisis, but its defence of liberty from subversion or attack occasionally involved the suppression of the very freedoms it claimed to uphold. If the balance between freedom and security is one that modern democratic governments find hard to strike, how much harder must it have been for the primitive and ill-informed parliaments of the early nineteenth century? 'The most that one can say', Paul Schroeder writes,

> is that there was a perceived crisis, possibly the preconditions for a
> potential revolution, but none of the forces necessary to make it reality,
> and no revolutionary movement that tried to do so. There was no union
> between the middle class and the workers for radical change; no general
> breakdown of the economy; no crushing military defeat; no fiscal crisis;
> no rebellion in the armed forces; no panic or loss of confidence in the
> ruling élite; no widespread alienation from the country's institutions.[16]

It is also worth remembering that wartime invariably brings a degree of repression, and that the defence of the realm legislation passed in Britain during the First and Second World Wars was more far-reaching than that passed by Pitt in the 1790s.[17]

The French Revolution had unleashed an ideological storm in late eighteenth-century Britain, which manifested itself most notably in two books: Edmund Burke's *Reflections on the Revolution in France* (1790) and Thomas Paine's riposte, *The Rights of Man* (1791). By 1792, the London Corresponding Society had been founded, to liaise with Paris, organize mass meetings, and demand universal male suffrage and annual elections. Similar bodies sprang up across the country, offering intellectual and material support to the French regime. This was a serious affront to the aristocratic oligarchy in a time of peace. After the French declared war in 1793, Pitt's government began to act against what it saw as an internal hostile force.

'The democratic agitation of the period of the French Revolution reached its peak in 1792', J. R. Dinwiddy writes,

> the year which saw the publication of the second part of Thomas Paine's
> *Rights of Man*, the [second, more radical] revolution of 10 August in
> Paris, and the first substantial working-class organizations devoted to
> the cause of parliamentary reform in Britain. There was a second peak
> during the subsistence [that is, food availability] crisis of 1795, but

at no stage in these years did the movement attract mass support …
After 1795, public agitation for reform encountered almost insuperable
obstacles: in particular, the repressive legislation passed by Pitt's
government, and the waves of loyalist sentiment which were aroused,
especially in 1796–8 and 1803–5, by the threat of French invasion.[18]

A good deal of legislation restricting freedom of speech and assembly was
passed in the last decade of the eighteenth century, certainly; and habeas
corpus – which requires that suspects be produced before a court after their
arrest – was suspended for acts of treason (loosely defined) between 1794 and
1795 and between 1798 and 1801. But whether this constituted 'Pitt's Terror', as
it came to be known, is debatable – after all, 20,000 people died in Robespierre's
version across the Channel.

In 1794, twelve republican intellectuals were arrested without the protection
of habeas corpus for 'compassing and imagining the King's death'. Three were
acquitted almost as soon as they were brought to court, and the others had
charges against them dropped. Lord Liverpool suspended 'that "ould Apias
Korkus"' (*LJ* VII. 49) again for a year in February 1817. Forty-four people
were eventually arrested on the charge of treason, of whom thirty-seven were
detained, two released immediately, and one died in custody. The remainder had all been released by the time habeas corpus was reinstated. Even the
infamous 'Six Acts' of 1819 were less repressive than their legend would suggest: they legislated against unauthorized public meetings and seditious libel,
it is true, and increased the stamp duty on newspapers, which was a restriction
on the freedom of speech. But they also expedited trials and forbade the carrying or stockpiling of arms in 'disturbed districts'. A year after their passage the
Cato Street conspiracy was uncovered, which intended the assassination of the
entire cabinet. Five of its leaders were hanged.

Still, there were many innocent victims. Some radical journalists and parliamentary reformers were imprisoned, while others fled the country. In 1813,
seventeen Luddite frame-breakers were executed in York. In March 1817,
a troop of working-class protesters known as the 'Blanketeers' set out from
Manchester to London to present their grievances to the Prince Regent; the
leaders were arrested and imprisoned, and the march broken up by troops. In
June of the same year, the town of Pentrich in Derbyshire witnessed a similar protest. Dragoons stopped that march, too, and its leaders were arrested –
many were transported to Australia and three were executed. On 16 August
1819, a squad of yeoman (volunteer) troopers, assisted by hussars, charged a
peaceful though illegal mass meeting at St Peter's Fields, Manchester, by order
of local magistrates, leaving eleven people dead and 400 injured. The 'Peterloo
Massacre' was a dreadful incident, but the central government could not risk

ostracizing the magistracy and yeomanry, which kept order in the country, and backed the authorities, though it played no part in the action that they had ordered.

Yet most social unrest in the period involved food and work rather than politics. A series of bad harvests at the beginning of the century, combined with an improved transport system that allowed producers to move corn to markets offering the highest price, caused real local shortages, and rioting was the quickest way of forcing the authorities to ensure the supply of bread. The government was fortunate that these agricultural and industrial problems rarely coincided either with each other or with failure in the war. The years 1811–12 were ones of crisis because food shortages from earlier lean years and unemployment coincided with the arrival of the Regency. But the war in the Spanish Peninsula was turning the corner, and harvests improved in the years that followed. No British monarch was reduced to suggesting, as the French queen Marie Antoinette in all innocent incomprehension once had, that his hungry people might eat cake as a substitute for bread.

Two hundred thousand soldiers and sailors were demobbed between 1814 and 1817, into a shrinking economy. The next political crisis was in 1819, as this profound post-war slump revived the radical cause. Byron in Italy was well aware of it: 'A revolutionary commission into Leicestershire would just suit me', he wrote; 'what colour is our cockade to be – and our uniform?' (*LJ* VI. 217.) His publisher John Murray wrote in November of that year, 'There is apprehension of Revolution I assure you – Reforms of various Kinds we ought & must have – & Ministers can not stand more in their own light than by opposing themselves to the March of the Intellect – the progress of Society.'[19] Murray's response is as significant as Byron's is facetious. Murray met fear of revolution not with dread of a working-class mob, but with the call for deeper ministerial responsibility. Together, these comments suggest how out of touch Byron had become with the actualities of British politics after his exile. His ideological contribution would be in another sphere.

Summary

To call Byron's attitude to the issues addressed here mercurial would be an understatement. Sir Walter Scott called him 'a patrician on principle', and Shelley regretted 'the canker of aristocracy' in him (Marchand, 530, 928), but neither comment is an adequate one. Politics, Byron wrote, 'with me is a *feeling* and I can't *torify* my nature' (*LJ* IV. 38), but that left plenty of room for man-oeuvre. His 1812 speech to the Lords on the Nottinghamshire frame-breakers was passionate but paternalistic, and the poem he wrote on the same subject sent an inflammatory accusation against the Parliament of which he was a member: 'That the frames of the fools may be first to be *broken*, / Who, when asked for a *remedy*, sent down a *rope*' (*CPW* III. 9). His poetry is famous for its liberal rhetoric, but his letters and conversation paint a complex picture of involvement and disenchantment.

Byron's ambivalence towards aristocracy was certainly genuine. 'If I was born, as the nurses say, with a "silver spoon in my mouth,"' he wrote, 'it has stuck in my throat, and spoiled my palate, so that nothing put into it is swallowed with much relish, – unless it be cayenne' (*LJ* IV. 153). But near the end of his life he defended the oligarchy he had left: 'There is not on earth a more honourable body of men than the English nobility,' he told listeners at Missolonghi, 'and there is no system of government under which life and property are better secured than under the British constitution.'[20] 'If we must have a tyrant,' he wrote, 'let him at least be a gentleman who has been bred to the business, and let us fall by the axe and not by the butcher's cleaver' (*LJ* VII. 44).

In the Lords – that 'hopeless & lethargic den of dullness & drawling' (*LJ* V. 19) – he described himself as 'a stranger not only to this house in general, but to almost every individual whose attention I presume to solicit' (*CMP* 22). But the library at Newstead was decorated from the pattern book of a Whig parliamentarian, with busts of Fox, Milton, and Cicero alongside a print of Trinity – at once the most aristocratic and most Whiggish of the Cambridge colleges. 'My parliamentary schemes are not much to my taste,' he told Augusta in 1813, within a year of returning to the Lords: 'I hate the thing altogether' (*LJ* III. 32). Byron's speeches were 'full of fancy, wit, and invective,' his political mentor, Lord Holland, noted in his memoirs, 'but not exempt from affectation nor well reasoned, nor at all suited to our common notions of Parliamentary eloquence' (Marchand, 322).

Though Byron played with the notion of returning to England in the crisis of 1819, play was all it was, covering a deep disillusionment with his native politics. As his friends Hobhouse and Kinnaird moved to the left, he moved to a kind of nihilism: 'I am and have been for *reform* always – but not for the *reformers*,' he told Hobhouse; 'I am not democrat enough to like a tyranny of blackguards' (*LJ* VI. 166, 229). 'Born an aristocrat, and naturally one by temper,' he wrote in an appendix to *The Two Foscari*, 'what have *I* to gain by a revolution?' (*CPW* VI. 223). By 1821, he had gone so far as to forgive the unforgiveable. The reviled Prince Regent, by then the gouty George IV, 'is not a bad king – and he *was* a fine fellow, – it is a great pity that he did not come to his crown thirty years before' (*CMP* 186). Byron's latter-day involvements with Italian and Greek movements for independence were welcome invitations to the sphere of pan-European liberalism, where the politics were black and white, rather than English grey.

Napoleonic Europe

For modern readers 'the Great War' means the First World War of 1914–18. But before that conflict the expression had been in use for 100 years to describe the French-Revolutionary and Napoleonic Wars fought between 1793 and 1815: 'a series of separate conflicts bound together by the permanent enmity that divided Britain and France'.[21] Those two superpowers of their time 'were like wrestlers, struggling on the edge of a precipice', Hazlitt wrote in 1814 (when he thought it was all over), 'one (or both) of whom must be certain of destruction'.[22] Seven million people died during the wars, and British losses were higher in proportion to the total population than those in the First World War. In 1809, one in ten British males of serviceable age was in uniform; one in six, if volunteers and militia are included.[23] No European nation preserved its neutrality – not even Switzerland – and the conflict was a near-global one, with associated hostilities in North and South America, the Caribbean, the Cape of Good Hope, Egypt, and India. A new style of warfare emerged, as the 'cabinet armies' deployed by the monarchs of the *ancien régime* gave way to the 'nation at arms',[24] with enormous implications for propaganda, ideology, and the home front.

Causes

Traditionally, the 'French wars' were thought to have had their source in the French Revolution and the reaction to that event among the crowned heads of Europe. There is some truth in this account, but not much. Two facts are significant. First, the conflict began before 1789: 'Europe in the 1780s was not heading inexorably toward revolution, but toward war, whether or not there was a revolution. Revolution was contingent; war systemic and structural.'[25] Second, Russia, Prussia, and Austria forged alliances with revolutionary and Napoleonic France as often as it suited them. Austria, for example, provided one princess (Marie Antoinette) for the French king Louis XVI; it provided another (Marie Louise) for Napoleon. The great autocracies were more frightened of France than of revolution.

As with the First World War the origins of the conflict lay not with developing strength, but developing weakness. To flex its slowly dying muscle, the Ottoman Empire declared war on Russia in 1787, bringing Austria in as Russia's ally – which distracted Austria from a political crisis in its territory in the Dutch Republic and gave Prussia the opportunity (encouraged by Britain, which at all costs wanted to avoid French domination in Holland, threatening India through Dutch East Indian colonies) to invade Holland to 'restore order'. This race was one in which France humiliatingly refused to take part, thus weakening the French monarchy and the army's loyalty to it, and laying the seeds of the Revolution to come.[26]

This chaotic pattern is a standard one in European conflicts during the eighteenth century, in which a set of powers nervously, unscrupulously, and blindly exploited small shifts in the 'balance of power' that were perceived in different terms by everybody involved. (Britain and France eyed each other off in this way for the whole 'long eighteenth century'. Of the 126 years between 1689 and 1815, they were at war for fifty-eight.) The entire process was futile, and disastrous for political cohesion and social progress, and perhaps the best single explanation of this period of warfare and of Napoleon's role in it is that both were needed to change the pattern of eighteenth-century conflict. The process took twenty-two years and cost millions of lives, but its result was that central Europe was reduced to a species of order that lasted more or less intact until 1914. Certainly, no British soldier fired a shot in earnest in Western Europe for ninety-nine years after Waterloo.

Conduct

The war between Britain and France – between 'the whale and the elephant', as it has been called – was one to the knife, like that between Churchill and Hitler. Like that later war it also was, as Hazlitt said, 'a war against an opinion, which could, therefore, never cease, but with the extirpation of that opinion'.[27] There were times in that war when Britain stood altogether alone. Fears of invasion were constant between 1797 and 1805, when the destruction of the Franco-Spanish fleet at Trafalgar at last allowed Britons to breathe more easily, and there were genuine invasion panics in 1801 and 1803–4.

Britain had few friends on the Continent, and spent huge sums of money paying its allies to continue the fight. After Napoleon made (temporary) accord with the Russians in 1807, Britain was completely isolated behind the wooden wall of its navy. If Britain then rehearsed the role it would play in 1940, it was also as economically committed to this conflict as the United States eventually was to the Second World War. In the years 1790 and 1850, British government expenditure was 12 per cent of gross national product (GNP); in 1800 and 1810 it was 22 per cent of GNP.[28] In 1815, government expenditure was £30 million while government income was £8 million. Over the period 1793–1815, the government spent the colossal sum of £64 million on foreign subsidies, with Portugal, Spain, and Sweden being particularly expensive.[29]

The war was an ideological struggle, too. It was only in 1803, when Napoleon resumed hostilities after the brief Treaty of Amiens, that the conflict was seen as a justified one even by those Britons with republican sympathies, and that Napoleon, as a contemporary said, was no longer 'worshipped as the Hero of Liberty; his actions have decidedly proved him the Military Tyrant'.[30] Even Byron, who was an ardent Napoleonist, wrote in November 1813: 'he has been a "Héros de Roman" [fictional hero] of mine – on the continent; I don't want him here' (*LJ* III. 210).

'All the wars after 1802 were Napoleon's wars.'[31] Napoleon was not quite the prototype of Hitler, but neither man had any idea what to do with peace. Again and again Napoleon found himself in a position of dominance on the Continent, with Britain abandoned by its fickle allies. In 1797, after the Treaty of Campo Formio, in 1802, after the treaties of Lunéville and Amiens, after the Treaty of Pressburg in 1805, after the Treaty of Tilsit of 1807, and in early 1812: on all these occasions peace and victory for France were achievable, and on each occasion Napoleon antagonized one power or another to bring the rest into a series of reluctant alliances, climaxing in the 'Fourth Coalition' of 1813, when Britain, Russia, Prussia, and Austria at last came together, and Britain's second front in the Spanish peninsula (opened in 1808, a year before Byron's visit) scored its decisive success at the battle of Vittoria. In October 1813, Napoleon (having retreated from Moscow in 1812) was shattered at Leipzig, and in April 1814 he abdicated and was sent to rule the tiny Mediterranean island of Elba. '''Tis done – but yesterday a King!', as Byron wrote in his 'Ode to Napoleon Buonaparte' (*CPW* III. 259).

Consequences

To bring that victorious coalition about the allied powers had to change the habits of a lifetime and *behave* like allies. Britain had to commit to the Continent, Austria and Prussia had to stop squabbling over German territories, and Russia had to stop leering opportunistically at Poland and the Ottoman Empire. When the curtain was finally run down on Napoleon's performance in his 'Hundred Days' (April–June 1815), Europe was 'like a catamaran, with the two outriggers (Great Britain and Russia) holding a vulnerable centre above the waves'.[32] That outcome was the result of the Congress of Vienna, convened in November 1814 and concluded a week before Waterloo. It has been easy to see that congress as Byron himself did: 'the triumph of tameness over talent' accompanying 'the restoration of the despicable Bourbons' (that is, the French royal family) and the general victory of repression throughout Europe 'in all the pomp and rabblement of Royalty' (*LJ* IV. 101, 100).

In hindsight we are able to say that Byron needed to look deeper. 'No attempt was made to turn back the clock at Vienna', Charles Esdaile argues, and the consensus there proved 'far more stable than that of 1918 or 1945, let alone those of earlier general peace settlements.'[33] 'If the people … called for anything *en masse* in 1815, it was for the same thing most princes and elites wanted, and what the congress gave them – peace and order under their traditional rulers.'[34] Vienna achieved peace in central Europe less by 'Cobbling at manacles for all mankind', as Byron argued (*DJ* 'Dedication', 110) than by pacifying the major powers' habit of picking fights over bits of territory, and by building a prospect of Europe in those terms, worked out in a succession of future congresses. The British foreign secretary, Robert Castlereagh, was a particularly effective contributor to this process.

But it is also true that the congress system found certain problems too difficult to solve, especially in the Mediterranean zone where Byron lived after 1815. Weak areas like Spain, northern Italy, and Greece were either left to sort themselves out or put under colonial occupation – which Byron witnessed in Italy, and fought against in Greece. 'That Dog Liverpool', he fumed, regarding Austrian rule in northern Italy (*LJ* VII. 183), 'to say that their subjects were *happy* – what a liar!' But even Byron was forced to admit that he could 'hardly be out of humour with a peace which has enabled me to see so beautiful a country as Italy' (*LJ* V. 202). Poland remained partitioned until 1918, but in other respects something prodigious was achieved, on the basis of which Paul Schroeder mounts a counter-intuitive but impressively documented case that it was Vienna in 1815, not Paris in 1789, which 'launched Europe on a century of genuine political social and economic progress'. 'A competitive balance-of-power struggle gave way to an international system of political equilibrium based on benign shared hegemony and the mutual recognition of rights underpinned by law.'[35]

From the nadir at Austerlitz in December 1805 – 'Roll up that map [of Europe]', Pitt said: 'it will not be wanted these ten years' – to the triumph of Waterloo, Britain lifted itself to an eminence no other European nation had ever achieved or ever would. Britain and France entered the wars as rivals, but whereas the conflict crippled the French economy it ultimately strengthened the British one, and prepared it for the Industrial Revolution in full spate during the 1830s. 'Spain in the Sixteenth Century, France in the Seventeenth and Eighteenth Centuries, Germany in the Twentieth Century, all strove to obtain the hegemony of Europe and on each occasion the English took the lead in preventing them. That hegemony was only once achieved, and by the country that had led in resisting it in others.'[36] We can see this, but only with the benefit of hindsight; for historical witnesses like Byron the picture was not so clear.

The War in the Lords

The *Journals of the House of Lords* indicate that Byron attended the House forty-eight times between 13 March 1809, when he took his seat, and his final visit on 2 April 1816, a fortnight before he left the country for good: seven times in 1809, twenty-six times in 1812, ten times in 1813, twice in 1814, once in 1815, and twice in 1816. It was 1812 that was the year of crisis and opportunity for the Whigs, but also the year in which *Childe Harold* changed Byron's life completely. After that he had clearly decided parliamentary politics – 'The struggle to be Pilots in a storm', as he later called it (*DJ* XIII. 43) – was not for him.

About two-thirds of the sittings Byron attended were given over to administrative matters. The House of Lords is a court as well as a legislative assembly, and it also passed a large number of bills on minor matters, typically processed in committees, on which Byron served a dozen times. The House dealt with personal cases, and in February 1813 Byron sat on a committee considering a baronet's desire to break legal succession and sell his estate (a matter close to his heart). It dealt with divorces, each of which required an Act of Parliament, and on 14 March 1809 Byron sat through some palpably inauthentic testimony from chambermaids and ostlers designed to establish an 'unlawful connexion' in a London hotel. (Small wonder he and his wife later sought a separation rather than a divorce.) It dealt with petitions, and the House took many of these in 1813 – dealing with Catholic emancipation, Christian missions to India, and the shady trading practices of the East India Company. It dealt also with the building of new roads (a huge enterprise at this time), and Byron sat on committees in February 1812 and April 1813 to consider such innovations in Dartmoor and Glasgow. It dealt with foreigners' applications to become naturalized citizens, and he served on such committees twice in 1812. Finally, the House dealt with enclosures – the absorption of smaller rural properties and common land into larger farms – which Byron considered in committee no fewer than six times, in April and May 1809 and February and March 1812. His last committee service was on 14 May 1813.

Byron was present in the House for fifteen major sittings, and spoke at three of them, always on domestic issues, and always from a Whig-cum-radical position. On 27 February 1812, he spoke in defence of rioting frame-breakers in the industrial north (*CMP* 20–7); on 21 April of that year, he spoke in favour of Catholic emancipation (*CMP* 28–43); and on 1 June 1813, he supported the request of a long-standing reformer, Major John Cartwright, to petition the House once more on constitutional reform (*CMP* 43–5). He was on the losing side on each occasion.

In January 1812, Byron was in the House when six of George III's physi-
cians – including Dr Matthew Baillie, who had examined Byron's club foot in
1799 – testified to the king's failing state of health, and when extra money was
drafted to the royal household to help manage that situation. On 18 February,
the Prince Regent assumed power, and one of his first acts was a 'Message
Respecting Lord Wellington', delivered to Parliament on 20 February, in Byron's
presence, requesting that Wellington be elevated to the earldom and given a
£2,000 per annum annuity as a reward for his recent success in the Peninsular
War. No modern politician would query the recognition of a military hero,
but the Whig Earl Grosvenor did his best to rain on Wellington's parade, split-
ting hairs over the Regent's description of the general's campaign as 'eminently
beneficial to the interests of the nation'.[37] His objection was politely ignored
and the proposal was passed unanimously.

On the day Byron spoke on Catholic emancipation (21 April 1812) the
other issue before the House was the 'Orders in Council', a set of restraints
on trade established by the Government in 1807 in response to Napoleon's
attempt to destroy the British economy by denying it markets in Europe. As
it happened, Napoleon's 'Continental System' failed in its aim, but the Orders
in Council infuriated the Americans, as they were denied access to European
ports. By 1812, it was apparent that they needed to be repealed, since even
British industrialists were objecting to them, and repealed they were in June
of that year – too late to prevent the Anglo-American war, a Napoleonic sideshow that dragged on until the end of 1814. The conflict was the first and will
presumably remain the last occasion upon which British troops burned down
the White House.

On 18 June 1813, Byron was in the Lords to hear about Indian missions,
more enclosures, and a treaty with Sweden, a mercurial ally in the fight against
Napoleon. On 14 January 1814, accordingly, Britain signed the Treaty of Kiel,
which involved Denmark giving Norway (then not an independent state)
to Sweden with British connivance. The Norwegians objected to this and
declared independence, thus producing another Napoleonic sideshow. On 10
May 1814, with Byron in the chamber, 'the Capo Politico of the remaining
whigs' (*LJ* VIII. 27) and future prime minister, Earl Grey, rose to support the
Norwegians and decry the Government's role in their betrayal. Grey's speech
was long on principle but short on realism. To attack a crucial ally six weeks
after war had been stopped with its help was hardly tactful, and Grey went so
far as to suggest that even if support for 'the honourable and glorious cause
of Norway' meant conflict with Sweden and Russia combined, that support
should be forthcoming. The Government Earl of Harrowby asked the Lords
'to admit a little practical common sense into the discussion'; the independent

Lord Boringdon sympathized with Grey's feelings and concurred with his principles, but could not vote with him; Lord Liverpool doggedly reiterated Government policy; the House divided; and Grey was defeated 34 to 115. He and his friends left a dissentient protest in the Lords' *Journal*, which Byron did not sign. Business for the next day included Wellington's elevation to a dukedom for his continued services in Spain, agreed to overwhelmingly – Byron did not attend.

Napoleon escaped his exile on Elba on 1 March 1815, and the Allies wearily returned to the fray. On 22 May, the Prince Regent wrote to Parliament to announce the collapse of the first Treaty of Paris of 1814 and the need 'of forming such a concert as present circumstances indispensably require, and as may prevent the revival of a system which experience has proved to be incompatible with the peace and independence of the nations of Europe'. The following day Byron was in the Lords to consider the government's response. Liverpool opened proceedings, noting 'the changes which had taken place in the relations and habits of the different states owing to these perpetual wars', and regretting their necessary recurrence, but insisting that Napoleon's 'character' and 'conduct' were such that peace could never be expected from him: 'no Treaty concluded by this person was observed for a moment longer than it suited his convenience'. It had been so difficult 'to produce a general confederacy of the great Powers of Europe' that while that confederacy existed it should be brought to bear on the French. On the basis of long experience, he proposed, 'the nations of Europe could say to France, not what government she should have, but what she should not have'.

Once again Earl Grey came to his feet, for a long disquisition on what we would now call 'just war' theory. He agreed the Treaty of Paris 'has been violated'; but as yet the French had not behaved aggressively, and the 'personal existence and personal character' of Napoleon surely could not constitute a just cause for war. 'Who can say that all change in his character is impossible?', Grey asked – when Napoleon was in fact behaving as he always had, aggressively. 'Has he not during his year of exile had ample opportunity of reflecting on his former errors?', he suggested – when Napoleon had demonstrably not changed his stripes. On the one hand, Grey argued, Britain had much to lose by resuming hostilities; on the other, its triumph had been so complete it had no need to do so. The Government had been warned France was in a disturbed state, but the truth of that might be subject to dispute. After all, was not the French government 'arming the whole population' from 20 to 60'? Was that a sign of social unrest? (Perhaps not; but neither was it a sign of pacifism.) Were not the minor powers looking forward to another round of the war, if only to get more 'of the golden eggs which the great goose of Europe' – that is,

Britain – 'has been laying for some time'? But then again, 'what shall be our situation if the events of the war should induce some of the Powers to fall off from the confederacy?' After which, with the greatest obsequiousness to His Royal Highness, and expressions of all-round patriotism, Grey proposed that the Allies 'may be established on a defensive principle' to await developments.

It was a remarkable performance, which even Grey's Whig partner Lord Grenville could not support. Britain could not desert its allies: 'it was with societies as with individuals, with governments as with men – when they stand in any relation to each other, they must be contented to see their rights regulated with a view to the natural rights of all' – the essence of the Vienna process. In the absence of a United Nations-style 'common authority or tribunal', the 'great transaction' of the Paris treaty must be defended. Napoleon's 'faithlessness and ambition' were proved in the very course he was now bent upon, and Grenville supported the Government – as did the House, 112 to 35, Byron being one of the minority. There is no mention of his decision in his correspondence. Some might call him a dove – others an appeaser.

Summary

The great war of 1793–1815 was a world-historical conflict, with implications for British history that we are only now beginning to fathom. Why then, does its progress figure so fleetingly in the English literature of the time? And why did Byron so signally misunderstand its conclusion and its aftermath?

It is humiliating to note the indifference Romantic writers could express regarding the sacrifice their countrymen were making. '*Nelson was* a hero', Byron was prepared to admit in 1821; but Wellington 'is a mere Corporal' (*LJ* IX. 48). The battle of Vittoria (June 1813) was a turning point in the war: 5,000 soldiers died on each side. All Byron could find to say to Lady Melbourne was: 'this victory! – sad work – nothing but Conquest abroad & High health at home' (*LJ* III. 90). Even Jane Austen, whose brothers served in the Navy, could only remark of another Peninsular battle, Fuentes de Oñoro: 'How horrible it is to have so many people killed! – And what a blessing that one cares for none of them!'[38] Indeed, members of the ruling class were not at all interested in the men fighting in their name. 'The subject of curiosity, of enthusiasm almost, one might say, of the moment [in 1812]', the Duchess of Devonshire wrote to her son in America, 'is not Spain or Portugal, Warriors or Patriots, but Lord Byron! … in short, he is really the only topic almost of conversation – the men jealous of him, the women of each other' (Marchand, 335).

There is a possible explanation for this degree of callousness, and it takes the form of a remarkable statistic: 'only *one* Oxbridge man died in battle during the entire 1792–1815 period: the Hon. Edward Meade of Wadham [College, Oxford], who was killed at the head of the flank company of the 40th Foot at the Aboukir landing on 8 March 1801.'[39] To be educated at either Oxford or Cambridge – as Wordsworth, Coleridge, Shelley, and Byron all were – was almost a precondition for gentility, and the genteel classes were not fighting this war. The British army, in Wellington's memorable phrase, was 'composed of the scum of the earth – the mere scum of the earth'. Their deaths were not recorded, nor did they leave countless bereaved families in the middle and upper classes as the great twentieth-century conflicts were to do.

Not only did the poets have little emotional investment in the outcome of the war; those who were engaged in hostilities were illiterate almost to a man. Betty Bennett claims that 'the war was the primary poetic preoccupation of the age',[40] but her anthology of war poetry in the Romantic age contains almost no poetry by serving men. It is a book of newspaper verse for and against the war, and there is no Edward Thomas, Isaac Rosenberg, or Alun Lewis lurking in its pages. All this speaks volumes about British society and the relation between the classes. Working men died on the battlefield as they did in the sheepfold or the coalmine. Nobody – or nobody with a public voice – cared.

That Byron misunderstood the outcome of the war is also understandable, and not only because he lived in a part of Europe that the settlement did not reach. Historical trends are always matters of hindsight, barely accessible to contemporaries. But in an era of politics without democracy, when governments hardly faced the people at all, when procedural transparency in government was non-existent, and the media were in their infancy, it is hardly surprising that opinion was under-informed. Even the educated classes had no intellectual access to the wars and treaties made in their names.

But there is another reason for Byron's attitude to events after 1815: a grievous sense of inter-generational disappointment. It is easy to note that the likes of Coleridge, Southey, and Wordsworth rejected their early radicalism, and it is easy to follow modern historians as they unpick the myths surrounding 'Pitt's Terror', Napoleon, and the Congress of Vienna. But unquestionably the events of 1789 had unleashed an immense surge of political idealism, to do with freedom, no doubt, but perhaps even more profoundly to do with *change*. 'How much the greatest event it is that ever happened in the world!' Charles James Fox wrote, 'and how much the best!' 'Nothing', said Southey, 'was dreamt of but the regeneration of the human race.' 'Bliss was it in that dawn to be alive,' Wordsworth joined in; 'to be young was very heaven.'

That immense desire for change transplanted itself to Napoleon, Europe's greatest ever self-made man, and outlived his collapse. 'The king-times are fast finishing', Byron wrote in 1821. 'There will be blood shed like water, and tears like mist; but the peoples will conquer in the end. I shall not live to see it, but I foresee it' (*LJ* VIII. 26). Byron's old Harrow schoolmate and future prime minister, Robert Peel, writing in March 1820, was at the centre of things, but even he knew it could not hold. 'Do you not think', he wrote to an associate in government,

> that there is a feeling … in favour of some undefined change in the mode of governing the country? It seems to me a curious crisis – when public opinion never had such influence on public measures, and yet never was so dissatisfied with the share which it possessed. It is growing too large for the channels that it has been accustomed to run through.[41]

The destruction of Napoleon and the restoration of the French royal family must have felt to many like a massive reverse in direction, even if in reality it was a continuation of the deeper trend in events since 1787. Napoleon had lost the war but he won the battle, for hearts and minds at least.

The Romantic movement

Alongside the ideological and military conflicts just described, there raged in Byron's lifetime another one, literary and philosophical, with at least as many implications for Western history: an aesthetic and cognitive revolution we call Romanticism. Byron is often seen as a roving freeshooter in that conflict because he wrote neoclassical plays, admired Pope, and abused Wordsworth and Keats. What does this mean? What is Romanticism?

'I perceive that in Germany as well as in Italy, there is a great struggle about what they call *Classical and Romantic*', Byron wrote in 1820,

> terms which were not subjects of Classification in England – at least when I left it four or five years ago. – Some of the English Scribblers (it is true) abused Pope and Swift – but the reason was that they themselves did not know how to write either prose or verse, but nobody thought them worth making a Sect of.   (*CPW* IV. 546)

So Byron himself knew that some such movement existed. But, as his comment implies, the nature of Romanticism is difficult to establish because it is so diverse. That diversity itself suggests that the movement is a negative reaction, taking many forms: a broad rejection of an existing state of affairs, rather than a development in harmonious accord with it. So definitions of Romanticism frequently start from comparisons with the eighteenth-century Enlightenment, and a conventional account normally begins by comparing rationalism with imagination, and intellect with feeling.

Such comparisons are problematic, however – first and foremost because those are the terms in which Romantic writers themselves wanted such comparisons to be expressed. 'The downfall of the French school of poetry [i.e., the neoclassical, Augustan one associated with poets like Dryden and Pope]', Leigh Hunt wrote in 1818, 'has of late been increasing in rapidity; its cold and artificial compositions have given way, like so many fantastic figures of snow; and imagination breathes again in a more green and genial time.'[42] Critics like Hunt, Wordsworth, Keats, and Hazlitt repeatedly attacked Pope's poetry accordingly, in terms of his perceived lack of imagination. Clearly Byron did not share this view. On the contrary, he held the work of Alexander Pope (1688–1744) in very high regard: not as a 'cold and artificial' writer, but as 'the moral poet of all Civilization' (*CMP* 150). While that remark is a polemical one, it is certainly important to remember that Pope is by no means a simple representative of neoclassical canons of poetry, like order, symmetry, and the hierarchy of genres. His imaginative idiosyncrasy and his ideological grip on his own society (from which he was something of an outsider as a Catholic, just as Byron was as a parvenu) were both too intense for a conventionally Romantic view of him to stand. Hunt's characterization of the 'French school' suggests that there is the danger of seeing Romanticism in terms chosen by itself – though there is also the question of whether we can do anything else, given that we are the intellectual inheritors of Romantic attitudes.

Such an account may be inadequate as well as tendentious. Swift and Pope are as imaginative as any writers in English, and we are now also aware of the seriousness with which eighteenth-century writers discussed emotion, feeling, and passion. Still: narrowing the discussion down either to semantics or particular intellectual categories can lead us into an intellectual thicket, in which we find ourselves agreeing that the Romantic reaction hardly even took place and that there is nothing left to discuss at all.

The rejection of the Enlightenment

Perhaps, considering Byron's work in its historical context, it is best to start with a broad distinction between the Enlightenment and the Romantic eras. The historian of ideas Isaiah Berlin is certainly a revolutionist rather than an evolutionist on this matter. For him, Romanticism is nothing other than 'the largest recent movement to transform the lives and the thought of the Western world.'[43] In his view the Enlightenment rested on three intellectual pillars – 'that all genuine questions can be answered', 'that all these answers are knowable', and 'that all the answers must be compatible with one another' – to which it added a fourth, that 'there is only one way of discovering these

answers, and that is by the correct use of reason,[44] as opposed to (say) tradition or religious belief.

This is not that hyper-rationalist principle of reason associated with
seventeenth-century philosophers like Descartes or Spinoza, but a more practical and socially engaged form of thought – associated with Locke and Hume
in Britain, and with the French group of *philosophes*: Voltaire, Montesquieu,
Diderot, Rousseau, and others. The latter group laid the foundations of social
analysis, in books like Montesquieu's *The Spirit of the Laws* (1748), Voltaire's
Essay on the Customs and Spirit of Nations (1756), and Rousseau's *Discourse on
the Origin of Inequality* (1755). The most momentous outcomes of the movement were the American Declaration of Independence (1776) and the French-
Revolutionary Declaration of the Rights of Man and the Citizen (1789), as well
as the thirty-five-volume *Encyclopédie* published in France between 1751 and
1772 – emphatically a book which claimed all questions to be answerable in
consistent and rational terms. The Enlightenment idea of reason was practical,
optimistic, and universalist, with a profound belief in the power of education
and the reform of social abuses like feudalism and religious superstition.

For Isaiah Berlin, the Romantic movement can be said to assert itself only if
and when those four intellectual convictions – that questions can be answered,
that answers can be known, that all knowledge is commensurate, and that reason is the clue to it – are actively rejected in their entirety. There can be no
smooth transition from one set of views to another, only outright rejection,
and this Berlin found first in the writings of an obscure Prussian cleric, Johann
Georg Hamann (1730–88), whose ideas he summarizes as follows:

> If you asked yourself what were men after, what did men really want,
> you would see that what they wanted was not at all what Voltaire
> supposed they wanted. Voltaire thought they wanted happiness,
> contentment, peace, but this was not true. What men wanted was for all
> their faculties to play in the richest and most violent possible fashion.
> What men wanted was to create, what men wanted was to make, and
> if this led to clashes, if it led to wars, if it led to struggles, then this
> was part of the human lot. A man who had been put in the Voltairean
> garden, pared and pruned, who had been brought up by some wise
> *philosophe* in knowledge of physics and chemistry and mathematics,
> and in knowledge of all the sciences which the Encylopaedists had
> recommended – such a man would be a form of death in life.[45]

The Enlightenment proposed that a linked set of significant questions existed
regarding nature and humanity, with a linked set of answers awaiting them.
Sometimes those answers would vary in detail, according to culture, as
Montesquieu suggested. Sometimes those answers demonstrated themselves

empirically, by experience, rather than rationally, within the intellect, as Hume pointed out. But the important questions were there, and the answers existed, all the same. The Romantic movement, by contrast, did not merely reject the function of reason in that intellectual process. *It rejected the process altogether.* The number of questions are illimitable, the answers various, obscure, and incommensurable, and the place of reason questionable, to say the least. The diversity of Romanticism is not incidental to its rejection of Enlightenment, but fundamental to it.

This led Romanticism to a profound intellectual conclusion: that *what* you believed mattered less than the intensity, integrity, and authenticity of your belief. This was an affront not only to religion and tradition – the Enlightenment had already affronted those – but to Renaissance and Enlightenment varieties of intellectual faith, too.

> Clearly something occurred to have shifted consciousness to this degree, away from the notion that there are universal truths, universal canons of art, that all human activities were meant to terminate in getting things right, and that the criteria of getting things right were public, were demonstrable, that all intelligent men by applying their intellects would discover them – away from that to a wholly different attitude towards life, and towards action.[46]

Berlin can explain a good deal on the basis of Hamann's example. First, he asks us to look deeper than literary or stylistic factors. So where some historians have argued that Romanticism had its origins in the England of the 1750s, Berlin asks us to test such writings by the degree to which they reject the principles of the Enlightenment, not the degree to which they merely mourn their failure. Such a test allows us to distinguish between the intellectual pessimism we see in mid-eighteenth-century English writers like Samuel Johnson and Thomas Gray and the intellectual rebellion we see in people like Hamann. It also allows us to distinguish writers in the Romantic period still loyal to the principles of the Enlightenment (say, William Godwin and Mary Wollstonecraft) from others who rejected them.

Second, Berlin's analysis sets a pattern. Hamann was an obscure writer, the product of the mid-century religious revival in Germany and a personal conversion. If we look in England for a comparable figure we can go nowhere else but to William Blake: the even more obscure product of a religious revival and a religious conscience, with an intellectual outlook strikingly similar to Hamann's own. When similar conditions arose elsewhere a similar result was brought about, and if there was a place where such conditions arose only in a partial way, then the local reaction would be fainter or more confused.

Furthermore, individuals of a pronounced spiritual turn, like Hamann and Blake, were allergenic to the Enlightenment, and reacted first, like canaries in a mineshaft. With the passage of time, others – like Goethe and Schiller, Wordsworth and Coleridge – also felt that reaction setting in, in intellectual and creative terms.

Britain, Germany, France

To see Romanticism in this way allows us to make comparisons between Germany, Britain, and France, and between the natures of three cultures so close to one another and yet so far apart as regards politics, religion, literature, and history. Eighteenth-century Britain and France possessed literary traditions similar in strength but different in kind, the former being gluttonous and lackadaisical, the latter being intensely self-conscious and much given to neoclassicism. By contrast, Germany in the time of Hamann felt itself hardly to have a literature at all. Its national identity was something it yearned for, whereas England was the first independent state of modern Europe. England had experienced a prolonged bout of religious radical sectarianism throughout the seventeenth century, and when a religious revival came at the end of the eighteenth century it was much gentler than that experienced by Germany forty years before. France, by contrast, went in a matter of years after 1789 from state Catholicism to state deism.

The resulting pattern permits us to say that, culturally speaking, eighteenth-century Britain was a country to be found somewhere between France and Germany. In political terms it was the inheritor of a strong tradition (compared to Germany) but a liberal one (compared to France). In religious terms it experienced a revival similar to but gentler than Germany's (whereas France took a headlong dive into secularism). In literary terms it retained a tolerance for novelty (compared to France) going along with a sense of traditional self-assurance (compared to Germany).

So the three countries' Romantic reactions played themselves out. The German movement is marked by that intensity we call German Idealism: philosophically as radical in its concept of the self as it was politically radical in its concept of the state. France experienced the opposite of a religious revival and underwent a massive political change based on Enlightenment principles that a series of monarchical restorations after 1815 never wholly extinguished. Its Romanticism is therefore delayed, depends greatly on external influences (Byron and Constable, for example), and is essentially formal: more a question of changing the guard at a tutelary academy than destroying the academy itself. The British experience appears to be that of deep-seated literary and intellectual traditions – particularly the empirical one, loosely defined, which includes not only Bacon, Hobbes, Locke, and Newton, but Chaucer and Shakespeare, too – given a profound stimulus by a reaction to Enlightenment values, even while those same traditions acted as a counterweight to the development of a German-style philosophical or political radicalism. 'France after 1789', art historian Andrew Graham-Dixon argues, 'was a revolutionary nation with a conservative culture. Britain after 1789 was a conservative nation with a revolutionary culture.'[47]

Britain: a reactionary revolution?

The historian Dror Wahrman has recently provided an examination of eighteenth-century English attitudes that adds a broader, cultural dimension to that intellectual rejection of the Enlightenment described by Isaiah Berlin, and helps solve Andrew Graham-Dixon's paradox of a conservative nation possessing a revolutionary culture. What he documents is the collapse in England of what he calls 'the *ancien régime* of identity'.[48] The modern, post-Romantic self is 'one that presupposes an essential core of selfhood characterized by psychological depth, or interiority, which is the bedrock of unique, expressive individual identity'. The eighteenth-century self, by contrast, 'could be imagined as unfixed and potentially changeable – sometimes perceived as double, other times as sheddable, replaceable or moldable'.[49]

In particular, Wahrman finds that the eighteenth century made few fixed or automatic links between the essences and the appearances of identity. The *ancien régime* of identity knew that men and women were different, but it was remarkably unconcerned by those individuals who flouted that boundary by cross-dressing or in other ways. In short, the connection between sex and gender was not automatic. The same applied to the connection between race and civilization, or that between class and politics. Every individual was a member of a given order – male or female, white or black, ruling or working class – but the individual could jump such boundaries more easily than we might expect. Precisely because the Enlightenment had a strong faith in humanity's ultimate access to reason, it was not too concerned about the paths individuals pursued. All roads would lead (so to speak) to Rome in the end.

Then the picture alters dramatically. There is a 'sea change in the last two decades of the eighteenth century', bringing with it a 'new, alternative identity regime ... defined by a fundamental emphasis on self', and initiating 'a far-reaching pattern of historical change, one that may even be described as a "cultural revolution"'.[50] There was a 'shift from mutability to essence, from imaginable fluidity to fixity, from the potential for individual deviation from general identity categories to an individual identity stamped indelibly on each and every person.'[51] Dramas featuring cross-dressing heroines, for example, popular in the *ancien régime*, practically disappear in the later period, or when they are revived they are met with disgust and disbelief. The virtues of modesty, chastity, and motherhood are almost hysterically asserted in advice-books for young women. Tolerantly curious attitudes to other peoples – visible, for example, in the Pacific journals of Captain Cook (written between 1769 and 1779) – are suddenly swallowed in missionary fervour to save 'dark races', or colonial fervour to control them. The mob and the ruling elite come to be seen as unbridgeably opposed.

This shift was a reactionary one: a mark of anxiety about social change, military failure, and loss of prestige. Wahrman finds the watershed for it in Britain's loss of its American colonies by 1783. Anxiety brought in its wake a political rigidification throughout the culture, from which Byron's Whigs, with their 'Regency' attitudes, would suffer acutely. 'In the half-century after the American war,' Linda Colley writes,

> there would emerge in Great Britain a far more consciously and officially constructed patriotism which stressed attachment to the monarchy, the importance of empire, the value of military and naval achievement, and the desirability of strong, stable government by a virtuous, able and authentically British élite.[52]

Colley provides a small but telling example of the response that she charts in her study as a whole: 'Between George III's accession in 1760 and 1781, the records of the London theatres show that "God Save the King" received only four formal performances. Over the next twenty years, however, it was to rise to more than ninety performances.'[53] 'In a nutshell', Boyd Hilton writes, 'the American debacle discredited the [Whiggish] aristocracy and created a moral vacuum, which the moralistic upper-middle classes were able to fill.'[54] Byron's aristocratic ethos and his cultural tolerance were indeed reminiscent of eighteenth-century culture (which makes him look like an anomalous Romantic). But the one he never really owned, and the other he converted into a far more radical position than that of Hume or Montesquieu.

The most prodigious result of this transformation in the final decades of the eighteenth century was the arrival of the British class system, and in particular its middle class. It was the period of the making of the working class, too, but middle-class consciousness arose first and more rapidly because the instruments of literacy and of communication (generally withheld from working people) expanded at an unprecedented rate at this time.

Behind the scenes where both the moral crisis after the American war and the middle-class agitation in response to it were concerned was the evangelical revival, dragging Britons out of the liberal world of the Enlightenment. 'Spirit of *Hume*, the subtil; spirit of *Rousseau*, the fanciful; spirit of *Voltaire*, the cowardly tho' daring', the Nonconformist divine Thomas Pentycross wrote in 1796: 'tell us, what can you suggest for the happiness of the World equivalent to the Gospel?'[55] People like Pentycross had a hatred of the Enlightenment as visceral if not as sophisticated as Hamann's, and wanted a complete religious regeneration.

For historian Gordon Rattray Taylor, this set of reactions is a matter of nothing less than a 'new moral attitude' in Britain, which we call 'Victorian' but which 'was achieved long before Victoria came to the throne in 1838'. 'Everything points to the fact', Taylor concludes, 'that the period of decisive moral change was not at the time of Victoria's accession, or even in the nineteenth century at all, but that it took place during the decade 1790–1800.'[56] Some Romantic writers (Wordsworth, Coleridge, Scott, Austen) swam with that tide; others (Blake, Hazlitt, Shelley, Byron) swam against it. But neither group reverted to the four pillars of Enlightenment thought described by Isaiah Berlin. Those beliefs had sunk beneath the waves, and if reform and republicanism were to be argued for it could not be on the basis of that suite of intellectual and political verities established by the American Declaration of Independence: 'We hold these truths to be *self-evident* … '. There was nothing self-evident in the Romantic world order.

In March 1820, we find Byron's emphatically middle-class publisher dropping a hint to his star author about the poet's moral drift from the standards of his readers. Byron's latter-day works, he pointed out – *Manfred, Beppo, Don Juan* – were in danger of becoming as anachronistic as Restoration drama. 'The Comedies of Charles Seconds days', John Murray wrote,

> are not tolerated now – and even in my Own time I have gradually seen my favourite Love for Love absolutely pushed by public feeling – from the stage – it is not affectation of morality but the real progress and result of refinement – and our minds can no more undergo the moral & religious grossness of our predecessors than our bodies can sustain the heavy Armour which they wore.[57]

A firmer claim could hardly be made for ownership of 'progress' and 'refinement': those quintessentially Victorian social values that Byron would flout so energetically in his later poetry.

With the exception of Blake, the first generation of English Romantic writers – not to mention the painter, John Constable – all came to take an identifiably middle-class view of the world, even if some had started out as radicals. It is a striking fact that the second generation tended to be either aristocrats like Byron and Shelley or 'classless' bohemians like Keats and Leigh Hunt. In the second generation we see an anti-middle-class reaction. But it sputtered out, the great poets of the second generation dying in obscurity, in exile, or (in Shelley's case) both. Byron's case is a particularly illustrative one of a poet doing everything in his power to bite the middle-class hand that had fed him at the outset of his career.

The practical, optimistic, rationalist centre in which the Enlightenment had taken its stand was exposed to a pessimist, individualist, and determinist reaction in both generations of British Romantic writers. 'We receive but what we give', Coleridge wrote (in 'Dejection: An Ode'), 'And in our life alone does Nature live.' 'Have I not reason to lament', Wordsworth added (in 'Lines Written in Early Spring'), 'What man has made of man?' Keats, too (in the 'Ode to a Nightingale'), lamented 'The weariness, the fever, and the fret / Here, where men sit and hear each other groan', and Shelley (in the 'Ode to the West Wind') was even more melodramatic: 'I fall upon the thorns of life! I bleed!' As we shall see, Byron played as great a role as any other Romantic writer in making this new world, and in coming to terms with it.

Summary

How is a phenomenon as various as Romanticism best approached? First, we should look deeper than styles and attitudes, or we will become ensnared on trivial issues, or confused by non-indicative markers. (Many Romantics disparaged Pope; Byron admired him. Both positions are consistent with a rejection of the Enlightenment, with which Pope himself was only half a fellow traveller.) Second, we must acknowledge that the Romantic movement is indeed a profound one, upsetting and inverting not just styles of art and literature but the entire European intellectual tradition since the Renaissance, with its emphasis on reasonable approaches to coherent problems. (Accordingly, we should not be surprised if Romantics fail to offer a united front, but argue with each other constantly.) Third, this deep-seated rejection of Enlightenment thought was accompanied in England by a reactionary cultural shift that was determinist, moralistic, anti-aristocratic, and patriotic – a shift that became entwined with Britain's entire attitude to France and the 'French Wars'. Fourth, there came in the second generation of English Romantic writers a reaction against the reaction, so to speak, as a group that saw the Allies as sources of oppression rather than a defence against the threat from France. But though writers like Byron, Shelley, and Hazlitt found much to favour in French Revolutionary ideals, there was not and could not be a return to the Enlightenment ethos. European radical politics would adapt to that fact in due course, and move from the language of Enlightenment idealism to the language of class struggle. But European art, literature, and thought had shifted away irreversibly from neoclassicism. Byron was not given to philosophical statements or acts of literary criticism (his attempts in that line are reprinted in *CMP* 88–183), but in creative terms his work is a rejection of the four pillars of Enlightenment thought as emphatic as that of Wordsworth or Coleridge.

Finally, to see the Romantic movement in the terms proposed by Berlin and Wahrman may prevent readers getting impaled on abstractions like Imagination and Nature, the terms of which hardly suit Byron's contribution. Byron is notorious for his comments on Keats, with his '*p-ss a bed* poetry', which he called 'a sort of mental masturbation – he is always f[ri]gg[in]g his Imagination' (*LJ* VII. 200, 225). He was similarly curt with the poet he liked to call 'Turdsworth': 'that pedlar-praising son of a bitch' (*LJ* XI. 198). But the feelings were mutual. Keats called Byron a 'careless hectorer in proud bad verse' in his 'Fall of Hyperion', and wrote to his brother and sister that Byron 'describes what he sees – I describe what I imagine – Mine is the hardest task.' 'What a monster is a Man of Genius whose heart is perverted', Wordsworth joined in.[58] These three Romantics need not agree with one another any more than with Coleridge, Shelley, Blake, or Austen; but for none of them was a return to the Enlightenment a possibility in intellectual, psychological, or political terms. What Byron made of that situation – and what it made of him – is what we must turn to next.

Chapter 3

The letters and journals

Even if Byron's poems had never existed he would remain a classic author. Alongside Pepys's diary (1660–9) and Boswell's journals (1762–95), his letters and journals constitute one of the three most significant informal autobiographies in English. There are other great letter-writers in English literature (such as John Keats, Charles Dickens, Henry James, Robert Louis Stevenson, D. H. Lawrence, and Virginia Woolf), and there are European writers whose correspondences match them (Madame de Sévigné, Gustave Flaubert, and Vincent van Gogh, to name but a few). But none of these possesses the range, vigour, and immediacy of Byron's informal prose.

Byron's formal prose, by comparison, is less successful. 'Byron's prose is bad', Hazlitt wrote; 'that is to say, heavy, laboured, and coarse'[1] – and, as a rule, he is right. (What Hazlitt knew were Byron's prefaces to his various poetical works, as well as his contributions to the 'Bowles/Pope' literary-critical controversy of 1821: see *CMP* 12–83.) When Thomas Moore published his *Letters and Journals of Lord Byron, with Notices of His Life* (1830), therefore, readers were surprised and (generally) gratified by what they found. 'The extracts from the journals and correspondence of Lord Byron,' the historian Thomas Babington Macaulay wrote in his review of Moore's biography, 'are in the highest degree valuable – not merely on account of the information which they contain respecting the distinguished man by whom they were written, but on account, also, of their rare merit as compositions.' 'If the epistolary style of Lord Byron was artificial,' Macaulay concluded, 'it was a rare and admirable instance of that highest art, which cannot be distinguished from nature.'[2]

Macaulay's commendation has gathered weight in the nearly 200 years since he offered it. 'There is no more Shakespearian writing in English', critic George Wilson Knight wrote, 'than the prose of Byron's letters and journals', and certainly when Ruskin said Byron wrote 'as easily as a hawk flies and as clearly as a lake reflects', it was his letters he had in mind as much as his poetry.[3] A reviewer of Leslie Marchand's twelve-volume edition of the *Letters and Journals* (1973–82) was emphatic: 'No one … need doubt', Michael Ratcliffe wrote in *The Times*, 'that the letters, perhaps even more than *Don Juan*, are the beginning, middle, and the end of Lord Byron.'[4]

'This other Byron'

Byron's letters raise a larger issue, which is also brought out in a review of Marchand's edition. 'The letter-writer and the author of *Beppo*, *The Vision of Judgment* and *Don Juan* are clearly the same person', the Australian poet Peter Porter wrote; 'but what of the Byron who thrilled his contemporaries and inspired poets in every European language – the legend-maker who wrote *Childe Harold*, *The Corsair* and *Manfred*?' 'Reading the letters in their full and uncensored texts', Porter went on,

> establishes the realistic Byron even more completely, and widens the gap between our appreciation of the man and of the romantic poet. But it also helps give shape to the otherwise haphazard pattern of his life – his true progress being the coming together of the man of the correspondence with the poet, until in *Don Juan* he writes poetry even more succinct, stylish and life-like than the prose he had always written in his letters.[5]

We should be cautious about divisions between the 'realistic' man and the 'romantic' poet, or between the 'haphazard pattern' and the 'true progress' of his life and art. But Porter had gone beyond Michael Ratcliffe's simple preference for the letters, and outlined a significant case: that there is a gap between the 'realistic' correspondent and the 'romantic' poet, and that the true progress of Byron's talent was one in which that gap eventually disappeared.

The Byron of the twenty-first century is not that of the nineteenth. As things stood when Moore's documentary biography was published, the public image of Byron was in marked conflict with many of the letters made available there. For most of his readers in 1830, Byron was Porter's 'legend-maker': a figure of gloom, introspection, and romantic affliction, trailing 'the pageant of his bleeding heart' across continental Europe (as Matthew Arnold put it in his

'Stanzas from the Grande Chartreuse') before meeting a heroic end in Greece. This was the source of his spell. Macaulay described the effect his poetry typically had on impressionable young people:

> The number of hopeful under-graduates and medical students who became things of dark imaginings, – on whom the freshness of the heart ceased to fall like dew, – whose passions had consumed themselves to dust, and to whom the relief of tears was denied, passes all calculation.[6]

This aspect of Byron's appeal was ruthlessly parodied by Dickens in the persons of Dick Swiveller, from *The Old Curiosity Shop*, and William Guppy, from *Bleak House*, as late as 1841 and 1853, respectively. ('My boat is on the shore and my bark is on the sea, but before I pass this door I will say farewell to thee', Swiveller murmurs gloomily to his chosen one, Sophy Wackles, channelling the poet's 'To Thomas Moore' of 1817.)

Byron's letters made the Guppy–Swiveller model of the poet as a man consumed by dark imaginings suddenly obsolete. Indeed, they provided evidence for a case made later in the nineteenth century by the Danish critic Georg Brandes. All that was in *Childe Harold*, he wrote, 'is certainly Byron, but there was in him, along with this, another and perfectly different man; and it was not until he wrote *Don Juan* that he succeeded in introducing this other Byron, as he lived and thought and spoke, into his poetry.'[7] To those raised on Byron's earlier verse, the author of the letters must indeed have seemed 'another and perfectly different man'.

Brandes was at the end of a long line of people who shared that experience of Byron – many of them at first hand. Again and again individuals making Byron's acquaintance recorded their surprise that the man who published such introspective and melodramatic poems was such an outgoing individual in real life. 'Byron's suavity of manner surprised and delighted me', recollected one such witness; 'my own previous conceptions, supported by common rumour, having prepared me to expect to find in him a man of morose temper and gloomy misanthropy, instead of which, from his fecundity in anecdote, he was a most delightful associate.'[8] In the preface to his poem about their relationship, *Julian and Maddalo*, Shelley commented on Byron's 'concentred and impatient feelings', while noting that 'in social life no human being can be more gentle, patient, and unassuming.'[9] Shelley's friend Edward Williams was similarly surprised: 'far from his being (as is generally imagined) wrapt in a melancholy gloom he is all sunshine, and good humour with which the elegance of his language and the brilliancy of his wit cannot fail to inspire those who are near him' (Marchand, 945).

'Of the sort of double aspect which he thus presented, as viewed by the world and by his friends,' Moore wrote, Byron 'was himself fully aware.'[10] 'I perceive by part of your last letter – that you are still inclined to believe me a very gloomy personage', he wrote to his future wife in November 1813; 'still I look upon myself as a facetious companion – well respected by all the Wits [of contemporary London] – at whose jests I readily laugh' (*LJ* III. 159). He puzzled an American visitor in 1821, 'from his having expected to meet a misanthropical gentleman, in wolf-skin breeches, and answering in fierce monosyllables, instead of a man of this world' (*LJ* VIII. 146).

A potential explanation of this 'double aspect' was that the facetiousness was a disguise for the gloom. 'People have wondered at the Melancholy which runs through my writings', Byron wrote (to himself, in one of his journals). 'Others have wondered at my personal gaiety.' He then recollected his wife telling him 'at *heart* you are the most melancholy of mankind, and often when apparently gayest' (*LJ* IX. 38). Thomas Moore was so perplexed by his friend's double aspect that he wondered if the poetry was in fact sincere. 'Finding him invariably thus lively when we were together, I often rallied him on the gloomy tone of his poetry, as assumed; but his constant answer was … that, though thus merry and full of laughter with those he liked, he was, at heart, one of the most melancholy wretches in existence.'[11]

The clichéd and hyperbolic qualities of this explanation make it unconvincing, but whether or not the one was only a disguise for the other, what Moore called 'the two extremes, between which his own character … so singularly vibrated'[12] were dominant polarities in his life and art, as any reader who turns from *Childe Harold* to *Don Juan* will soon discover. No reader of Byron can ignore the powerful contrasts between those two poems (despite their profound aesthetic affinities), or those between the poems that made him famous, and the worldly and humorous letters that shared houseroom with them. Nor will many readers deny that by the end of his career the author of the letters and the author of the poetry were in large measure reconciled, and that the site of that reconciliation was *Don Juan*.

Two principles of Byronism?

Byron's imagination, it seems, was governed by, and in turn provokes in his readers, considerations of two kinds. On the one hand, we see him or his fictional alter egos as individuals afflicted by a sense of social isolation, in personal, political, and sexual terms. This condition is dramatized intermittently but insistently throughout *Childe Harold's Pilgrimage* (especially in Cantos I–III), in the Eastern Tales set in the Mediterranean, in *Manfred* (1816–17), and in other writings right up to *Cain* (1821) and *The Island* (1823). In such writings the poet and his chief protagonists feel themselves to be cursed by an inexpiable fate or destiny, producing an ongoing sense of crisis and moral tension.

But Byron also reveals himself to be someone possessing attitudes more or less the reverse of those just described: as someone who saw human life in terms of moral and cultural diversity – a state of affairs suggesting that individuals and their inevitable moral failings should be regarded with acceptance and toleration. Here the stress falls not on what marks out the individual as such but on what individuals have in common with humanity at large. This latter principle asserts itself up to a point and in certain ways in the fourth canto of *Childe Harold* and his neoclassical dramas; almost completely in his later comic masterpieces, *Beppo*, *The Vision of Judgment*, and *Don Juan*; and in most of his letters. Byron's output grew towards that tolerant, humane, morally lenient point of view, even as it was occasionally punctuated or perforated by the earlier, 'Byronic' disposition, which was not something that ever disappeared.

If readers were looking for a period in Byron's writing life when both these principles manifested themselves, I would suggest the year 1817 and the poems *Manfred* and *Beppo*. Both works concern sexual misdemeanours, but there the similarities between them end. The Alpine drama is a tormented and guilt-ridden confession of sexual crime; the Venetian tale is a light-hearted and indulgent depiction of an incipient *ménage-à-trois*. The first poem nearly ends in suicide, the second ends in a cup of coffee. Indeed, *Mazeppa* (also 1817) contrives to fold one sort of narrative inside the other: a story of adulterous love and revenge is framed by its protagonist nostalgically and humorously recounting it to his monarch after a defeat in battle.

The one way of looking at the world is tragic and melodramatic, the other is comic and tends to burlesque – but both are complicated. The tragic mode, for example, makes much of social isolation and misanthropy, but at the same time it exploits a deep sense of theatrical complicity and authorial display as far as readers are concerned. Byron knows he is being seen within and behind his fictional creations in *Childe Harold* and the Eastern Tales, and exploits this situation for maximum effect, even as he warns his readers that the dark secrets his poems contain are too scandalous to tell. The comic mode, too, can come up against the realization that it is too morally tolerant to be fully convincing as a way of life or a comment on it. It is a position that underwrites humour and understanding in particularly successful ways – as we shall see in discussing *Don Juan* in Chapter 8 – but it is tested by Christian virtues as well as by psychological reality.

These two principles will manifest themselves in the poetry to be discussed in chapters to come, but there are two remarks worth making immediately. First, these two 'positions' are themselves symbiotic and mutually dependent. On the one hand, there is a tragic sense of personal dread and inescapable fatality; on the other, there is a comic assertion of human solidarity and exoneration. Each position is the antithesis of the other, and each comments on and delimits the other. Second, it is important to remember that this distinction is not a key to all the poet's mythologies, or a short cut, or an open sesame. Byron is too complicated a personality and a writer for any neat formulas to catch him. But these two ways of understanding his experience (between melodramatic dread and comic relief, as one might say) do recur, alternate, and merge in his work. To study his letters and journals at the outset is to get a sense of that aspect of his writing as a whole.

'The absolute monarch of words'

The 'most conspicuous quality' of Byron's letters, it has been said, 'is their spontaneity. Never, we feel, can written utterance have been less premeditated, less rehearsed, less inhibited, less controlled.'[13] But the impression Byron's letters leave, even at their most exuberant, is not exactly that of unpremeditated, unrehearsed, uninhibited, uncontrolled utterance. 'I am not a cautious letter-writer', he suggested, 'and generally say what comes uppermost at the moment' (*LJ* X. 33). Significantly, he made the same remark with respect to *Don Juan*, of which he said, 'I write what's uppermost, without delay' – indeed, 'I rattle on exactly as I'd talk / With any body in a ride or walk' (*DJ* XIV. 53, XV. 151–2). But 'rattling on' hardly testifies to Byron's preternatural capacity to *transform* 'what comes uppermost' into a rhetorical pattern preserving both spontaneity and design, in his letters and his poetry alike. His letters share with his poetry – all of it, and not just his comic output – an extraordinary talent for what I can only call 'phrase-making': an intuitive ability rhetorically to produce, repeat, and explore verbal patterns.

Consider a letter from the 19-year-old in London to his young friend, Elizabeth Pigot ('My dear *Elisabat*'), at home in Southwell, Nottinghamshire, which shows that ability at full pelt. 'The Intelligence of London', he wrote, 'cannot be interesting to you who *have rusticated* all your life':

> the annals of Routs, Riots, Balls & Boxing matches, Dowagers &
> demi-rep[utable]s, Cards & Crim-con ['criminal conversation': a legal
> euphemism for adultery], Parliamentary Discussion, Political Details,
> Masquerades, Mechanics, Argyle Street Institution & Aquatic races,

Love & Lotteries, Brookes's & Buonaparte, Exhibitions of pictures with Drapery, & *women without*; Statues with more *decent dresses*, than their *originals*, Opera-singers & Orators, Wine, Women, Wax works, & Weathercocks, cannot accord with your *insulated* Ideas, of Decorum & other *silly expressions*, not inserted in our *Vocabulary*.   (*LJ* I. 127)

The percussive alliterative rhythm builds to an absurd climax in 'Wine, Women, Wax works, & Weathercocks', and so the writer's assertion of cosmopolitan social exclusivity – 'you who *have rusticated* all your life' – collapses into bathos. The effect is poetic: highly contrived but leaving an impression of spontaneity – 'that highest art,' in Macaulay's words, 'which cannot be distinguished from nature.'

Such patterns, rhetorical and poetic, were Byron's creative addiction. At the other end of his life, a matter of weeks before he died, his prose still falls into poetic rhythms at will, just as his poetry falls into prosaic ones. 'Excuse haste', he wrote to his Greek banker from Missolonghi; 'It is late – and I have been several hours on horseback – in a country so miry after the rains – that every hundred yards brings you to a brook or a ditch – of whose depth – width – colour – and contents – both my horses and their riders have brought away many tokens' (*LJ* XI. 141). *Of whose dépth, wídth, cólour and cóntents* is almost an octosyllabic tetrameter: four stressed sounds tripping neatly (if irregularly) across nine syllables – like *wíne, wómen, wáxworks, and wéathercócks*, in fact.

Byron's vernacular prose style was an element in which his view of the world floated throughout his writing life: 'I see not much difference between ourselves & the Turks', he wrote at sea in May 1810,

> save that we have foreskins and they none, that they have long dresses and we short, and that we talk much and they little. – In England the vices in fashion are whoring & drinking, in Turkey, Sodomy & smoking, we prefer a girl and a bottle, they a pipe and pathic [a boy employed for homosexual sex].   (*LJ* I. 238)

This passage – in which syntactic and musical patterns rise, fall, and recur with prodigious ease – employs what we might call the rhetoric of reductionist egalitarianism. There is no meaningful difference between the items listed, as their phonemic similarity itself demonstrates. Differences between 'we' and 'they', 'they' and 'we', are similarly superficial. Whoring and sodomy, drinking and smoking, girl and pathic, pipe and bottle are all the same in terms of utility and in the light of experience. *Don Juan* is largely built out of such acts of moral and cultural deflation:

> Well – well, the world must turn upon its axis,
>   And all mankind turn with it, heads or tails,

And live and die, make love and pay our taxes,
    And as the veering wind shifts, shift our sails;
The king commands us, and the doctor quacks us,
    The priest instructs, and so our life exhales,
A little breath, love, wine, ambition, fame,
Fighting, devotion, dust, – perhaps a name.   (*DJ* II. 25–32)

Crucially, Byron employs this rhetoric to affront and confront moral complacency and cultural ethnocentrism – particularly that of his countrymen. It comes as no surprise, therefore, that he associated that rhetoric with the reality of worldly experience and the poem that celebrated it: *Don Juan*. When one of John Murray's editorial cronies objected to *Don Juan* that in reality 'we are never scorched and drenched at one time' – whereas the poem goes out of its way to celebrate the coincidences and contradictions of daily life – Byron delivered an astonishing broadside:

> Blessings on his experience! Ask him these questions about 'scorching and drenching'. – Did he never play at Cricket or walk a mile in hot weather? – did he never spill a dish of tea over his testicles in handing the cup to his charmer to the great shame of his nankeen breeches? – did he never swim in the sea at Noonday with the Sun in his eyes and on his head – which all the foam of ocean could not cool? did he never draw his foot out of a tub of too hot water damning his eyes & his valet's? did he never inject for a Gonorrhea? – or make water through an ulcerated Urethra? – was he never in a Turkish bath – that marble paradise of sherbet and sodomy?   (*LJ* VI. 207)

And so forth. Comic escalation and deflation competes here with an increasing degree of imaginative specificity, and a rampant appeal to experiences inherently unlikely to be shared by the critic he is lampooning: namely, Francis Cohen, scholar of medieval history, and later the editor of Palgrave's *Golden Treasury* of English verse (1861), stored on every Victorian parlour bookshelf. (The *Golden Treasury* contains a good deal of Byron – but nothing from *Don Juan*.)

Don Juan and this particular element in the letters coalesce again when Byron defended the comic mode in which he was writing for the benefit of his friend, Douglas Kinnaird:

> As to 'Don Juan' – confess – confess – you dog – and be candid – that it is the sublime of *that there* sort of writing – it may be bawdy – but is it not good English? – it may be profligate – but is it not *life*, is it not *the thing*? – Could any man have written it – who has not lived in the world? – and tooled in a post-chaise? in a hackney coach? in a Gondola? against a wall? in a court carriage? in a vis a vis? on a table? and under it?   (*LJ* VI. 232)

Byron's act of literary-critical self-defence is provocatively coarse, but that is not all it is. Many wheeled vehicles are listed here, presenting all sorts of challenges to sexual congress, from a humble hackney-cab to a court carriage (with a two-person vis-à-vis and a public post-chaise thrown in for good measure), so the claim is based on the author's social experience as well as his sexual history. Like its author, *Don Juan* presents itself as a poem familiar with all such things, and more besides: 'you have so many *"divine"* poems,' Byron protested; 'is it nothing to have written a *Human* one?' (*LJ* VI. 105.)

'One should see every thing once'

Catalogues such as these remind us of Lady Byron's comment to the effect that Byron 'is the absolute monarch of words, and uses them, as Bonaparte did lives, for conquest'.[14] If this were all Byron's prose amounted to its appeal would be deep but narrow. He also possessed a striking capacity for moral insight, again giving the supremely artistic effect of unmediated, unpondered transparency. 'The day before I left Rome I saw three robbers guillotined', he told John Murray in May 1817:

> the ceremony – including the *masqued* priests – the half-naked executioners – the bandaged criminals – the black Christ & his banner – the scaffold – the soldiery – the slow procession – & the quick rattle and heavy fall of the axe – the splash of the blood – & the ghastliness of the exposed heads – is altogether more impressive than the vulgar and ungentlemanly dirty 'new drop' & dog-like agony of infliction upon the sufferers of the English sentence.

This is an instance of Byron's appetite for cultural comparison, which we shall see in full-scale operation in works like *Beppo* (in Chapter 6) as well as *Don Juan*. It is also an instance of his prodigious mimetic gift in turns of phrase like 'quick rattle and heavy fall' – expressions which render the action of a guillotine almost audible. 'Two of these men', Byron went on,

> behaved calmly enough – but the first of the three – died with great terror and reluctance – which was very horrible – he would not lie down – then his neck was too large for the aperture – and the priest was obliged to drown his exclamations by still louder exhortations – the head was cut off before the eye could trace the blow – but from an attempt to draw back the head – notwithstanding it was held forward by the hair – the first head was cut off close to the ears – the other two were taken off more cleanly … The pain seems little – & yet the effect to the spectator – & the preparation to the criminal – is very striking

& chilling. – The first turned me quite hot and thirsty – & made me shake so that I could hardly hold the opera-glass (I was close – but was determined to see – as one should see every thing once – with attention) the second and third (which shows how dreadfully soon things grow indifferent) I am ashamed to say had no effect on me – as a horror – though I would have saved them if I could. – – It is some time since I heard from you – the *12th April* I believe.   (*LJ* V. 229–30)

As a meditation on 'how dreadfully soon things grow indifferent' the passage could hardly be improved upon – right down to the shocking detail of the opera-glass at its climax, and the cursory change of subject at its end. The letter is *about* things growing indifferent, and becomes so itself; it possesses a candour travelling along the verge of the repellent, but never quite crossing it.

'There is something so incomprehensible about death,' Byron wrote, 'that I can neither speak or think on the subject' (*LJ* II. 69) – which was by no means true. Death was an event and phenomenon that his humanism was always troubled by – even when the victim was an escaped elephant in Venice:

I saw him the day he broke open his own house – he was standing in the *Riva* [degli Schiavoni] & his keepers trying to persuade him with *peck-loaves* to go on board a sort of Ark they had got. – I went close to him that afternoon in my Gondola – & he amused himself with flinging great beams that flew about over the water in all directions – he was then not *very* angry – but towards midnight he became furious – & displayed the most extraordinary strength – pulling down every thing before him. – All Musquetry proved in vain – & when he charged the Austrians threw down their musquets & ran. At last they broke a hole & brought a field-piece the first shot missed the second entered behind – & came out *all but* the Skin at his Shoulder. – I saw him dead the next day – a stupendous fellow. – He went mad for want of a She it being the rutting month.   (*LJ* VI. 108)

What is typical about this passage is its almost surreal combination of engagement and objectivity: the writer gets close to an elephant, but on a gondola, of all things. Keepers attempting to tempt a wild beast onto a boat unexpectedly take us to the Ark in Genesis, only the biblical context is completely absent. The animal is anthropomorphized ('his own house', 'amused himself', 'not *very* angry'), but also seen in hyperrealist terms ('*all but* the Skin at his Shoulder'). Byron's final position – itself typically of that morally lenient attitude to the world that his later comic poems strike – is an unostentatiously sympathetic expression of solidarity: the dead beast is 'a stupendous fellow', an individual like ourselves, driven by the sexual dependency that every mammal shares.

An elephant shot with a cannon is one thing, but Byron's greatest such meditation involved, naturally enough, a fellow human: the military commandant of Ravenna, shot in the street outside Byron's residence by patriots on 9 December 1820. His servants did not want him to get involved,

> but I ran down into the Street – Tita the bravest of them followed me – and we made our way to the Commandant who was lying on his back with five wounds – of which three in the body – one in the heart. – – There were about him – Diego his Adjutant – crying like a Child – a priest howling – a Surgeon who dared not touch him – two or three confused & frightened Soldiers – one or two of the boldest of the mob – and the Street dark as pitch – with the people flying in all directions. – As Diego could only cry and wring his hands – and the Priest could only pray – and nobody seemed able or willing to do anything except exclaim shake and stare – I made my Servant & one of the mob take up the body – sent off Diego crying to the Cardinal – the Soldiers for the Guard – & had the Commandant carried up Stairs to my own quarters. – But he was quite gone. – I made the Surgeon examine him & examined him myself. – He had bled inwardly, & very little external blood was apparent. – One of the Slugs had gone quite through – all but the Skin, I felt it myself. – Two more shots in the body – one in a finger – and another in the arm. – His face not all disfigured – he seems asleep – but is growing livid.   (*LJ* VII. 247)

'I shall never be deterred from a duty of humanity by all the assassins of Italy – and that is a wide word', Byron wrote, before adding a postscript: 'The poor Man's wife is not yet aware of his death – they are to break it to her in the morning. – The Lieutenant who is watching the body is smoking with the greatest Sangfroid – a strange people' (*LJ* VII. 247–8). By the end of the year Byron had converted this letter into one of the most profound and brilliant passages in *Don Juan* (V. 257–312), where the meditation it provides on sangfroid versus the duty of humanity is spelled out in a very particular dramatic context. But even here we can see the strange harmony between those things in the author himself: a good Samaritan, but one who can't resist examining exit wounds – 'all but the Skin' – the very expression he had used of the unfortunate rogue elephant in Venice.

Characters

Byron could be unerring on human life as well as death. In his early days on the literary scene in London he visited the 'banker-poet', Samuel Rogers, fifteen years his senior, and captured the author of *The Pleasures of Memory* (1792) inimitably:

> Rogers is silent, – and, it is said, severe. When he does talk, he talks well; and, on all subjects of taste, his delicacy of expression is pure as his poetry. If you enter his house – his drawing-room – his library – you of yourself say, this is not the dwelling of a common mind. There is not a gem, a coin, a book thrown aside on his chimney-piece, his sofa, his table, that does not bespeak an almost fastidious elegance in the possessor. But this very delicacy must be the misery of his existence. Oh the jarrings his disposition must have encountered through life!   (*LJ* III. 214)

It is a remarkably knowing portrait to be painted by a 25-year-old, full of ambivalent insight into a person as unlike the letter-writer as could be: the realization that delicacy could be a source of misery, for example. Byron's prose is as poised and fastidiously elegant as Rogers' drawing room itself, until the tension snaps and the understanding bursts its banks in the last two lines.

Years later, Byron's long letter to John Murray describing a favourite Venetian lover, Margarita Cogni (*LJ* VI. 192–8), is an evocative triumph: unsentimental and proprietorial, but charged also with respect and admiration. On one occasion Byron was caught in a squall in his gondola, and was in some danger: 'hats blown away – boat filling – oar lost – tumbling sea – thunder – rain in torrents – night coming – & wind increasing':

> On our return – after a tight struggle: I found her on the open steps of the Mocenigo palace on the Grand Canal – with her great black eyes flashing through her tears and the long dark hair which was streaming drenched with rain over her brows & breast; – she was perfectly exposed to the storm – and the wind blowing her hair & dress about her tall thin figure – and the lightning flashing round her – with the waves rolling at her feet – made her look like Medea alighted from her chariot – or the Sibyl [sorceress] of the tempest that was rolling around her – the only living thing within hail at that moment except ourselves.   (*LJ* VI. 196)

(Medea was a fatal witch of Greek myth, who flew from Corinth to Athens in a magic golden chariot, having murdered her two children by the hero, Jason.) The series of verbal past continuous constructions here ('flashing … streaming … blowing', etc.) itself tumbles and coalesces, like stormy wind and water.

From Ravenna, in 1821, Byron recalled his experiences at the Drury Lane Theatre management subcommittee, and the authors who trapped him there, whom he retrospectively lists and converts into a dramatic chorus from every corner of the British Isles:

Then the scenes I had to go through! – the authours – and the authoresses – – the Milliners – the wild Irishmen – the people from Brighton – from Blackwell – from Chatham – from Cheltenham – from Dublin – from Dundee – who came in upon me! – to all of whom it was proper to give a civil answer – and a hearing – and a reading – – Mrs. Glover's father an Irish dancing Master of Sixty years – called upon me to request to play '*Archer*' [in Farquhar's comedy, *The Beaux' Stratagem* (1707)] – drest in silk stockings on a frosty morning to show his legs – (which were certainly good & Irish for his age – & had been still better) – Miss Emma Somebody with a play entitled the 'Bandit of Bohemia' – or some such title or production – Mr. O'Higgins – then resident in Richmond – with an Irish tragedy in which the unities could not fail to be observed for the protagonist was chained by the leg to a pillar during the chief part of the performance.   (*LJ* IX. 35–6)

The fluent, vivid, and economical characterizations we find in *Don Juan* have their origin in passages like these and the view of the world they illustrate: beady-eyed, humane, evocative, and celebratory.

So close were such evocations to the dramatic that Byron not only incorporated a passage from his letters seamlessly into *Don Juan*; he invented letters in the *Don Juan* style. When John Murray sought Byron's editorial help on a tragedy he had received from Byron's quondam travelling companion, Dr William Polidori, the poet was happy to offer it. 'You want a "civil and delicate declension" for the medical tragedy?', he said: 'Take it – '

> Dear Doctor – I have read your play
> Which is a good one in it's way
> Purges the eyes & moves the bowels
> And drenches handkerchiefs like towels
> With tears that in a flux of Grief
> Afford hysterical relief
> To shatter'd nerves & quickened pulses
> Which your catastrophe convulses.
> Your plot too has such scope for Scenery!
> Your dialogue is apt & smart
> The play's concoction full of art –
> Your hero raves – your heroine cries
> All stab – & every body dies;
> In short your tragedy would be
> The very thing to hear & see –
> And for a piece of publication
> If I decline on this occasion
> It is not that I am not sensible

> To merits in themselves ostensible
> But – and I grieve to speak it – plays
> Are drugs – mere drugs, Sir, nowadays.
>
> (*LJ* V. 258–9) ['drug': a commodity hard to sell]

In June 1818, Byron pulled off a similar feat of ventriloquism and wrote to his friend Hobhouse as his own valet, William Fletcher, announcing his employer's demise:

> Sir – With great grief I inform you of the death of my late dear Master – my Lord – who died this morning at ten of the Clock of a rapid decline & slow fever – caused by anxiety – sea-bathing – women & riding in the Sun against my advice. – He is a very dreadful loss to every body, mostly to me – who have lost a master and a place – also I hope you – Sir – will give me a charakter [i.e. reference]. – I saved in his service as you know several hundred pounds – God knows how – for I don't, nor my late master neither – and if my wage was not always paid to the day – still it was or is to be paid sometime & somehow – you – Sir – who are his executioner [i.e., executor of his will] won't see a poor Servant robbed of his little all. My dear Master had several phisicians and a Priest – he died a Papish [i.e., Papist – Catholic] but is to be buried among the Jews in the Jewish burying ground.   (*LJ* VI. 44–5)

'If a sparrow come before my window', Keats wrote in a famous letter of 22 November 1817, 'I take part in its existence and pick about the gravel.' Byron had just the same mercurial capacity dramatically to project himself into other forms of correspondence and other forms of life.

'My own wretched identity'

Peter Porter's 'legend-maker' is not as visible in Byron's informal prose. Only to Thomas Moore among his male friends would he admit to having 'a mountain of lead upon my heart', or write that, apart from influenza-style infections, 'What I find worse, and cannot get rid of, is the growing depression of my spirits, without sufficient cause' (*LJ* VIII. 230, 236). Men of his time rarely shared confidences of an emotional nature.

But there were two people to whom Byron did write in this vein: his sister and himself. 'As for me', he wrote to Augusta from Switzerland in 1816, 'I am in good health – & fair – though very unequal – spirits – but for all that – she – or rather – the Separation – has broken my heart – I feel as if an Elephant had trodden on it – I am convinced I shall never get over it – but I try' (*LJ* V. 91). In the Alpine journal he wrote for her a few weeks later he welcomed the change of scenery,

> But in all this – the recollections of bitterness – & more especially of recent & more home desolation – which must accompany me through life – have preyed upon me here – and neither the music of the Shepherd – the crashing of the Avalanche – nor the torrent – the mountain – the Glacier – the Forest – nor the Cloud – have for one moment – lightened the weight upon my heart – nor enabled me to lose my own wretched identity in the majesty & the power and the Glory – around – above – & beneath me.   (*LJ* V. 105)

The prose rhythms here are very different from the passages quoted earlier: slower and more deeply orchestrated (using elaborate subordinate phrases and powerful syntactic arrangements like 'neither … nor'). The *Childe Harold* note in prose is audible here because losing 'my own wretched identity' in that of others (from lovers to valets, and elephants to commandants) was precisely the experience offered in 'comic' letters like those quoted from above. This inability to *escape* – and to escape oneself above all – was the quintessential 'Byronic' experience.

But then again such trains of thought (again from a journal) can amount to a form of moral commentary on the 'realist', 'comic' *Don Juan* disposition:

> Why, at the very height of desire and human pleasure, – worldly, social, amorous, ambitious, or even avaricious, – does there mingle a certain sense of doubt and sorrow – a fear of what is to come – a doubt of what *is* – a retrospect to the past, leading to a prognostication of the future? … Why is this? or these? – I know not, except that on a pinnacle we are most susceptible of giddiness, and that we never fear falling except from a precipice – the higher, the more awful, and the more sublime.   (*LJ* VIII. 37)

Such passages amount to an underwriting of varieties of fatality and moral justice that are ineluctable and cannot be diverted by comic tolerance or 'understanding'. Doubt, sorrow, and fear can never be entirely charmed away. Some passages written for his own eyes suggest that Byron saw that fatality at work within himself:

> I took my gradations in the vices – with great promptitude – but they were not to my taste – for my early passions though violent in the extreme – were concentrated – and hated division or spreading abroad. – I could have left or lost the world with or for that which I loved – but though my temperament was naturally burning – I could not share in the common place libertinism of the place and

time – without disgust. – – And yet this very disgust and my heart thrown back upon itself – threw me into excesses perhaps more fatal than those from which I shrank. (*LJ* IX. 37)

It is time to turn towards Byron the legend-maker, and consider the poem that would broadcast such sentiments to the nineteenth century: *Childe Harold's Pilgrimage.*

Chapter 4

The poet as pilgrim

Childe Harold's Pilgrimage: A Romaunt (transparently entitled 'Childe Burun's Pilgrimage' in its first draft) could be called the most original English long poem of its age – especially as Wordsworth's autobiographical *The Prelude* remained unpublished until 1850. But topographical poems had appeared long before it was published. Wordsworth himself started his poetic career with items like 'An Evening Walk', set in the Lake District, and *Descriptive Sketches*, set in the Alps, and Byron had read Waller Rodwell Wright's *Horae Ionicae* ('Greek Hours', 1809) before setting off on his travels. The form Byron chose, too – the stanza first used in English by Edmund Spenser in *The Faerie Queene* (1596) – had remained in use since the great Elizabethan's day, most effectively by James Beattie (*The Minstrel*, 1774) and James Thomson (*The Castle of Indolence*, 1748). It was what Byron did with these traditions that 'combined to make the world stark mad about *Childe Harold* and Byron', as his contemporary Samuel Rogers put it.[1]

Readers of Byron's poem normally confront it in its entirety, and that is how I shall treat it here. But it should be kept in mind that *Childe Harold* was begun in October 1809 and completed in March 1818. It dominated the first half of Byron's poetic career just as *Don Juan* (July 1818–May 1823) dominated the second. Being intermittent projects for eight and five years, respectively, the two poems incorporate a good deal of change over their length, and are punctuated by other works of very different kinds (see Table 2). Four years elapsed between the publication of Cantos I and II of *Childe Harold* in 1812

Table 2. *Dates of composition and publication of Byron's major poems*
All published by John Murray except as indicated

Title	First full draft	Publication
Childe Harold I	31 Oct.–30 Dec. 1809	10 Mar. 1812
Childe Harold II	New Year–28 Mar. 1810	10 Mar. 1812
The Giaour	late 1812–Mar. 1813	5 June 1813
The Bride of Abydos	1–11 Nov. 1813	2 Dec. 1813
The Corsair	18–31 Dec. 1813	1 Feb. 1814
Lara	15 May–12 June 1814	early Aug. 1814
The Siege of Corinth	Jan.–Dec. 1815	13 Feb. 1816
Parisina	mid-1815–Dec. 1815	13 Feb. 1816
Childe Harold III	25 Apr.–8 June 1816	18 Nov. 1816
The Prisoner of Chillon	mid-June–2 July 1816	5 Dec. 1816
Manfred Acts I–II	Aug. 1816–15 Feb. 1817	16 June 1817
Manfred Act III	late Apr.–5 May 1817	16 June 1817
Childe Harold IV	19 June–19 July 1817	28 Apr. 1818
Beppo	9–10 Oct. 1817	24 Feb. 1818
Mazeppa	2 Apr. 1817–26 Sept. 1818	28 June 1819
Don Juan I	3 July–6 Sept. 1818	15 July 1819
Don Juan II	13 Dec. 1818–mid-Jan. 1819	15 July 1819
Don Juan III–IV	17 Sept.–30 Nov. 1819	8 Aug. 1821
Marino Faliero	4 Apr.–16 July 1820	21 Apr. 1821
Don Juan V	10 Oct.–27 Nov. 1820	8 Aug. 1821
Sardanapalus	13 Jan.–27 May 1821	19 Dec. 1821
The Two Foscari	12 June–mid-July 1821	19 Dec. 1821
Cain	16 July–9 Sept. 1821	19 Dec. 1821
The Vision of Judgment	20 Sept.–4 Oct. 1821	15 Oct. 1822 (*The Liberal*)
Heaven and Earth	9 Oct.–late Oct. 1821	1 Jan. 1823 (*The Liberal*)
Werner	18 Dec. 1821–20 Jan. 1822	23 Nov. 1822
The Deformed Transformed	Jan. 1822–early 1823	20 Feb. 1824 (Hunt)
Don Juan VI–VIII	Jan.–late July 1822	15 July 1823 (Hunt)
Don Juan IX–XI	Aug.–mid-Oct. 1822	29 Aug. 1823 (Hunt)
Don Juan XII–XIV	Oct. 1822–Feb. 1823	17 Dec. 1823 (Hunt)
The Island	11 Jan.–10 Feb. 1823	26 June 1823 (Hunt)
Don Juan XV–XVI	8 Mar.–6 May 1823	26 Mar. 1824 (Hunt)
Don Juan XVII	May 1823	1903

and Canto III in 1816: years dominated by the 'Eastern Tales' discussed in the following chapter. But Byron clearly saw both *Childe Harold* and *Don Juan* as ongoing wholes, built upon earlier instalments, and the account offered here attempts to honour that intention.

Early starts, true and false

Jerome McGann's seven-volume edition of Byron's *Complete Poetical Works* (*CPW*) reprints 404 poems, great and small. In choosing to start detailed discussion with *Childe Harold's Pilgrimage* I am going to all but pass over 173 of them: over 40 per cent of his output, numerically speaking. (Byron wrote excellent short poems throughout his career, but as they are not as complex as the major lyrics of, say, Wordsworth and Keats, I have chosen to concentrate on his longer works. Still, a reader of Byron will want to read poems like 'Lines to Mr. Hodgson', 'Written after Swimming from Sestos to Abydos', 'She Walks in Beauty', 'Stanzas for Music', 'Churchill's Grave', 'Epistle to Augusta', 'Darkness', 'To Thomas Moore', 'So, We'll Go No More A Roving', 'Epistle from Mr Murray to Dr Polidori', and 'To the Po'.)

When Byron started work on *Childe Harold* in Albania he was the author of a large number of lyric poems, about half of which had been published in an evolving collection: *Fugitive Pieces* from August 1806, *Hours of Idleness* from June 1807, and *Poems Original and Translated* from March 1808. These poems are on a variety of themes, but three predominate: adolescent love poems; translations-cum-imitations, direct from his classical education at Harrow and Cambridge; and nostalgic lyrics about his Scottish childhood, Newstead, and his time at school.

Most of these lyric poems are conventional in theme and expression. Couplets and quatrains are the preferred medium, just as they had been in the eighteenth century. There is little consensus about their quality nowadays, but they demonstrate a force of personality and a lyrical gift that is profound, though intermittent. The sixth poem in the *Complete Poetical Works* was written in the summer of 1805, when Byron was seventeen:

> Hills of Annesley, bleak and barren,
>   Where my thoughtless childhood stray'd,
> How the northern tempests, warring,
>   Howl above thy tufted shade!
>
> Now no more, the hours beguiling,
>   Former favourite haunts I see;
> Now no more my Mary smiling
>   Makes ye seem a Heaven to me.
>
>   (*CPW* I. 3; by permission of Oxford University Press)

However early a work, 'Hills of Annesley' demonstrates a pronounced tendency towards retrospection, nostalgia, and exile – associated on this occasion with lost landscape (Annesley is between Newstead and Nottingham) and lost love (Mary Chaworth, a cousin, who married in August 1805).

Retrospection, nostalgia, and exile recur in a significant number of Byron's early poems (all from *CPW* I): 'Remembrance' ('Chill'd by misfortune's wintry blast, / My dawn of life is overcast'; 6), 'On Leaving Newstead Abbey' ('your descendant, departing / From the seat of his ancestors, bids you, adieu!'; 35), 'Song' ('I left my bleak home, and my visions are gone, / The mountains are vanish'd, my youth is no more'; 48), 'To the Duke of D[orset]' ('Tho' ev'ry Error stamps me for her own / And dooms my fall, I fain would fall alone'; 67), 'Lachin Y Gair' ('Years have roll'd on, Loch na Garr, since I left you, / Years must elapse, e'er I tread you again'; 104), 'Elegy on Newstead Abbey' ('In thee, the wounded conscience courts relief, / Retiring from the garish blaze of day'; 107), 'On a Distant View of the Village and School, of Harrow, on the Hill' ('Ye scenes of my childhood, whose lov'd recollection, / Embitters the present, compar'd with the past'; 138), 'Childish Recollections' ('World! I renounce thee! all my hope's o'ercast; / One sigh I give thee, but that sigh's the last'; 158), and, finally, 'The Adieu' ('Hall of my Sires! a long farewell – / Yet why to thee adieu? / Thy vaults will echo back my knell, / Thy towers my tomb will view'; 183).

Retrospection, nostalgia, exile, and guilt form a particularly powerful combination in two poems written around Byron's nineteenth birthday, during one of his terms away from Cambridge. The first, originally entitled 'My Character', and strongly reminiscent of Alexander Pope, is called 'Damaetas' (a name from the classical tradition, implying a shepherd or pastoral simpleton):

> In law an infant, and in years a boy,
> In mind a slave to every vicious joy,
> From every sense of shame and virtue wean'd,
> In lies an adept, in deceit a fiend;
> Vers'd in hypocrisy, while yet a child,
> Fickle as the wind, of inclinations wild;
> Woman his dupe, his heedless friend a tool,
> Old in the world, though scarcely broke from school;
> Damaetas ran through all the maze of sin,
> And found the goal, when others just begin:
> Ev'n still conflicting passions shake his soul,
> And bid him drain the dregs of pleasure's bowl;
> But, pall'd with vice, he breaks his former chain,
> And, what was once his bliss, appears his bane.

(*CPW* I. 51–2; by permission of Oxford University Press)

This is demonstrably autobiographical, however melodramatic its expression may be – the young Byron made neither the women he knew dupes nor his friends tools, but he would like to have us think he did.

The second poem, 'Oscar of Alva: A Tale' (*CPW* I. 54–66), is autobiographically more obscure and aesthetically more Romantic. Once again we have an abandoned feudal pile, apparently in Scotland. Once again there is an exhausted noble line. But this time there are two male heirs, the eponymous hero and his younger brother, Allan. (The 'childe' in *Childe Harold* means a youth of noble birth, an eldest son and heir.) When another laird's daughter visits, Oscar claims her, but on the day of his wedding the groom mysteriously disappears – a circumstance for which Allan has no explanation. After three years' wait Allan takes his turn with the laird's daughter, another marriage is planned, and this time completed – only there is a strange and sinister guest at the celebration:

> But, who is he, whose darken'd brow
>   Glooms in the midst of general mirth?
> Before his eye's far fiercer glow,
>   The blue flames curdle o'er the hearth.   (*CPW* I. 61)

The stranger proposes a toast to the long-lost brother, which Allan is unable to drink, then reveals himself to be the usurped heir. Allan dies of horror, and the action fades over his 'lonely tomb', isolated from the 'noble grave' of the rest of his clan as punishment for fratricide.

'Oscar of Alva' is not autobiographical in a straightforward way; in it the author's sense of himself takes an almost mythic form as inheritor and outcast. In Damaetas, Oscar, and Allan we have the same 'conflicting passions' and 'inclinations wild' seen from different points of view and compacted into a mysterious but violent destiny.

Within six months of *Hours of Idleness* being published, Byron had weaned himself off lyric juvenilia and started a satire called 'British Bards'. Stung by a condescending notice of his lyric collection in the *Edinburgh Review*, he expanded this later project into *English Bards and Scotch Reviewers*, eventually published in March 1809, a few months before his departure for Europe.

Byron finished a first draft of *Childe Harold* I–II in Turkey on 28 March 1810, and revised it early the following year, at which time he also wrote a second satire, *Hints from Horace*. *English Bards* and *Hints from Horace* belong together, formally speaking (both being in rhyming couplets), but they also offered Byron a choice of poetic career after *Hours of Idleness*. On the one hand, he had his highly personal travel poem; on the other, he could remain in the impersonal role of disinterested satirist, awarding brickbats and bouquets to fellow poets while remaining behind a Horatian screen. The travel poem was urgently innovatory in terms of content; the satires were as traditional as could be.

On his return to London in July 1811, Byron played ducks and drakes with *Childe Harold* and *Hints from Horace*, introducing the latter to his friend

Robert Dallas with the comment he 'believed Satire to be his *forte*' (Marchand, 278). Only when Dallas raved about the travel poem did Byron commit to it, though he remained worried that his track record with both *Hours of Idleness* and *English Bards* would bring the critics down on the new venture. Certainly there is hardly anything in the earlier poems to suggest that *Childe Harold* was in the offing, and Bernard Blackstone is right to speak of 'the catalytic agency of Greece and the Levant … to unlock Byron's unique poetic potential, and make him into a writer of European stature', just as Caroline Franklin is right to suggest that the *Edinburgh Review*'s rubbishing of *Hours of Idleness* 'galvanised Byron into declaring himself a serious writer with a moral purpose' in the first place.[2]

In his poem 'Childish Recollections' Byron noted 'Let keener bards delight in Satire's sting, / My Fancy soars not on Detraction's wing' (*CPW* I. 161). *English Bards* has its moments – when Byron mocks the contemporary fad for working-class poets, for example:

> Ye tuneful cobblers! still your notes prolong,
> Compose at once a slipper and a song;
> So shall the fair your handy work peruse,
> Your sonnets sure shall please – perhaps your shoes
> …
> While punctual beaux reward the grateful notes,
> And pay for poems – when they pay for coats.   (ll. 790–3, 797–8)

But he never consistently attained Pope's capacity for focused invective, imaginative idiosyncrasy, or poetic momentum. *Hints from Horace* is even more placid, though it does contain an authentically Popean portrait of an Oxbridge graduate:

> Launch'd into life, extinct his early fire,
> He apes the selfish prudence of his sire;
> Marries for money, chooses friends for rank,
> Buys land, and shrewdly trusts not to the Bank!
> Sits in the senate, gets a son and heir,
> Sends him to Harrow, for himself was there;
> Mute, though he votes, unless when call'd to cheer,
> His son's so sharp – he'll see the dog a peer!   (ll. 241–8)

This is not quite a self-portrait. Byron was already a peer, and however selfish his father was no one could accuse 'Mad Jack' Byron of being prudent. But the references to Harrow and to 'early fire' being extinguished by a conventional career in Parliament suggest that this is yet another sketch of an alter ego: someone Byron might become if he allowed his talent to wither and accepted the cosy embrace of his social class and political role. *Childe Harold* would ensure that fate would never be his.

Form and function

Childe Harold is a narrative poem, but unlike the *Iliad, Paradise Lost,* or *The Prelude* it is composed in stanzas rather than blank verse. Blank verse is a form that puts almost as little formal constraint on content as can be, and therefore prioritizes the flow of narrative or argument; a stanza format, on the other hand, tends towards both artistic self-consciousness and digression. Even if syntax, narrative, and punctuation propel onward movement in a stanzaic long poem, its visual layout shifts the balance from content towards form. 'This effect', as prosodist Catherine Addison suggests, 'comprises an additional stylization of language over and above the basic markers of poetry [metre, rhyme, etc.].'[3]

What is so for the reader is so for the writer: 'discourse shapes its segments to fit into the formal pattern of the verse',[4] so content adapts itself to the container into which it is poured. And the Spenserian stanza is an unusual container:

> Yet oft-times in his maddest mirthful mood
> Strange pangs would flash along Childe Harold's brow,
> As if the memory of some deadly feud
> Or disappointed passion lurk'd below:
> But this none knew, nor haply car'd to know;
> For his was not that open, artless soul
> That feels relief by bidding sorrow flow,
> Nor sought he friend to counsel or condole,
> Whate'er his grief mote be, which he could not control.   (I. 64–72)

The first thing to say about this form (rhyming *ababbcbcc*) is that it commits the poet to finding three rhymes at least twice, which in a rhyme-poor language like English (compared to Italian, for example – and all major English stanza forms have their origin in Italian Renaissance literature) is not easy. The word the poet chooses at the end of line two must be rhymed three more times, which is a serious constraint on sense. But, more importantly, the rhyme structure manages to be both convoluted and involuted, extended and elaborate. The first four lines are a quatrain: *abab*. But then the last line of the quatrain becomes the first line of a couplet: *abab–b*. But that rhyme has itself been anticipated at line 2, so the couplet is not what prosodists call 'alienated'. It does not function as couplets in complex stanzas frequently do, as a marked change or conclusion to a pattern.

And the stanza is not over yet. The second line of the couplet is also the first line of a second quatrain (*abab–bcbc*); and the last line of that quatrain is once again the first line of a second couplet (*ababbcb–cc*), also anticipated at line 6. So in the Spenserian stanza couplets and quatrains merge into one another in a way that has been called 'interlaced', 'musical', and 'reflective'.

Controlling the emphases within this suite of rhymes produces a great deal of variety. If rhyming lines are end-stopped by punctuation, the rhyme is strong. If syntax carries the reader over the line, without pausing at the rhyme-word, the rhyme is weak. Spenser tended to punctuate regularly at the end of each line, but Byron is more adventurous. So in the stanza just quoted the 'mood / feud' rhyme is weak. So is the anticipation of the final couplet, since the reader cannot pause on the word 'soul' before going on to 'condole' and 'control' at the stanza's end. (When two lines form an 'eye-rhyme', as in 'brow / below', the rhyme is weaker still.) 'While losing Spenser's sustained, patient sense of explaining everything', Catherine Addison points out, Byron 'gain[s] the ability to express a passionate intensity quite foreign to Spenser's more classical, even-tempered narrator.'[5] Byron was able to gallop or stroll as he saw fit towards the stanza's last important feature: the twelve-syllable final line, in contrast to its eight ten-syllable predecessors – the flourish which brings the stanza to a powerful close, thus breaking up forward progress yet more emphatically. In *Childe Harold*, then, we have a combination of Spenserian rumination and Romantic force, themselves values in conflict, contributing to the poem's unique mood.

I have dwelt on this feature of *Childe Harold* for a reason. Though he wrote lyrics, odes, satires, and plays, it is on Byron's narrative poems that his claim to greatness stands. These poems form three groups: the Spenserian *Childe Harold*, the *ottava rima* of his later comic poems (*Beppo*, *Don Juan*, and *The Vision of Judgment*), and the couplets (however irregular) that dominate the other tales, from *The Giaour* (1812) to *The Island* (1823). *Childe Harold* and *Don Juan* repay careful consideration in these terms because they are so similar in other important respects, and because they almost overlapped in the year 1818, when the first poem made room for the second.

Both *Childe Harold* and *Don Juan* are open-ended and apparently incomplete. Both were apparently unplanned. *Childe Harold*, Byron wrote, 'was intended to be a poem on *Ariosto's* plan that *is* to *say* on *no plan* at all' (*LJ* II. 63), and he said of *Don Juan*, 'I *have* no plan – I *had* no plan – but I had or have materials' (*LJ* VI. 207). In both poems the hero is a young aristocratic male turned loose into Europe for the purposes of moral education in the form of travel. Both exploit the relationship between hero and narrator. Both are attempts to make sense of the world, but from different perspectives, related to the 'two principles of Byronism' discussed in Chapter 3: reflective versus comic, solipsistic versus dramatic. Both are given to digression, but in different manners: *Childe Harold* is disciplined and focused; *Don Juan* is radically diverse. Still, reading *Childe Harold's Pilgrimage*, it has been well said, 'will always be the most helpful preparation for reading *Don Juan*.'[6]

Prospects of Europe

Childe Harold is one poem, in four cantos, based on three pilgrimages: from Newstead to Athens, from Waterloo to Lake Geneva, and from Venice to Rome. A pilgrimage is a special form of travel: the destination is known beforehand and dominates the expedition, and as readers we expect a distinct moral contrast between the point of departure and the point of arrival. The pilgrim travels from darkness to light, blindness to insight, confusion to order, and from worldly values towards spiritual ones.

Byron's three pilgrimages also relate to different periods of European history. The first is a journey through contemporary Napoleonic Europe, the Peninsular War, and the British-dominated Mediterranean to Greece as a 'sad relic' of its former greatness. The second starts at Waterloo and follows the Rhine upstream to its source in the Swiss Alps. In doing so it pursues the history of the French Revolution and Napoleon's empire to its source, in the persons of three representative Enlightenment intellectuals, all of whom had lived on the shores of Lake Geneva: Rousseau, Voltaire, and Edward Gibbon, author of the *Decline and Fall of the Roman Empire* (1776–88). The third journey looks back further yet, from Renaissance Italy to its origins in classical Rome. The tours get shorter but the temporal perspectives get longer. All three are attempts to make sense of Byron's Europe in its chaos and violence, but also in its beauty, natural and man-made.

What unites these three prospects of Europe is the outlook of the hero-cum-narrator, formed by the English classical education Byron had received – itself an attempt to make sense of the world in terms of an inherited experience. 'Byron's early power', Ruskin pointed out, 'was founded on a course of general reading of the masters in every walk of literature, such as is … unparalleled in any other young life, whether of student or author.'[7] (Evidence for Ruskin's comment is provided by Byron's 1807 'Reading List' and the sale catalogues of his libraries in *CMP* 1–7 and 231–54.) 'The Greek and Roman classics', Hazlitt wrote, were 'a sort of privileged text-books'[8] for university graduates like Byron, particularly in the sense that they conferred access to European topography as well as history – and to the one seen in terms of the other. Napoleon made the conventional Grand Tour through France to Florence, Rome, and Naples impossible; but Byron brought with him on his version of that aristocratic rite of passage the sense of access to Europe and its past that his education had given him.

Newstead to Athens

From the moment Harold arrives in Portugal, therefore, the landscape is a subject for moralizing or historical reflection, on the basis of what he sees but also of what he knows from his education. 'It is a goodly sight to see / What heaven has done for this delicious land', certainly, 'but man would mar' the 'goodly prospects' spread out before him 'with an impious hand' (I. 207–11). The native Portuguese are 'poor, paltry slaves! yet born 'midst noblest scenes', surrounded by 'views more dazzling unto mortal ken' even than those depicted for the English genteel reader in *Paradise Lost* (I. 234, 240).

Such contrasts between humanity and its environment are traditional in classical poetry, but in Byron's hands they are subject to a Romantic sense of discontinuity. When Harold approaches the border with Spain there is no bucolic pastoral in prospect:

> More bleak to view the hills at length recede,
> And, less luxuriant, smoother vales extend:
> Immense horizon-bounded plains succeed!
> Far as the eye discerns, withouten end,
> Spain's realms appear whereon her shepherds tend
> Flocks whose rich fleece right well the trader knows
> Now must the pastor's arms his lambs defend:
> For Spain is compass'd by unyielding foes,
> And all must shield their all, or share Subjection's woes.   (I. 351–9)

If little sense can be made of a pastoral landscape threatened by war, none whatsoever is available on the battlefield itself, where

> The foe, the victim, and the fond ally
> ...
> Are met – as if at home they could not die –
> To feed the crow on Talavera's plain,
> And fertilize the field that each pretends to gain.   (I. 445, 447–9)

Military conflict amounts to feeding on carrion, and it is only 'Ambition's honour'd fools' who fall victim to patriotic delusions, while tyrants 'pave their way / With human hearts – to what? – a dream alone.' (I. 450, 454–5.) 'The

Pilgrim prick'd his steed', we are told; 'Full swiftly Harold wends his lonely way' (I. 460, 477). There is nothing to be learned or recovered here.

But the Peninsular War is only the latest in a long series of such conflicts. 'Moorish turrets' look down on the 'wounded ground' of modern Andalusia, where the 'bold peasant' points with pride 'to yonder cliffs, which oft were won and lost' (I. 514–21). Seen in the light of the Moorish occupation of Spain between the eighth and fifteenth centuries AD the French one seems a minor affair. All Byron can voice is a Romantic dissent taking the form of rhetorical questions: 'And must they fall? the young, the proud, the brave, / To swell one bloated Chief's unwholesome reign?' (I. 549–50). It seems they must, but there is no purpose, logic, or outcome of this war that history does not render ironic from its seat among the gods. Men die for reasons, but in time the reasons disappear.

If the landscape is historically unknown to the peasants who occupy it, the people are dislocated, too. 'Spain's maids are no race of Amazons,' Byron says, 'But form'd for all the witching arts of love' (I. 585–6); only now the heroic Maid of Saragoza has 'unsex'd' herself and 'dar'd the deed of war' to fight the French (I. 560–1). From masculine Seville we travel to feminine Cadiz, where women form the majority of the audience for that 'ungentle sport', the bull-fight – itself the symbol of ruined Spain, 'nurtur'd in blood' (I. 794):

> Flows there a tear of pity for the dead?
> Look o'er the ravage of the reeking plain;
> Look on the hands with female slaughter red;
> Then to the dogs resign the unburied slain,
> Then to the vulture let each corse remain;
> Albeit unworthy of the prey-bird's maw,
> Let their bleach'd bones, and blood's unbleaching stain,
> Long mark the battle-field with hideous awe:
> Thus only may our sons conceive the scenes we saw!   (I. 900–8)

The problem is that the bones and the bloodstains of the Napoleonic era will indeed disappear, just as those of the Moorish era have done. If humanity could see the signs of conflict, perhaps it would abjure it; but history and landscape suggest the scars will heal and the struggle will recommence on some other pretext.

The ultimate origin of Byron's education was Athens. But it, too, is a place of radical discontinuity, and when he invokes Athena and Apollo on the Acropolis it is with his tongue in his theological cheek: 'Even gods must yield – religions take their turn: / 'Twas Jove's – 'tis Mahomet's', and humanity, the 'Poor child of Doubt and Death' will find no Pythagorean point of departure or illumination here any more (II. 23–4, 27).

But the sense of pan-European conflict truly comes into focus at the Eastern end of the Mediterranean, so the second canto of the poem is able to discover more in Athens than the first could in the war-torn anarchy of Spain. There is still a note of Romantic protest that not even 'Fancy's eye' can 'restore what Time hath labour'd to deface' in Greece, and at the total apathy of Turks and Greeks alike to its decline (II. 87–90). But there is also the perspective attained when Harold leaves mainstream Christian Europe and penetrates its Muslim fringe in Albania: 'the cross descends, thy minarets arise' (II. 340). 'The scene was savage, but the scene was new' (II. 385). Now the human conflict is graphic and visibly historical in its origins. Being so, it has produced an outcome of its own: not an ethnic melting pot, but a hypnotically alluring multiculturalism. Ali Pasha's palace is a latter-day version of the *Pax Romana*, upheld by the threat of armed retribution:

> Richly caparison'd, a ready row
> Of armed horse, and many a warlike store
> Circled the wide extending court below:
> Above, strange groups adorn'd the corridore;
> And oft-times through the Area's echoing door
> Some high-capp'd Tartar spurr'd his steed away:
> The Turk, the Greek, the Albanian, and the Moor,
> Here mingled in their many-hued array,
> While the deep war-drum's sound announc'd the close of day.
>
> (II. 505–13)

If Byron could see no sign of a just war in the Iberian Peninsula, and if he found the 'many-hued array' of the contemporary Ottoman Empire attractive, neither of these things prevented him accusing the Greeks of living through 'years of shame' while they waited for outsiders to deliver them from colonialism. The first two cantos of *Childe Harold* revolve around this dilemma, between historically informed scepticism about the purposes of war and rhetorical idealism about freedom that can (presumably) be won only by means of it. After all, if the Greeks do not fight for their freedom again, as they did in their heroic age, what will that freedom be worth?

In the meantime, the pilgrim can meditate upon the gulf between his own classically trained sense of Greece and its contemporary state:

> Thy vales of ever-green, thy hills of snow
> Proclaim thee Nature's varied favourite now:
> Thy fanes, thy temples to thy surface bow,
> Commingling slowly with heroic earth,

Broke by the share of every rustic plough:
So perish monuments of mortal birth,
So perish all in turn, save well-recorded Worth.   (II. 803–9)

So Harold leaves us with a prospect of Europe revealed as a meaningless cycle of imperialisms, layered each over the other like Shelley's 'Ozymandias', the happiest occupants in the end being those who understand the least. One may protest, certainly – but against what? Dissent can itself be a form of resignation, even passivity, if it is unfocused.

Waterloo to Geneva

Six years later, in 1816, the Napoleonic experiment was over, but the pilgrim is back where he was before, with 'Albion's lessening shores' behind him (III. 9), driven on by the force of winds, waters, and personal impulse. In the first instalment of *Childe Harold* the French empire had been exerting itself in Spain. At Waterloo it is the same empire's dust we tread upon (III. 145). History hasn't inched any further towards human liberty, so the rhetoric of Romantic protest is still attractive: 'Gaul may champ the bit / And foam in fetters; – but is Earth more free?'; 'shall reviving Thraldom again be / The patched-up idol of enlightened days?' (III. 163–8).

Is this purposeless cycle of power and decline the product of history or, as a classical education might lead one to suspect, something inherent in humanity? Napoleon's case as a latter-day Caesar provides evidence for the latter view:

An empire thou couldst crush, command, rebuild,
But govern not thy pettiest passion, nor,
However deeply in men's spirits skill'd,
Look through thine own, nor curb the lust of war,
Nor learn that tempted Fate will leave the loftiest star.   (III. 338–42)

We see here the arrival in Byron's poetry of a fully fledged and conscious stoicism – though elements of it were present in the Eastern Tales he had written between 1812 and 1816. Bonaparte's 'soul hath brook'd the turning tide' of history, 'With that untaught innate philosophy' that looks out upon the world 'With a sedate and all-enduring eye' (III. 343–9) that is itself a classical, time-honoured way of making sense of fortune. Whether the Childe should imitate it remains to be seen, but for the first time stoic self-reliance is registered as a possible reaction to the chaos of contemporary history.

To travel up the Rhine is to escape the nightmare of Napoleonic Europe to a landscape where violence and aristocracy have receded into the historical past and become harmonized with nature:

> There Harold gazes on a work divine,
> A blending of all beauties; streams and dells,
> Fruit, foliage, crag, wood, cornfield, mountain, vine,
> And chiefless castles breathing stern farewells
> From gray but leafy walls, where Ruin greenly dwells.   (III. 410–14)

At the Rhine's source in the Alps, among 'the palaces of Nature' (III. 591), Byron can distinguish battles for freedom (like Marathon and Morat) from those of imperial aggression (like Cannae and Waterloo). 'With its crystal face', Lake Geneva (in point of fact the source of the Rhône, not the Rhine, which originates in Lake Constance) offers the possibility of a clear focus: 'The mirror where the stars and mountains view / The stillness of their aspect in each trace / Its clear depth yields of their far height and hue' (III. 644–7).

Seen in these terms, Alpine nature is a point of vantage on the war-ravaged lowlands Byron has left behind. He discusses it as such at some length before lighting on Switzerland as a source not only of the Rhine but of the Enlightenment, in whose name the French Revolution was carried out. In Voltaire, Gibbon, and Rousseau the Enlightenment divides itself into its satirical, intellectual, and passionate components: the first 'breathed most in ridicule', the second 'Sapping a solemn creed [i.e., Christianity] with solemn sneer', and the last – the most complicated of all – 'phrenzied by disease or woe, / To that worst pitch of all, which wears a reasoning show' (III. 992, 999, 759–60). So the 'crystal face' of rationalism is an illusion; the storm clouds of recent European history still hover undischarged:

> How the lit lake shines, a phosphoric sea,
> And the big rain comes dancing to the earth!
> And now again 'tis black, – and now, the glee
> Of the loud hills shakes with its mountain-mirth,
> As if they did rejoice o'er a young earthquake's birth.   (III. 873–7)

The lucid certainties of Voltaire, Gibbon, and Rousseau are lifeless by comparison: attractive, certainly, from the perspective of 1815, but also irrecoverable. Perhaps Italy, 'the throne and grave of empires' (III. 1027), will hold the clue to Europe's destiny in a still-revolutionary age.

Venice to Rome

Each instalment of *Childe Harold* prepares its reader for the next, and so, whereas the fourth canto is by far the most detailed part of an ambitious poem,

perhaps enough has already been said to help readers see how Byron converts the objects he encounters to his intellectual purpose. As an object of pilgrimage, Rome (compared to Athens and Geneva) is not only an emphatically
human artefact but also a historically consistent one in that it has not been
severed from its classical past as modern Greece had. Here is an indescribably
rich culture – 'the projection of Greece in art' as the critic Bernard Blackstone
puts it[9] – in place long enough, perhaps, to answer the questions Byron has put
to Europe about its current state. This enterprise is shown, moreover, not only
as a re-run of Byron's earlier travels but also those of a Roman pilgrim, Servius
Sulpicius, who had visited Greek ruins in the Aegean before returning to a
Roman civilization itself laid waste since Sulpicius' time (IV. 388–414). That is,
Byron acknowledges that pilgrimages such as his are themselves classical, and
that ruin is not the unique experience of modernity.

He starts with the old question re-proposed: in Venice, with 'A palace and a
prison on each hand' (IV. 2). No city is more palatial; no city is more secretive
and cruel – but Venice is in its dotage anyway, after France and Austria have
occupied it:

> empty halls,
> Thin streets, and foreign aspects, such as must
> Too oft remind her who and what enthrals,
> Have flung a desolate cloud o'er Venice' lovely walls.   (IV. 132–5)

As in Athens, only interim answers are available here.

The tour to Rome is immensely detailed, and Byron goes to great lengths
to marshal his material and to 'track / Fall'n states and buried greatness' (IV.
219–20) along the way. A visit to Petrarch's tomb at Arqua, for example, brings
to mind the three other great poets of Renaissance Italy: Dante, Ariosto, and
Tasso. Do these four writers, so different in style and temperament, hold
between them a clue to Italian history – or indeed to Byron's own? In the church
of Santa Croce in Florence another eminent foursome is buried – Machiavelli,
Michelangelo, Galileo, and the neoclassical dramatist Alfieri – blending, one
might say, the arts and the sciences 'like the elements, [which] / Might fur-
nish forth creation' (IV. 487–8). But the same city exiled Dante, Petrarch, and
Boccaccio, much as London had exiled Byron. Was the Tuscan capital a
worthy receptacle, then?

If literature and science cannot realize humane ideals or consistently illu-
minate the course of history, then perhaps 'triumphal Art' can (IV. 445). The
Venus de Medici (dragged off to the Louvre by Napoleon, and returned by the
Allies in 1815) in Florence (IV. 433–77), and the Apollo Belvedere in Rome
(IV. 1441–67) constitute one statuary group. So do Pompey and Romulus and
Remus, as icons of republican Rome (IV. 775–92). So do the Dying Gaul and

the Laocöon (IV. 1252–70, 1432–40) as images of human suffering. Ancient war at Lake Thrasimene is contrasted with modern peace at Clitumnus – though even that river plunges over 'the wave-worn precipice' at the falls of Velino (IV. 550–648). The masculine and public values of literature, art, and war are contrasted with feminine and private ones embodied in the nymph Egeria, who loved a Roman king and 'blend[ed] a celestial with a human heart' (IV. 1064), or in the Roman lady and idealized wife (Lady Byron please note), Cecilia Metella (IV. 883–945). There seem to be patterns in such groupings – but what do they imply?

These means of access to the past are so contradictory that Byron comes close to intellectual despair:

> we but feel our way to err:
> The ocean hath his chart, the stars their map,
> And Knowledge spreads them on her ample lap;
> But Rome is as the desart, where we steer
> Stumbling o'er recollections; now we clap
> Our hands, and cry 'Eureka!' it is clear –
> When but some false mirage of ruin rises near.   (IV. 723–9)

Three colossal Roman buildings provide a means of coming to terms with the problem of time by doing more than simply posing it: the Coliseum, the Pantheon, and St Peter's (IV. 1144–296, 1306–23, 1369–431). All are temples of one kind or another: to human suffering, to 'a holiness appealing to all hearts' by virtue of its pagan antiquity, and to Renaissance humanism, 'all musical in its immensities'. All are either round or domed: images of perfection and harmony produced by, but apparently inconsistent with, human aspiration.

A view of the Palatine Hill, however, should not breed complacency or cynicism:

> There is the moral of all human tales;
> 'Tis but the same rehearsal of the past,
> First Freedom, and then Glory – when that fails,
> Wealth, vice, corruption, – barbarism at last.
> And History, with all her volumes vast,
> Hath but *one* page …   (IV. 964–9)

But to adopt this view is dangerous: it would be to return to the empty pose of the epigraph to Canto I, from Louis Charles Fougeret de Monbron's *The Cosmopolitan, or The Citizen of the World* (1753): 'The world is a kind of book, of which you've only read the first page if you've only seen your own country. I've read quite a few, and found them equally disappointing' (*CPW* II. 3). That is no longer a position Byron can occupy with any certainty. From Rome he escapes to the coast and the sea, where humanity's control ends (IV. 1603–11). There may be no historical development from the Armada to Trafalgar, from Assyria, Greece, and Rome to Carthage, but 'Time writes no wrinkle on thine azure brow', he tells the Mediterranean: 'The image of Eternity – the throne / Of the Invisible' (IV. 1637, 1644–5). The riddle of modern Europe remains unsolved, but three potential answers to that riddle – a university-derived classical education, the stoicism displayed by Napoleon, and the cosmopolitanism of de Monbron – have suggested themselves, but also been found wanting.

Chapter 5

The orient and the outcast

A final draft of *Childe Harold* I–II was handed to John Murray in October 1811, but Byron did not start work on his next significant poem until a year later: an unusual state of affairs for a poet who is a byword for prolificacy. Certainly 1812 was a busy year: *Childe Harold* was published in March and made Byron famous overnight. On other fronts he was involved with both the House of Lords and his relationship with Lady Caroline Lamb. There was a hiatus at this time, not surprising in an author contemplating the follow-up to a massive success.

There is evidence (*CPW* III. 479–80) that Byron started work during this period on a verse tale which was later broken into two and completed separately as *The Siege of Corinth* and *Parisina*, published in February 1816. Some lines associated with the first poem survive, originally entitled 'The Stranger' (*CPW* III. 356–7). There is evidence, also, of two songs for what Byron called 'an unfinished Witch drama' (*CPW* IV. 463–4), later used in *Manfred*, published in June 1817. And there is a satire, *Waltz*, about the dance craze of the Regency. Then, in late 1812, this period of indecision was resolved by a 344-line narrative poem, *The Giaour*, 'born, phoenix-like', as Jerome McGann describes it (*CPW* III. 414), from the ashes of two other projects. The first was 'The Monk of Athos', dating back to early 1811, about 'The hopeless Exile's Anguish and Despair'

> As he still lingers near his native Land,
> Or drags a weary load of Grief and Care
> From clime to clime astray, forlorn, and reckless where.   (*CPW* I. 286)

The second was 'Il Diavolo Inamorato' ['the lovesick fiend'], dating from August 1812, and involving another mysterious wanderer, encountered at the Venetian Carnival:

Heedless – yet marked of many – stalked he by,
For in his garb and gesture something strange
And wild seemed foreign to this Revelry.
His front [i.e., forehead] was veiled, all saw that eye, when change
Flashed as with long-desired – but still-deferred Revenge!

(CPW III. 16)

Both these poems are in Spenserian stanzas, and both these gloomy out-casts are evidently related to Childe Harold, but in them and the anonymous Giaour, Byron's reflective tourist in Eastern climes was suddenly transformed into a fatal and fated protagonist who pursues a violent career there. As Harold had been labelled almost immediately as a self-portrait, and as these new tales haunted the same region of the Mediterranean that he had, Byron's readers made the identification that has kept its place in some form or another ever since: that 'The Giaour, the Corsair, Childe Harold, are all the same person', as Hazlitt put it, 'and they are apparently all [Byron] himself.'[1] That the tales were delayed for as long as they were, came as swiftly as they did once the sequence was initiated, and demonstrate the intensity they do, clearly suggests the weight they carried for the author.

The pressures converging on Byron during this entire period – financial, sexual, emotional, and political – were considerable, and certainly he saw this series of poems as a reflection of and relief from almost intolerable depression and disappointment. 'In the last three days I have been quite shut up,' he wrote to Lady Melbourne in November 1813;

> my mind has been from *late* and *later* events in such a state of fermentation that as usual I have been obliged to empty it in rhyme – & am in the very heart of another Eastern tale … this is my usual resource – if it were not for some such occupation to dispel reflection during *inaction* – I verily believe I should very often go mad.   (*LJ* III. 157)

The Bride of Abydos, for example, 'was written to drive my thoughts from the recollection of' – Augusta, Frances Wedderburn Webster, or both; Byron would not say (*LJ* III. 205).

Nor were these pressures only personal. A detailed case has been made by Daniel Watkins that 'the Eastern Tales dramatize powerfully the world into which Byron awoke to find himself famous in 1812,'[2] and that they were polit-ically as specific as they were psychologically so, analysing as best they could his sense of frustrated purpose. Byron's Orient was a place of authenticity com-pared with the shams of English social and political existence, and Bernard Blackstone might almost speak for the poet when he says that within his Eastern poems 'passions are lived without concealment, without shame and without dilution; life and death hang on the lifting of an eyebrow, the folding of a turban, the cadence of a flattering phrase.'[3]

In any event, and for whatever reasons, the cork was pulled: *The Giaour* was the first of five such tales written and published between late 1812 and early 1816 (the others being *The Bride of Abydos*, *The Corsair*, *Lara*, and *The Siege of Corinth*), which extended Byron's fame to levels unprecedented in English literature. Later in his career Byron tended to disparage what he called 'the exaggerated nonsense' of his outpourings, 'which has corrupted the public taste' (*LJ* IX. 161). Nearer the time of their composition he regretted 'that I called some of my own things "Tales," because I think that they are something better' (*LJ* V. 186). But their commercial success has never been disputed. John Murray printed 6,000 copies of *Childe Harold* I–II in 1812, which was already a large run. (He printed only 750 copies of Jane Austen's *Mansfield Park* in 1816, for example, of which 490 copies were remaindered in 1820.) The firm printed 12,500 copies each of *The Giaour* and *The Bride of Abydos* in 1812, and no fewer than 25,000 copies of *The Corsair* in 1814. (Percy Shelley, by contrast, printed 750 copies of *The Revolt of Islam*, at his own expense, in 1818; as late as the 1840s, that edition was still being remaindered at sixpence a copy.)[4]

Without doubt, Murray was a key figure in this story. A quiet but sophisticated publicist, he was 'the first publisher in a modern sense', according to print historian William St Clair: 'an entrepreneur who selected and put together packages of text, finance and marketing', all carefully under the Byron brand, exclusive to the company.[5] Murray played the market assiduously, reprinting poems with extra contents, and sometimes inventing editions that never existed to exaggerate circulation (there is a first edition of *Lara*, for example, and a fourth – but no evidence of a second or third coming in between).[6] We can see Murray repeatedly wheedling product from Byron after his self-imposed exile. 'May I hope', he wrote in July 1819, with Christmas sales in mind, 'that yr Lordship will favour me with some work to open my Campaign in November with … [?]'.[7] In his lordly way Byron liked to point out that he 'care[d] nothing about what you call "the Season"' (*LJ* IX. 159), but, careless or not, he was in part Murray's creature as well as his patron: an object of circulation and exchange in a marketplace of celebrity and notoriety, as well as the artist he rightly believed himself to be.

We can get a sense of the notoriety these poems of 1812–16 conferred on Byron from a clergyman he met in Cephalonia in 1823. 'The poet seemed to delight', James Kennedy wrote in his *Conversations on Religion with Lord Byron and Others*, 'in imagining and delineating all that was bad in human nature.'

Impetuous, stormy, and violent passions; insatiable revenge, unconquered pride, ferocity, and the ungovernable and unlawful omnipotence of love, seem subjects which engaged his thoughts and his pen: in them were mixed expressions of discontent with all earthly enjoyments; with the established order of things; with feelings of contempt for all that man takes pride in; the vanity of ambition, of rank, of warlike or scientific glory. He pourtrays the misery which man brings on man, from the exercise of unruly passions; the evils of tyranny and war; the disorders in the physical, as well as the moral world; he tries in vain to penetrate the inscrutable mysteries of Providence; and, failing in his attempt to account for what he sees, he throws out doubts against the Divinity of the Scriptures. He is not the poet of virtue.[8]

It is easy to imagine both the appeal and the scandalousness of such a writer in a period of widespread moral repression. We have the testimony of Susan Ferrier, future author of novels with titles like *Marriage* (1818) and *Destiny* (1831), for example. 'Did you ever read anything so exquisite as the new Canto of Childe Harold[?]', she wrote to a friend in 1816: 'It is enough to make a woman fly into the arms of a *tiger*.'[9]

The Aegean matrix

The primary feature of the tales is their location, in the Graeco-Turkish bad-lands of the Eastern Mediterranean: 'the blue waters and dazzling skies – the ruined temples and dusky olives – the desolated cities, and turbaned popula-tion', as one of Byron's reviewers put it, 'of modern Attica'.[10] *Childe Harold* II had already discovered this territory, but in these poems Byron exploited the region for every ounce of exoticism and romance it could offer. The besieging forces gathered outside Corinth are typical:

> The tent is pitched, the crescent shines
> Along the Moslem's leaguering lines;
> And the dusk Spahi's bands [of Turkish cavalry] advance
> Beneath each bearded pasha's glance;
> And far and wide as eye can reach
> The turban'd cohorts throng the beach.   (*Siege* 30–5)

The stress is on perennial conflict between Islam and Christianity. 'The shock – the shout – the groan of war' is the norm (*Giaour* 640), and destruction is the rule:

> Leave not in Corinth a living one –
> A priest at her altars, a chief in her halls,
> A hearth in her mansions, a stone on her walls.   (*Siege* 665–7)

Seyd's Muslims may plan to 'flesh their growing valour on the Greek', but Christian Conrad has much the same plans for them: 'Their galleys blaze', he points out during his gang's attack on Seyd's headquarters; 'why not their city too?' (*Corsair*, II. 17, 195.)

Violence underwrites a life of primitive authenticity. 'In hours of love or strife', the Giaour boasts, 'I've scap'd the weariness of life' that consumes the rest of the human species (984–5). Conrad and his piratic followers have 'No dread of death – if with us die our foes':

> Save that it seems even duller than repose:
> Come when it will – we snatch the life of life –
> When lost – what recks it – by disease or strife?
> Let him who crawls enamoured of decay,
> Cling to his couch, and sicken years away.   (*Corsair* I. 26–30)

The 'too long afflicted shore' of Greece (*Siege* 984) is a place for 'man as himself' (*Corsair* I. 248), and a powerful sexual dimorphism is in operation. Chivalry is at once a weakness and a saving grace, a 'softer feeling' (*Corsair* I. 281) that redeems a life of crime.

These men are natural leaders, often in exile from a social system elsewhere. The Giaour – 'some stray renegade' (812) – is also the possessor of 'A noble soul, and lineage high' (869). Like him, Alp, the hero of *The Siege of Corinth*, is a Venetian,

> From Venice – once a race of worth
> His gentle sires – he drew his birth;
> But late an exile from her shore,
> Against his countrymen he bore
> The arms they taught to bear.   (70–4)

'Commanding, aiding, animating all' under his command, Lara, too, is 'Cut off by some mysterious fate from those / Whom birth and nature meant not for his foes' (II. 368, 234–5).

But Byron's protagonists are apostates as well as aristocrats. Certainly Alp 'refused to sign / The cross he deemed no more divine' (*Siege* 493–4); the Giaour is no Christian ('never at our vesper prayer, / Nor e'er before confession chair / Kneels he': 802–4); and Selim is 'From unbelieving mother bred' (*Bride* I. 82), and hence a kind of religious half-breed in his (supposed) father's eye. For Conrad, too, any form of prayer is only 'the coward crouching of despair' (*Corsair* II. 481).

As figures of authority, however tormented, these men attract loyalty. Selim has his 'lawless brood' of henchmen,

> But rough in form, nor mild in mood;
> And every creed, and every race,
> With them hath found – may find a place;
> But open speech, and ready hand,
> Obedience to their chief's command;
> A soul for every enterprize,
> That never sees with terror's eyes;
> Friendship for each, and faith to all,
> And vengeance vow'd for those who fall.   (*Bride* II. 364–72)

Conrad's gang is almost identical:

> In scattered groups upon the golden sand,
> They game – carouse – converse – or whet the brand;
> Select the arms – to each his blade assign,
> And careless eye the blood that dims its shine.   (*Corsair* I. 47–50)

Conrad dominates his pirate crew with 'arts that veil, and oft preserve the proud': a 'lofty port', 'solemn aspect', and a 'high-born eye' that 'lacks not courtesy' (*Corsair* I. 540–4). Alp is a leader, too, but isolated as a Christian among Muslims:

> He stood alone – a renegade
> Against the country he betrayed;
> He stood alone amidst his band,
> Without a trusted heart or hand.   (*Siege* 261–4)

Two ideals offer forms of escape from this war zone: nature, and the love of women. The tales are studded with descriptions of natural beauty, in contrast to the violence that takes place in front of it:

> Strange – that where Nature lov'd to trace,
> As if for Gods, a dwelling-place,
> And every charm and grace hath mixed
> Within the paradise she fixed –
> There man, enamour'd of distress,
> Should mar it into wilderness …

This is from the opening of *The Giaour* (46–51), where the poet looks out over a seascape as beautiful as it is dangerous, bristling with pirate vessels. In *The Bride of Abydos*, the stress is the same. 'Know ye the land', the poem begins, 'where the cypress and myrtle / Are emblems of deeds that are done in their clime'? (That is, emblems of death and love.)

> Where the tints of the earth, and the hues of the sky,
> In colour though varied, in beauty may vie,
> And the purple of Ocean is deepest in die;
> Where the virgins are soft as the roses they twine,
> And all, save the spirit of man, is divine …

Often enough these poems pause climactically on a moment of peace before all hell is let loose. 'Again the Aegean, heard no more afar,' at the beginning of the third canto of *The Corsair* (49–50), 'Lulls his chafed breast from elemental war':

> Who that beheld that Sun upon thee set,
> Fair Athens! could thine evening face forget?
> Not he – whose heart nor time nor distance frees,
> Spell-bound within the clustering Cyclades!   (59–62)

Lara is not set in the clustering Cyclades but in Spain, though Byron acknowledged it to be a sequel to *The Corsair* (*CPW* III. 453), in which (presumably) Conrad has returned home after his Mediterranean sojourn, with his guilty love Gulnare disguised as a page, Kaled. Certainly Lara speaks to Kaled in a language unknown in Spain, and points significantly to the East in his dying moments (II. 444, 467). *Lara*, too, has a breathless night, 'so still, so soft in earth and air, / You scarce would start to meet a spirit there', which is a mockery of the hero's turbulent emotions (I. 167–8, 180). In *The Siege of Corinth* a starlit night looks down before the horrors of the next day: 'Who ever gazed upon them shining,' the narrator wonders, 'And turned to earth without repining, / Nor wished for wings to flee away, / And mix with their eternal ray?' (203–6).

The other ideal that Byron proposes as an escape from a regime of violence is love. Every one of these tales is built upon the traditional fatal triangle. Sometimes the forbidding, proprietary male is a father, sometimes a husband of some kind or another; often he is of another religion. Always the mistress is idealized to the highest degree, precisely because she represents the avenue of escape from the hero's social and psychological torments. 'Oh! who young Leila's glance could read,' the Muslim narrator of *The Giaour* remarks, 'And keep that portion of his creed / Which saith, that woman is but dust, / A soulless toy for tyrant's lust?' (487–90). Zuleika is the same:

> The light of love – the purity of grace –
> The mind – the Music breathing from her face!
> The heart whose softness harmonized the whole –
> And, oh! that eye was in itself a Soul!   (*Bride* I. 178–81)

'With thee all toils are sweet – each clime hath charms,' Selim assures her; 'Earth – sea alike – our world within our arms!' (II. 452–3). The Byronic beloved, that is to say, levels the earth and relieves her lover from the set of conflicts around which his existence rotates. On the night before the destruction of Corinth, Alp encounters his Venetian love, Francesca – though unbeknownst to him what he sees is her spirit, come to beg him to save the city, for she is already dead. 'None, save thou and thine, I've sworn', he tells her,

> Shall be left upon the morn:
> But thee will I bear to a lovely spot,
> Where our hands shall be joined, and our sorrow forgot.
>
> (*Siege* 540–3)

In *The Corsair* this pattern of sexual idealization is brought to a feverish climax. On the one hand there is Conrad's true love, Medora. On the other hand is Gulnare, who rescues him from Seyd's prison tower – tellingly more active and less feminine than his sedentary and secluded lover at home:

> Thou lov'st another – and I love in vain;
> Though fond as mine her bosom, form more fair,
> I rush through peril which she would not dare.   (III. 297–9)

Gulnare treacherously kills Seyd to effect Conrad's escape, and it seems Medora dies at the moment Seyd does. That is, with the loss of Conrad's honour comes the loss of his love, and Conrad is chained forever to a person 'at once above – beneath her sex' (III. 514), whose claim on him emasculates him: 'his mother's softness crept / To those wild eyes, which like an infant's wept' (III. 648–9). Polarized versions of masculinity and femininity are the nearest that nature comes to culture in this otherwise anarchic landscape; the nearest society (such as it is) submits to a form of control. If the opposition between the sexes collapses, the occupants of the landscape must follow suit.

'The Scorpion girt by fire'

The figure at the centre of the Aegean matrix – leader, exile, aristocrat, apostate, lover, tragedian – is one of the most recognizable figures in European literature: the Byronic Hero. We saw 'strange pangs' flashing 'along Childe Harold's brow' in the previous chapter – 'As if the memory of some deadly feud / Or disappointed passion lurk'd below' (*CHP* I. 65–7) – but the Eastern Tales develop this symptom into a fully blown pathology. Sometimes we are given inklings that seem directly autobiographical: that Lara's father died or abandoned him when he was young, for example (I. 13), or that Conrad's 'heart was formed for softness – warped to wrong; / Betrayed too early, and beguiled too long' (*Corsair* III. 662–3). Mostly, the psychological history is shrouded in the secrecy of closely guarded memories:

> o'er his soul
> Winters of Memory seemed to roll,
> And gather in that drop of time
> A life of pain, an age of crime.   (*Giaour* 261–4)

'Though smooth his voice, and calm his general mien,' we learn of Conrad,

> Still seems there something he would not have seen:
> His features' deepening lines and varying hue
> At times attracted, yet perplexed the view,
> As if within that murkiness of mind
> Worked feelings fearful, and yet undefined;
> Such might it be – that none could truly tell –
> Too close enquiry his stern glance would quell.   (*Corsair* I. 207–14)

Around Lara 'some mysterious circle thrown / Repell'd approach, and showed him still alone' (I. 107–8), despite the hypnotic fascination he produces in everyone who sees him. 'Who thundering comes on blackest steed?', the narrator asks at the beginning of *The Giaour* (180). 'Who is that CHIEF?' is the question on everybody's lips at the beginning of *The Corsair*: 'they ask and know no more' (I. 61–2). 'Oft will his glance the gazer rue', the narrator says of the Giaour,

> For in it lurks that nameless spell
> Which speaks – itself unspeakable –
> A spirit yet unquelled and high
> That claims and keeps ascendancy,
> And like the bird whose pinions quake –
> But cannot fly the gazing snake –
> Will others quail beneath his look,
> Nor 'scape the glance they scarce can brook.   (838–45)

Frequently enough, the Byronic man's sanctuary from public exposure is the same as Napoleon's would be in the third canto of *Childe Harold*: stoicism. 'Still in his stern and self-collected mien / A conqueror's more than captive's air is seen' (*Corsair* II. 300–1). But in the Eastern Tales stoicism is seen as a pose and a screen. Like Hamlet – whose gloomy and tortured aura pervades the first two cantos of *Childe Harold* and the Eastern Tales – the moment Byron's bravos are alone their inner torment bursts through:

> His trance was gone – his keen eye shone
> With thoughts that long in darkness dwelt –
> With thoughts that burn – in rays that melt.   (*Bride* I. 329–31)

'He, who would see, must be himself unseen', Byron says:

> Then – with the hurried tread, the upward eye,
> The clenched hand, the pause of agony
> …
> Then – with each feature working from the heart,
> With feelings loosed to strengthen – not depart;
> That rise – convulse – contend – that freeze, or glow,
> Flush in the cheek, or damp upon the brow;
> Then – Stranger! if thou canst, and tremblest not
> Behold his soul.
>
> (*Corsair* I. 235–6, 239–44)

All of which, in effect, constitutes an advertisement for the Eastern series as a whole. Soul beholding was the vicarious and guilty pleasure Byron and Murray had for sale, and they soon discovered between them that a secret never revealed was even more compelling than Selim's admission that he is not Zuleika's brother after all, or the Giaour's confession to his wondering Abbot. Lara disturbs his household with 'A sound – a voice – a shriek – a fearful call' (204), but that is all his readers ever get from him, as regards his guilty past:

> Could he who thus had suffered, so forget
> When such as saw that suffering shudder yet?
> Or did that silence prove his memory fix'd
> Too deep for words, indelible, unmix'd
> In that corroding secrecy which gnaws
> The heart to show the effect, but not the cause?   (279–84)

All there is in the world is fate, as inscrutable as the Mediterranean man himself. What you want you cannot have; what you have will be taken from you; what you fear and dread will never leave your side. The melodrama is directly related to Byron's paranoid sense of himself in his years of fame, with infamy coming around the bend:

> bound and fixed in fettered solitude,
> To pine, the prey of every changing mood;
> To gaze on thine own heart; and meditate
> Irrevocable faults, and coming fate –
> Too late the last to shun – the first to mend –   (*Corsair* III. 222–6)

If it is true that *The Siege of Corinth* was conceived before *The Giaour*, then Byron's comment on *Lara* is accurate: 'the last completes the series' (*LJ* IV. 165). Daniel Watkins has argued that the Byronic hero does not fight vaguely against society at large but against the Islamic merchant culture of the Aegean world – and, by analogy, against the bourgeois culture of Byron's (and John Murray's) England: the 'nation of shopkeepers' famously derided by Napoleon. The poet's gangs of desperados are all in league against domesticity and commercial civilization. 'A body of men associated for purposes of robbery', so the myth goes, 'shall be animated by perfect affection, and every member of it be ready to lay down his life for the life of his chief.'[11] In *Lara*, Byron ultimately puts this part-aristocratic, part-communistic myth of feudal and anti-capitalist loyalty to the test in the most chivalric nation in modern Europe, among the 'knights and dames' of Spain (383). Lara fails, and like Oscar of Alva is buried 'not where his fathers sleep' (520), an exile even in death.

With the failure of that myth of the robber band and its noble leader, Byron came up against a barrier like the one he had met at the end of the first instalment of *Childe Harold* in 1811 (and still in place at the end of the fourth canto of the poem in 1818): the failure of landscape, art, and history to make sense of modern Europe. But before leaving the Eastern sequence I want to look at two poems in more detail. The first begins the group. The second abstracts its themes so pointedly as to remove them even from Spain, and into the Alps, and to exchange narrative for dramatic form.

The Giaour

The first Eastern Tale is exactly what James Kennedy described: 'Impetuous, stormy, and violent passions; insatiable revenge, unconquered pride, ferocity, and the ungovernable and unlawful omnipotence of love'. It is a paean to violence, and purportedly a product of the Islamic cultural zone vicariously laid on for the inquisitive Western reader. To that extent, it is a classic instance of 'Orientalism': the Western habit of presenting the East not as it is but as the West would, for colonial and imperial reasons, like the East to appear – even to itself.[12]

But that is not the only de-familiarizing feature of the poem. *The Giaour* started its life in late 1812 as a manuscript of 344 lines; by the time of the poem's seventh edition – barely a year later – 'this snake of a poem' (*LJ* III. 100) had lengthened to its present 1,334 lines by the addition of nearly three dozen extra passages, long and short (see Table 3). The poem's fragmentary quality makes for demanding reading. But it breaks more fundamental rules of narrative, too. Events are narrated out of sequence, and the identity of the narrator at any given moment is far from clear. So the longitude and latitude of efficient narration are continuously flouted. Moreover, a peculiarly intrusive poet controls access to the entire presentation. The title is notoriously unpronounceable (as the heroine complains in Jane Austen's *Persuasion*); the subtitle

Table 3. *Additions to* The Giaour, *taken from the manuscript to the final edition* (References are to line numbers in the final version of the poem)

MS L (344 ll.)	MS M (375 ll.)	Proof (453 ll.)	1st edn (684 ll.)	2nd edn (816 ll.)	3rd edn (1,014 ll.)	4th edn (1,048 ll.)	5th edn (1,215 ll.)	7th edn (1,334 ll.)
1–6								
				7–20	21–45			
				46–102				
							103–67	
168–99								
					200–50			
							251–2	
					253–76			
277–87								
					288–351			
352–87								
		388–421						
422–4								
	425							
426–72	473–89							
	491–503	490						
					504–18			
519–602								
604–19				603				
				620–54				
655–8								
						689–722		
723–32								
735–8		733–4						
			739–45					
		748–86						
787–831								
								832–915
			916–98					
				999–1,023				
								1,024–8
			1,029–79					
					1,080–98			
			1,099–126					
								1,127–30
							1,131–91	
								1,192–217
							1,218–56	
			1,257–318					
1,319–34								

Slightly simplified version of Table C in Byron, *Complete Poetical Works*, ed. Jerome J. McGann, 7 vols. (Oxford University Press, 1980–93), III. 411. By permission of Oxford University Press.

tells us it is a 'fragment' of foreign extraction perhaps not even original to the author; and the elements modern publishers call 'prelims' (the epigraph, dedication, and 'advertisement') all contribute to a sense of the reader being welcomed among the cultural cognoscenti – who know that 'Moore' is the poet's friend Thomas Moore, and who recognize his baronial condescension to 'Samuel Rogers, Esq.' – but also of being excluded by precisely those things, as well as by his or her ignorance of the historical context 'at the time the Seven Islands were possessed by the Republic of Venice' in the late 1770s (*CPW* III. 39–40).

Readers are adept at bypassing authorial self-indulgences of this kind, but with *The Giaour* their work has only begun once the title-page is negotiated. First, there is a long scene-setting passage (1–179) to complete. Even thereafter, the story is punctuated by three dozen endnotes, some of which gloss Turkish terms the British reader would be unfamiliar with, others which themselves constitute lengthy discussions of Islamic life and custom, or which interrupt the drama in more unexpected and extended ways. At the beginning of the climactic fight between the protagonists, for example, we are told of Hassan that 'then curl'd his very beard with ire' (593): Byron's note describes this as 'a phenomenon not uncommon with an angry Mussulman', before adding a recollection of Ali Pasha's court in 1809. Such interruptions make smooth progress almost impossible.

Yet the poem contains all the compelling ingredients from the Aegean matrix, listed earlier. The net effect is twofold and contradictory. First, a sense that no well-ordered narrative, or stable and Archimedean position of 'truth' accompanying such a narrative, could or should be expected from a place as violently disordered as this, where 'passion riots in her pride, / And lust and rapine wildly reign, / To darken o'er the fair domain' (59–61). Second, that, compelling as it is, this is a *story*: a printed object from John Murray's firm in Mayfair, introduced and perforated by reminders and reassurances of that fact. Even as readers flick to the back of the book to learn the meaning of a Turkish expression they are reminded that this is a work of fiction contrived and controlled by a classically educated aristocrat whose ultimate adherence to Anglophone civilization is (presumably) beyond dispute.

This latter consideration is the reason *The Giaour* remains 'a picture of Turkish Ethics' (*LJ* XI. 186), as well as an Arabian Nights' entertainment, and why Byron can smuggle into this 'string of passages' (*LJ* III. 182) one as significant as this:

> The steed is vanished from the stall,
> No serf is seen is Hassan's hall;

The lonely Spider's thin grey pall
Waves slowly widening o'er the wall;
The Bat builds in his Haram bower;
And in the fortress of his power
The Owl usurps the beacon-tower;
The wild-dog howls o'er the fountain's brim,
With baffled thirst, and famine, grim,
For the stream has shrunk from its marble bed,
Where the weeds and the desolate dust are spread.
'Twas sweet of yore to see it play
And chase the sultriness of day –
As springing high the silver dew
In whirls fantastically flew,
And flung luxurious coolness round
The air, and verdure o'er the ground.
    …
And oft had Hassan's Childhood played
Around the verge of that cascade;
And oft upon his mother's breast
That sound had harmonized his rest;
And oft had Hassan's Youth along
Its bank been sooth'd by Beauty's song;
And softer seemed each melting tone
Of Music mingled with its own. –
But ne'er shall Hassan's Age repose
Along the brink at Twilight's close –
The stream that filled that font is fled –
The blood that warmed his heart is shed! –
And here no more shall human voice
Be heard to rage – regret – rejoice –
The last sad note that swelled the gale
Was woman's wildest funeral wail –
That quenched in silence – all is still,
But the lattice that flaps when the wind is shrill –
Though raves the gust, and floods the rain,
No hand shall close its clasp again.   (288–304, 308–27)

This is a vision of what the Giaour's revenge has brought about: not just an eye for an eye and a tooth for a tooth, but the extinction of an outpost of civilization. With brilliant appropriateness that solitary insect the spider 'weaves' a pall not just for Hassan but for a shattered household, as Islam traditionally requires a family without its head to relocate to the nearest patriarchal male. The harem was the set of apartments where Hassan's family slept; now it is home to a tribe of bats. The watchtower is occupied by the most watchful of birds. Wild animals come to exploit the benefits of civilization, but these are now broken and dried up. The fountain – even more emphatically the centre of a Muslim home than the hearth is of a Christian one, and the accompaniment of all phases of Hassan's life until its end – is as lifeless as his now-dead heart. The most mundane act of domestic care, to close a window against stormy weather so as to protect both the window and the building itself, is one that will never be carried out here again. The passage is the reverse of Orientalist exploitation, bringing home to attentive Western readers the vitality of Islamic civilization even as the next scene – the 'honour killing' of Leila – reminds them of its cruelty. (The beauty of Islamic culture is evoked again in Zuleika's chamber: *Bride* II. 63–86.) *The Giaour* provides no 'position' above and beyond culture by which to judge it in simple terms; any such judgement will have to comprehend the beauty and the ugliness together, in order to comprehend anything at all.

Manfred

'The Mind, that broods o'er guilty woes,' Byron suggested in *The Giaour*, 'is like the Scorpion girt by fire': eventually it will destroy itself with the very 'sting she nourish'd for her foes' (422–9). Byron liked to joke about suicide; but many a true word is spoken by him in jest. 'I should, many a good day,' he wrote from Venice in 1817, 'have blown my brains out, but for the recollection that it would have given pleasure to my mother-in-law' (*LJ* V. 165). The critic Bernard Beatty suggests that Byron 'had a peculiar horror of suicide,'[13] but horror is not inconsistent with fascination. The Giaour's confession is a kind of extended suicide note before what he calls 'the final goal' (1,282) of death, and Conrad even tries to electrocute himself in his captivity during a thunder storm (*Corsair* III. 264–5).

Manfred was begun in the Alps in September 1816, but was a long time achieving completion. Byron finished a first draft in January 1817, but was dissatisfied with the original third act and rewrote it by May that year. He saw its connection to his earlier poems when he told Murray *Manfred* was 'too much in my old style' (*LJ* V. 185). Once again we have a hero 'of high lineage' (II. I. 7) who exerts a magnetic appeal on strangers, and whose beloved, Astarte, meets a tragic end. Once again human deformity is contrasted to natural beauty (I. II. 36–47). Like *The Giaour*, *Manfred* involves a lengthy act of confession, but there is no desire for atonement in the Giaour's and Manfred's testimonies. Both are mixtures of defiance and despair (*Giaour* 908); both desire 'Oblivion, self-oblivion' above all things (*Manfred* I. I. 144, *Giaour* 997–8); both insist on the guiltlessness of their beloveds (*Giaour* 1,144, *Manfred* II. II. 116); and both protagonists are 'fatal and fated in [their] sufferings' (*Manfred* II. II. 36).

One key difference between the two guilty self-tormentors, however, is that there is no third party to carry the blame in the later poetic drama. Manfred is Giaour and Hassan combined, lover and murderer both. The other difference is the consanguinity of Manfred and Astarte, and the blatantly incestuous nature of their relation – the drama was based on a despairing but defiant Alpine journal that Byron kept for his half-sister (*LJ* V. 96–105), ending 'love me as you are beloved by me'. The theme of incest may be blatant – Manfred and Astarte 'loved each other as we should not love' (II. I. 27) – but the facts surrounding Astarte's demise remain shrouded in mystery. 'I have shed / Blood', Manfred tells the Witch of the Alps, 'but not hers – and yet her blood was shed – / I saw – and could not staunch it' (II. II. 119–21).

'I have always found *Manfred* the most baffling of Byron's works', Bernard Beatty remarks, 'and have never felt that I fully understand it.'[14] Certainly the drama betrays a lack of human interest in comparison with the earlier tales, but that is because it is an abstraction from them. Successively and impressively, the hero cuts himself free from any form of moral claim except the guilt he carries with him but is unable to discharge. 'Earth, ocean, air, night, mountains, winds, thy star' are all evoked in spiritual form in the first scene, and are all sent packing; a suicide attempt is foiled by a Chamois Hunter, embodiment of mundane human aspiration: 'cheerful old age and a quiet grave' (II. I. 69); Manfred is too proud to gain enlightenment from the Witch of the Alps at the cost of subservience (II. II. 155–60); and even three Destinies, fresh from the work of 'repairing shattered thrones, / Marrying fools, [and] restoring dynasties' (II. III. 62–3) in mainland Europe are not powerful enough to deny Manfred the vision of Astarte that is raised for him by Nemesis itself. 'To-morrow ends thy earthly ills', Astarte tells Manfred (II. IV. 152), and inevitably in the third act he returns home to confront his demons, confessing like the Giaour to a representative of organized religion. Manfred's agnosticism proves indestructible, just as the Giaour's did ('this grief / Looks not to priesthood for relief'; *Giaour* 1207), and in the final scene we find him in the tower he and Astarte used to share, on yet another breathlessly still evening, going over those same impressions of Imperial Rome that Byron had recently put to use in *Childe Harold* IV.

As in that poem, there is no answer in the Eternal City. The Abbot returns to join Manfred in defying a Satanic spirit come to claim the hero's soul on the basis of his 'many crimes' (III. IV. 121), while Manfred denies any such obligations but death itself, which can only touch his physical integument. 'The mind which is immortal makes itself / Requital for its good or evil thoughts' (III. IV. 129–30), Manfred insists, which would serve as the epitaph for the entire fraternity of Byronic over-reachers. 'The hand of death is on me', he tells this demon (III. IV. 141), 'but not yours!' To be utterly consumed by fate, it seems, confers a kind of freedom.

Chapter 6

Four philosophical tales

'Byron', it has been said, 'is the poet of liberty'[1] – which is like saying Wordsworth is the poet of nature; in each case there is a complicated relationship between the writer and his theme. We saw that the Byronic hero purchased freedom at the cost of cutting himself off from the world by rejecting its moral claims on him. (His avatar, Mr Rochester, in Charlotte Brontë's *Jane Eyre* (1847), does much the same thing as regards his plans for a bigamous marriage with the novel's heroine.) 'But Byron's concept of the free hero … is not monolithic', the critic Drummond Bone suggests, and freedom in his poetry 'is not simply a matter of a central character's struggle … but of explicit and implicit examination of historical and other fictional examples of its existence, or more often its failure to exist.'[2]

Four of Byron's medium-length verse narratives – *The Prisoner of Chillon* (1816), *Beppo*, *Mazeppa* (both 1817–18), and *The Island* (1823) – treat the issue of liberty with close attention. Each is a masterpiece of a different kind, and as a group they also differ from the earlier Eastern Tales. The origins of that set of poems are highly specific, in terms of both Byron's state of mind at the time of their composition and their setting within the 'Aegean matrix' where Islam and Christianity meet. The later group is more diverse. *The Prisoner of Chillon* concerns a sixteenth-century Swiss Protestant martyr; *Beppo* is an entirely fictitious Venetian shaggy dog story; *Mazeppa* relates an incident in the early life of a 70-year-old ally of King Charles XII of Sweden, on retreat in the Ukraine in 1709; and *The Island*, set in Polynesia, is based on the *Bounty* mutiny of 1789. Three are historical, therefore, but only in the loosest sense; and whereas every work of literature is to some extent personal to its author, these stories contain little of the confessional element tangible in *Manfred* or *The Bride of Abydos*.

This degree of abstraction is why 'philosophical' seems the right word to use of them. Yet these stories are also more *realistic* than the Eastern Tales: more plausible and less melodramatic. It is an important literary-critical paradox that a realistic specificity in the depiction of character produces a general applicability in human terms. In stories like *The Prisoner of Chillon* and *Mazeppa*, critic Mark Storey suggests, Byron 'manages to present us with plausible characters placed in fully realised settings, particularised and detailed, whilst at the same time implying that such characters are not outside the pale of our knowledge' – as the exotic Eastern heroes clearly are intended to be. 'There is in fact', he goes on,

> a very strong sense in which they become fully representative of their condition. In other words *The Prisoner of Chillon* is not just about Bonnivard, it is about the nature of imprisonment; *Mazeppa* is not just about a rather humorous old Pole with a good story to tell, it is about the nature of passion and freedom.[3]

So these stories extended Byron's artistic palette in a significant way, in terms of realism, objectivity, and creative purpose.

Though they form no sequence, the four poems approach a set of issues related to the overarching theme of liberty: imprisonment, personal and political self-hood, passion versus experience, and innocence versus guilt. It is no surprise, therefore, that sexual relations are the focus of three of these poems – no longer idealized, as they were in the Eastern Tales, but actualized and dramatic.

Byron's work is an unfolding project, like that of any other great writer, and themes from the Eastern Tales and from *Childe Harold* retain a place alongside his new interests. *Beppo* is an exercise in cultural relativism, much as *The Prisoner of Chillon* and *Mazeppa* are studies in stoicism, and even the Byronic hero returns (briefly) as Fletcher Christian in *The Island*. Moreover, this group anticipates as much as it recapitulates: *Beppo* and *Mazeppa*, in particular, are vital steps in Byron's 'true progress' towards *Don Juan*, as Peter Porter described it in Chapter 3.

A cell: *The Prisoner of Chillon*

The Prisoner of Chillon is subtitled 'A Fable', perhaps to distinguish it from the sequence of tales which preceded it. The *Oxford English Dictionary* defines fable as something explicitly fictional (whereas François Bonivard was an authentic historical figure, albeit a mythologized one, born in 1493 and imprisoned between 1530 and 1536), often involving supernatural or extraordinary persons or incidents (whereas Byron's Bonnivard is, if anything, a mundane being in comparison with the melodramatic heroes of the earlier stories), devised to convey some useful lesson (whereas the poem is strikingly undidactic). Why, then, did Byron choose the word fable to describe his story?

Perhaps its 'philosophical' qualities are what led Byron to entitle the story as he did. The historical Bonivard is not named in the narrative poem at all, only in the sonnet that Byron later attached to it. When Byron visited the castle of Chillon with Shelley on 25 June 1816, and throughout his composition of *The Prisoner of Chillon* thereafter, he 'had not heard any stories suggesting that Bonnivard suffered in the cause of liberty',[4] only that he was imprisoned for his religious beliefs. In fact the poem was originally entitled 'The Captive' (*CPW* IV. 4). Only after its completion did Byron write the 'Sonnet on Chillon', as well as a footnote regretting the opportunity he had lost to celebrate Bonivard's 'courage and virtues' in his fable (*CPW* IV. 453). The sonnet is a rhetorical reflection on liberty: 'Eternal spirit of the chainless mind! Brightest in dungeons' (*CPW* IV. 3), and so forth. The fable is a realistic reflection on the mental effects of incarceration – itself an immense theme in Romantic art, from Beethoven's *Fidelio* (1805) and Delacroix's 'Tasso in the Asylum' (1824), to Stendhal's *The Charterhouse of Parma* (1839). Perhaps 'fable' seemed to be the right word to use because of the story's aim: both to concentrate and to generalize the experience of imprisonment as much as possible.

This concentration is achieved in the first place by first-person narration, of which *The Prisoner of Chillon* is a classic instance – not only because it is an account of solitary confinement, which, by definition, cannot be witnessed, but also because the central figure's state of mind is the sole object of interest. In the prisoner's monologue Byron made a significant artistic advance on the florid account of himself that the Giaour offered in the second half of that earlier story.

Bonnivard begins with a chillingly matter-of-fact inventory of his cell's contents:

> There are seven pillars of gothic mold,
> In Chillon's dungeons deep and old,
> There are seven columns, massy and grey,
> Dim with a dull imprisoned ray
> …
> And in each pillar there is a ring,
> And in each ring there is a chain.   (27–30, 36–7)

What makes this account disturbing is our recognition that it is retrospective: a testimony written after the events described. This is not only a fable of which incarceration is the topic; it is the *product* of incarceration and of a man broken by that experience. The cell is still real for him, and there is nothing 'chainless' about Bonnivard's mind:

> That iron is a cankering thing,
> For in these limbs its teeth remain,
> With marks that will not wear away.   (38–40)

In Byron's later play, *The Two Foscari*, the imprisoned hero's wife suggests at one point that the mind should make its own liberty, to which her husband replies:

> That has a noble sound; but 'tis a sound,
> A music most impressive, but too transient:
> The mind is much, but is not all.   (*TF* III. I. 85–7)

At its heart, *The Prisoner of Chillon* has a simple but dreadful moral: that the mind is much, but it is not all, and that physical imprisonment eventually becomes a mental one from which the captive can never escape. Bonnivard and his two younger brothers are imprisoned together but can neither see each other nor speak in voices that they recognize: 'They never sounded like our own' (68). Incarceration severs even the closest human relationships, not through confinement or harsh treatment as such, but through the loss of liberty that is the prerequisite for those relationships to germinate and continue. 'My brother's soul was of that mould', the prisoner tells us, 'Which in a palace had grown cold, / Had his free breathing been denied' (140–2). After the death of his brothers, Bonnivard says, 'I had no thought, no feeling – none – / Among the stones I stood a stone' (235–6). Bonnivard's mental breakdown into catatonia is itself broken by the song of a bird, and not the least impressive element in the poem is Byron's refusal to treat Bonnivard's visitor in symbolic terms, as a messenger of freedom, for example, or an embodiment of his dead brother's soul. The bird's departure leaves the prisoner completely alone: a being 'That hath no business to appear / When skies are blue, and earth is gay' (298–9). His abjection is made clear when he interprets his new-found ability to move around his cell – having broken his chain in a passionate attempt to aid his dying brother – as 'liberty' (306), and when he carves out a footing in the prison wall 'not therefrom to escape' (319) but to discover instead that 'the whole earth' he can now see through the bars 'would henceforth be / A wider prison unto me' (322–3). The prison has triumphed over the prisoner; the sight of birds and fish, free agents of sky and water, now only troubles his broken will and makes him regret his 'recent chain' (358). He loses track of time, and when he is released he betrays no interest in the event: 'It was at

length the same to me, / Fettered or fetterless to be' (372–3). There is none of
the rhetorical defiance celebrated in Byron's accompanying sonnet in the bleak
conclusion of the prisoner's account:

> My very chains and I grew friends,
> So much a long communion tends
> To make us what we are: – even I
> Regain'd my freedom with a sigh.   (391–4)

In one of his last poems, 'Thoughts on Freedom', Byron comforted himself
with the notion that 'They only can feel freedom truly who / Have worn long
chains' (*CPW* VII. 77). Perhaps that was his hope for Greece. Bonnivard's case
is a less uplifting one: once to have worn long chains is never to feel freedom
again.

A society: *Beppo*

The Prisoner of Chillon is so bleak a vision of deprivation that it is hard to conceive of *Beppo* being connected to it thematically. Yet it, too, is about liberty –
only from a different point of view. Byron said the poem contained 'politics &
ferocity' (*LJ* VI. 9), but the poem is not at all ferocious, which is why it has the
impact that it does. Had Byron conducted his argument in a confrontational
style his audience would have rejected it entirely. As it was, readers like Francis
Jeffrey at the *Edinburgh Review* were entirely taken in. *Beppo* was, Jeffrey pla-
cidly concluded, 'absolutely a thing of nothing – without story, characters, sentiments, or intelligible object – a mere piece of lively and loquacious prattling,
in short, upon all kinds of frivolous subjects, – a sort of gay and desultory
babbling about Italy and England, Turks, balls, literature, and fish sauces'.[5] In
fact, *Beppo* marks another crucial advance for Byron, and a vital step in his
'progress' towards *Don Juan*: the realization that comic art could be profound.
It may look like desultory babbling, but it is a carefully focused analysis of freedom and the social ethos from which it is inevitably derived.

   Beppo is a product of the Venetian carnival, and of liberty and licence before
the period of Lenten abstinence. The whole world is collected in the city, albeit
in disguise – 'Greeks, Romans, Yankee-doodles, and Hindoos' (20) – and it is a
mundane world, the occupants of which entertain themselves, 'However high
their rank, or low their station, / With fiddling, feasting, dancing, drinking,
masquing, / And other things which may be had for asking' (6–8). This, the
poem suggests, is how the world goes on and sexually restocks itself, and only
one rule remains in place: although the influence of religion is diminished, the

clergy is exempt from ridicule (23). The carnival is an example of the Catholic faith's traditionally tolerant attitude to everyday irregularity. If the Church requires an extended period of abstinence, that is best inaugurated by a briefer one of chartered licence, humans being what they are.

Gender hierarchies go the way of class and religion during this holiday. 'Prudery flings aside her fetter' (12) for a time, and Venetian women assert their preponderance accordingly:

> They've pretty faces yet, those same Venetians,
>   Black eyes, arch'd brows, and sweet expressions still,
> Such as of old were copied from the Grecians,
>   In ancient arts by moderns mimick'd ill;
> And like so many Venuses of Titian's
>   (The best's at Florence – see it, if ye will)
> They look when leaning over the balcony,
> Or stepp'd from out a picture by Giorgone.   (81–8)

The carnival is a specifically feminine celebration, and hence a licensed, lingering farewell to the pleasures of the flesh.

Any time of the year 'less liked by husbands than by lovers' (11) is potentially dangerous, and Byron reminds us of a famous – albeit mistaken – case of Venetian adultery, dramatized in *Othello* by the quintessential English author. 'Shakespeare described the sex in Desdemona', the poet innocently remarks, 'As very fair, but yet suspect in fame' (129–30). So we are prepared for a time-honoured storyline, involving both adultery and murder – only to be disappointed. There is neither Othello nor Iago here, and no one will be stifled with a pillow by way of a tragic climax. Laura (jestingly named after Petrarch's platonic mistress) is no Desdemona, but as suave, sophisticated, and worldly as Venice itself. 'Blooming still', she 'looked extremely well where'er she went' (177, 180). Her husband has been lost at sea for some years, and, as is the Italian custom, Laura has taken 'a vice-husband, *chiefly to protect her*' (232). Every married lady is 'permitted to have *two* men … and no one notices, nor cares a pin' (283, 286), provided appearances are kept up. It is a negotiation built on social tolerance and moral permissiveness – at the opposite end of the spectrum, of course, from Byron's earlier, Orientalist (408), Mediterranean poems of fatal conflict and romantic prohibition.

This dramatic account of Laura's 'sinful doings' (321) – *Beppo* is an English poem for Protestant readers, after all – unexpectedly produces a much larger set of cultural comparisons, between Italian and British weather, language, and women at large,

From the rich peasant-cheek of ruddy bronze,
…
To the high dama's brow, more melancholy,
But clear, and with a wild and liquid glance,
Heart on her lips, and soul within her eyes,
Soft as her clime, and sunny as her skies.   (354, 357–60)

The pleasures of Italy are those of the flesh: carts loaded with grapes, not dung (334–5); sophisticated dining (337); a sunrise that is predictably clear and glorious (338–44); and a language that 'melts like kisses from a female mouth' (346) – unlike 'our harsh northern whistling, grunting guttural, / Which we're oblig'd to hiss, and spit, and sputter all' (351–2). The freedoms of Italy, accordingly, are personal ones, and it is not hard to imagine the narrator – 'a broken Dandy, lately on my travels' (410) – taking advantage of the situation, and requesting the extension of Catholic tolerance and permissiveness to him, too, should he have need of them.

England can hardly compete with Italy on grounds such as these. But Italy's personal freedoms, Byron reminds us, are balanced by Britain's political ones:

'England! with all thy faults I love thee still,'
  I said at Calais, and have not forgot it;
I like to speak and lucubrate my fill;
  I like the government (but that is not it);
I like the freedom of the press and quill;
  I like the Habeas Corpus (when we've got it);
I like a parliamentary debate,
Particularly when 'tis not too late;

I like the taxes, when they're not too many;
  I like a seacoal fire, when not too dear;
I like a beef-steak, too, as well as any;
  Have no objection to a pot of beer;
I like the weather, when it is not rainy,
  That is, I like two months of every year.
And so God save the Regent, Church, and King!
Which means that I like all and every thing.

Our standing army, and disbanded seamen,
  Poor's rate, Reform, my own, the nation's debt,
Our little riots just to show we are free men,
  Our trifling bankruptcies in the Gazette,
Our cloudy climate, and our chilly women,
  All these I can forgive, and those forget,
And greatly venerate our recent glories,
And wish they were not owing to the Tories.   (369–92)

The British government may have suspended habeas corpus on some occasions during Byron's lifetime, but early nineteenth-century Italians possessed no such legal protections at all. (Talking of 'the freedom of the press and quill': in Milan in 1816 Byron had met the nationalist poet and editor Silvio Pellico, a year younger than him. In 1820, Pellico would be arrested and arbitrarily incarcerated for ten years, before publishing his classic *My Prisons* in 1832. Pellico was imprisoned by Austrian authorities, it is true; but Teresa Guiccioli's family was bullied from house and home during the period of her association with Byron by Italian governments in Tuscany and the Papal States.) The Church of England may be a lacklustre institution compared to the Church of Rome, but its capacity to exercise legal powers over everyday English existence had been broken in the days of Henry VIII, and 'quizzing the clergy' (23) had been an English pastime ever since. English freedom is a social freedom, with all that that implies in terms of both legal protection and public exposure ('Our trifling bankruptcies', reported in the weekly papers, for example). There is personal liberty and there is social liberty, and in England the latter exists at the expense of the former, generating moral intrusiveness from the same soil as legal immunity. 'In *Beppo* we encounter two whole societies in miniature'[6] and must choose one or the other – we can't have both.

Wherever Enlightenment explorers went in the eighteenth century they regarded the status of women as an index of civilization. As the stronger sex, men can put women to work for them. So for a culture to treat women with civility is, from the European perspective, for it to advance out of savagery. Byron's position in *Beppo* is typically contrary. The Venetian carnival is feminine throughout, and Laura is its presiding deity; the English state, on the other hand, is a wholeheartedly masculine affair, with its standing army, its media, and its parliament.

This being so – and contrary to appearances and the national self-image, Byron implies – the British imprison their womenfolk in a regime more repressive even than the Turks, let alone the Italians. Turkish women are more free in the harem than their English counterparts in a modern, Protestant society, which constrains women even in the act of educating them according to its (masculine) standards:

> No chemistry for them [the Turks] unfolds her gasses,
>   No metaphysics are let loose in lectures,
> No circulating library amasses
>   Religious novels, moral tales, and strictures
> Upon the living manners, as they pass us;
>   No exhibition glares with annual pictures;
> They stare not on the stars from out their attics,
> Nor deal (thank God for that!) in mathematics.   (617–24)

English freedom, in Byron's view, is freedom for women not to be women at all – as nature had intended them to be, at any rate – but a miserably unhappy population of self-conscious would-be intellectuals, like Lady Byron, coddled and stifled by a Protestant moral code inculcated through the engines and organs of ideology and literary discourse. The sexual ethic of Venice is one of *vive la différence*, and no one could be more conventionally feminine than Laura, coolly re-encountering her lost husband while on her lover's arm. The sexual ethic of England is one where *la différence* is eradicated altogether, and femininity and masculinity are eradicated along with it.

'In England', Byron wrote in an unfinished sketch from 1823, 'An Italian Carnival',

> We … have seen many a splendid and dull Masquerade – dull – because they attempted to support Characters under a piece of paste-board without having even any of their own. – But the Italians pretend to nothing of the kind … A masque is merely a dress – or a disguise – but not an attempt at farce or Comedy. – Their parts are not studied. – On the contrary … it may be observed – that a woman, at least a Continental woman is never less a Masque than when a Masque.   (*CMP* 192)

The Italian woman is never more free than when in disguise; the social world has no final claim on her. Englishwomen, on the other hand, suffer acutely from their attempt to support a role and by that means to preserve the social norm. 'Perhaps, the Italians would but ill exchange their Carnival for a Parliament', Byron concluded: 'but they long for the latter' (*CMP* 193). Given the choice between nature and culture, humanity always chooses the second, and it always chooses wrongly.

A psyche: *Mazeppa*

English Romantic literature is rightly associated with lyric poetry, but its successes in narrative verse are just as remarkable. Wordsworth's 'The Ruined Cottage', Coleridge's 'The Rime of the Ancient Mariner', and Keats's 'The Eve of St Agnes' are flawless examples, and *Mazeppa* belongs with them: a story so spontaneous and so fluent that it appears to tell itself.

The poem had its origin alongside the first instalment (Cantos I–II) of the greatest Romantic narrative poem, *Don Juan*. In both, an *ingénu* falls in love with a married woman in a cultured environment (Poland, Spain), is torn from her by her husband, undergoes exposure to the elements (on horseback or via shipwreck), and is restored to life in a natural environment (Ukrainian steppe or Greek island) by a maiden lover.

Byron suggests in both *Don Juan* and *Mazeppa* – as poets have suggested since their medium was invented – that the motive force behind Juan's and Mazeppa's trials and tribulations is 'fortune'. 'Such was the hazard of the die' (15), he says in *Mazeppa*, 'When fortune left the royal Swede' (2), Charles XII, at the battle of Poltava, and sent him packing out of Russia as Napoleon would be sent 100 years later in 1812 (8–14). But 'the hazard of the die' is a half-truth only, as *Don Juan* and *Mazeppa* make clear. It is the way in which we *respond* to such hazards that matters.

In the hands of Enlightenment commentators like Samuel Johnson ('The Vanity of Human Wishes', 1749) and Voltaire (*History of Charles XII*, 1732) the career of Charles XII was interpreted in terms of defeated (and therefore misplaced) ambition. Johnson's comment is particularly relevant:

> A Frame of Adamant, a Soul of Fire,
> No Dangers fright him, and no Labours tire;
> O'er Love, o'er Fear, extends his wide Domain,
> Unconquered Lord of Pleasure and of Pain;
> No Joys to him pacific Scepters yield;
> War sounds the Trump, he rushes to the Field.[7]

It is typical of Johnson to wonder about a person such as this (impetuous, insatiable, self-destructive), and it is typical of Byron to choose a morally less direct mode of commentary on Charles's case: his Ukrainian ally, Mazeppa. Mazeppa is older and wiser than Charles; no longer the tortured possessor of a 'soul of fire' and therefore, perhaps, authentically that 'lord of pleasure and of pain' Johnson had described. What is it, Byron asks, to be such a thing? So Mazeppa presents us with a further treatment of stoicism: not the aristocratic-cum-Napoleonic variety we have seen so far in *Childe Harold* and the Eastern Tales, but something more spontaneous and less self-assertive (as we shall see it again in *Don Juan*).

Lying under 'a savage tree' (33) and seriously wounded, Charles is in pointed contrast to his unflappable lieutenant, who calmly makes his bivouac 'in an old oak's shade' (54), sees to his mount, services his weaponry, and feeds himself and others before his leader comments on the phenomenal relationship Mazeppa has with his horse – 'spirited and docile too' (68), just as he is. 'Ill betide / The school wherein I learn'd to ride!' (107–8) is the opening for Mazeppa's reminiscence, designed to take Charles's mind off his sufferings but, of course, completely relevant to them and to their perpetrator (that is, Charles himself).

Mazeppa's offence was against a ruler very different from Charles:

> A learned monarch, faith! was he,
> And most unlike your majesty:

He made no wars, and did not gain
New realms to lose them back again.   (131–4)

John Casimir of Poland is an alternative, then, but no more an ideal ruler than
Charles himself. His is a cultured court 'of jousts and mimes' (151), peaceably
corrupt and recognizably modern, and Mazeppa fell victim to its troubadour-
style ethos, falling in love with the wife of a Count Palatine thirty years older
than his bride. Casimir's Poland – unknown territory to Byron, of course –
is not a society of the kind depicted in *Beppo*, but an operatic backdrop for
an emblematic passion, just as Chillon is the location for an emblematic
incarceration.

As in any troubadour romance, Mazeppa's love affair is chivalrously pre-
ordained ('For I had strength, youth, gaiety'; 187), and Theresa is the eternal
mistress of the eternal squire: 'I loved her then – I love her still; / And such as
I am, love indeed / In fierce extremes – in good and ill' (225–7.) Such a comment comes directly out of Byron's own restless and dissatisfied speculations
on the sources of human sufficiency – like this from his 1814 journal:

> There is ice at both poles, north and south – all extremes are the
> same – misery belongs to the highest and the lowest only, – to the
> emperor and the beggar, when unsixpenced and unthroned. There is,
> to be sure, a damned insipid medium – an equinoctial line – no one
> knows where … (*LJ* III. 257)

An ethic of extremes might be preferable to an 'insipid medium'; but it is possible to see existence in terms more measured and more ambivalent – that is
to say, more like Mazeppa's world view than Charles's. 'He who would make
his way in the world,' Byron wrote (only two months before the journal entry
quoted above), 'must let the world believe that it made it for him, and accom-
modate himself to the minutest observance of its regulations' (*LJ* IV. 69). An
'equinoctial' accommodation is another reputable form of making your way in
the world, therefore. But how might it be achieved, and at what cost?

An ethic of fierce extremes implicitly comments on Charles's case, though
the Swede is no lover: 'They tell me, Sire, you never knew / Those gentle frailties' (283–4). Charles's frailties are martial, not amatory. Should he cultivate
Mazeppa's stoical indifference to defeat, and if so, how? Were he to do so,
would he remain himself? The nature of self-control is the freedom-related
'philosophical' issue of the poem, concentrated – and generalized – again in
the case of one individual.

Mazeppa's passion certainly wasn't a 'gentle frailty' when it had him in its
grip, but rather 'a form of imprisonment, a giving-up of one's own will and
destiny'.[8] The punishment meted out to him by Theresa's husband, therefore, is

the corollary of his crime: an all-absorbing passion which has branded his life in perpetuity, but from which he has emerged, marked but unscathed – able to speak of the passions in terms of 'gentle frailties', in fact, from the ironic perspective of experience. Mazeppa is already bound to a raging sexual passion, but now his predicament will be physically actualized. Inevitably the guilty couple are discovered almost as soon as they have become lovers. Within moments, Mazeppa is strapped to a wild horse – 'A Tartar of the Ukraine breed' (360) – which carries him back to its own wild origins, far from Casimir's toy court. The animal is utterly untamed and sensitively terrified, and the landscape they traverse is blatantly symbolic: 'a wild plain of far extent, / And bounded by a forest black' (430–1), through which they are chased by an implacable pack of wolves, whose 'stealing, rustling step' (502) is furiously punitive. A deathly climax passes and the horse plunges into a river the 'unknown and silent shore' (586) of which is not death but new life. 'My stiffen'd limbs were rebaptized', Mazeppa says: 'I scarcely knew / If this were human breath I drew' (589, 599–600).

In effect, Mazeppa survives an ordeal that destroyed Bonnivard. His twenty-four hour (643) exposure comes to an end as his mount is absorbed into a herd of horses, 'the wild, the free' (684) before expiring (quite undramatically; it is important that the horse is given no character, but represents only Mazeppa's passionate temperament). Instinctively, the herd retreats 'from a human eye' (708) that has tasted passion, witnessed death, and recovered its humanity:

> For he who hath in turn run through
> All that was beautiful and new,
> Hath nought to hope, and nought to leave;
> And, save the future, (which is view'd
> Not quite as men are base or good,
> But as their nerves may be endued),
> With nought perhaps to grieve.   (741–7)

This is a far stronger variety of stoicism than Bonnivard's abjection; life is a matter of nerves, not morality, and the secret is to command your passions lest they command you. Accordingly, Mazeppa awakes to his reward: a pair of 'black eyes so wild and free' (812), that embody legitimate but untaught love; a victory over the 'vain fool' (848), Theresa's husband, who had sought to extirpate (rather than temper) the hero's lust for life; and, years later, revenge, when his Ukrainians return to the Count's castle 'with twice five thousand horse' in place of one (411): 'For time at last sets all things even' (417).

The story is replete with morals for the defeated emperor, therefore. But he is oblivious to them, not only because such lessons must be learned at first hand if they are to be learned at all – but also because he is asleep. Mazeppa's is a triumph of temperament over experience, and such things cannot be taught.

A culture: *The Island*

The Island concerns an indigenous people and the exercise of British sea power. It is tempting, therefore, to see it as critic Nigel Leask does, as 'one of Byron's deepest indictments of European colonialism'.[9] But Byron trod a more careful line than such a comment suggests. 'I have two things to avoid,' he told Leigh Hunt: 'the first that of running foul of my own "Corsair" and style … and the other *not* to run counter to the reigning [loyalist, authoritarian] stupidity altogether – otherwise they will say that I am eulogizing *Mutiny*' (*LJ* X. 90). The poem is a study of two islands at opposite ends of the earth – Toobonai and Britain – and Peter Graham is right to bring *The Island* alongside *Beppo* in that regard. Both poems, he suggests, 'demonstrate more clearly than do any of the other tales Byron's ambivalent or relativist sense of different codes for different places – but also his concurrent understanding that some human truths transcend, or underlie, all such local difference'.[10]

That larger issue of relativism and truth is one to which we shall return in discussing *Don Juan*. Where *The Island* is concerned it is important to note that (as the poet warned Leigh Hunt) Byron had no intention of adding to the Romantic hagiography on Fletcher Christian. His grandfather, Admiral John Byron, was himself the victim of a famous mutiny on board HMS *Wager* in South American waters in 1741. So the hero of the story is carefully suspended between Bligh and Christian, duty and freedom.

Few later writers have called the historical Bligh 'gallant' or 'bold', as Byron does (I. 17, 51), and we first encounter him, 'Secure in those by whom the watch was kept' and dreaming 'of Old England's welcome shore' (I. 18–19). His crew has a very different set of loyalties:

> Men without country, who, too long estranged,
> Had found no native home, or found it changed,
> And, half uncivilized, preferred the cave
> Of some soft savage to the uncertain wave.   (I. 29–32)

Like Conrad's gang from *The Corsair*, the men of the *Bounty* aspire to 'the freedom which can call each grot a home' and to have no master but their mood (I. 42, 38). Theirs is a negative Utopia, defined solely in terms of what it lacks – above all, lords and masters. Christian's insurgency is a 'reign of rage and fear' (I. 54), and a 'Saturnalia of unhoped-for power' (I. 84), in which the ship's brandy supply is distributed immediately, 'lest passion should return to reason's shoal' (I. 100). Indeed, the *Bounty* becomes 'a moral wreck' (I. 128) immediately the mutiny takes place. Christian and his comrades may seek to bury their crimes in 'lands where, save their conscience, none accuse' (I. 212), but the 'roused discipline' (I. 203) of Georgian England is not far behind. Byron's attitude is the reverse of the Romantic-rebellious here.

After the first canto Bligh and Christian disappear, and we are taken directly to Toobonai itself, with the mutineers well established. But the island is no Polynesian idyll. The flowers that bloom best here grow out of dead warriors' skulls (II. 8) and memories of peace 'ere Fiji blew the shell of war' (II. 35) are remote. Conflict with the Fijians has left Toobonai's fields 'rank with weeds':

> Forgotten is the rapture, or unknown,
> Of wandering with the moon and love alone.
> But be it so: – *they* taught us how to wield
> The club, and rain our arrows o'er the field;
> Now let them reap the harvest of their art!   (II. 39–43)

The South Sea islanders have the same appetite for war and conquest as their North Sea counterparts, and the only difference between the two is the Pacific islanders' lack of hypocrisy – 'The prayers of Abel linked to the deeds of Cain' (II. 72) – which is the moral speciality of Europeans.

The Romeo and Juliet of these conflict-addicted peoples are a Hebridean boy, Torquil ('A careless thing, who placed his choice in chance'; II. 175), and a Polynesian princess, Neuha (whose 'hopes ne'er drew / Aught from experience, that chill touchstone'; II. 146–7). As Torquil (a 'truant mutineer'; II. 209) is held clear from involvement with Bligh's fate, so is Neuha (a 'gentle savage'; II. 123) from Toobonai's warlike preparations. Torquil's 'heart was tamed to that voluptuous state, / At once Elysian and effeminate' in which 'Caesar's deeds and Caesar's fame' are petty irrelevancies (II. 312–13, 320), and Neuha is free from the pettinesses conventionally visited upon women in the West:

> With no distracting world to call her off
> From love; with no society to scoff
> At the new transient flame; no babbling crowd
> Of coxcombry in admiration loud.   (II. 334–7)

Together, each has achieved a freedom that neither the islanders nor the mutineers could find: a freedom from inherited culture.

Naval culture breaks in upon Torquil's idyll in the form of Ben Bunting, who travels the world wreathed in tobacco smoke, and therefore hardly travels the world at all. Ben announces the arrival of a ship come to arrest the mutineers and Torquil springs to his duty immediately: 'We'll make no running fight,' he says, 'for that were base; / We will die at our quarters, like true men' (II. 517–18). This elliptical poem then jumps to Christian's defeat and his retreat to a rocky cape and a Byronic mood of gloom: 'Silent, and sad, and savage' (III. 141). Islanders come to their rescue, and Neuha escapes with Torquil to an underwater cave; but Christian's compromised bid for freedom ends with defiance and a suicidal death. It is, Byron comments, 'the *cause* makes all, / Degrades or hallows courage in its fall' (IV. 261–2), and their birthplace extends no homage to traitors – 'no fame', 'no grateful country' (IV. 263, 265):

> No nation's eyes would on their tomb be bent,
> No heroes envy them their monument;
> However boldly their warm blood was spilt,
> Their life was shame, their epitaph was guilt.   (IV. 267–70)

All Christian leaves behind him on Toobonai is 'A fair-haired scalp, besmeared with blood and weeds' (IV. 345), while the sea, which protects Torquil and Neuha, looks on indifferently: 'calm and careless heaved the wave below, / Eternal with unsympathetic flow' (IV. 367–8). The following morning the Navy sails away, and for the young people 'all was Hope and Home' and 'Peace and Pleasure, perilously earned' on this island fastness in a 'yet infant world' (IV. 404, 418, 420). The dream of guiltless freedom, self-abandonment, and the shedding of 'this fond and false identity' (II. 392) that Byron pursued so restlessly in his poetry has come to pass – and *The Island* is the last major poem he wrote.

Chapter 7

Histories and mysteries

After leaving England, in 1816, Byron became increasingly interested in the study of history, and as a result increasingly sceptical about both Enlightenment beliefs in human progress and Wordsworthian beliefs in human integrity. *Childe Harold* III illustrated these shifts of emphasis and their interrelation, but in *Childe Harold* IV Byron responded with particular intensity to the historically multifaceted arena of contemporary Italy – more complex than the 'sad relic' of modern Greece – and began to see that just as geography, culture, and religion relativize human affairs, so does the passage of time. His three neoclassical dramas, *Marino Faliero, Sardanapalus*, and *The Two Foscari* – written between April 1820 and July 1821, and interrupted only by the composition of the fifth canto of *Don Juan* – are a profound extension of this interest. But in them Byron also pursued historical analogues for his current political concerns (political leadership, revolution, exile, and 'the state's safety'; *TF* I. I. 85). So these dramas present theories of history and politics alongside one another – much as Shakespeare's Roman plays do.

Byron was fascinated, too, by what we might call the opposite of history, so we also have a more diverse group of works which emerge from a collision between the historical and the timeless – two biblical 'mysteries', *Cain* and *Heaven and Earth*, and the uncategorizable fantasies, *The Vision of Judgment* and *The Deformed Transformed* (all written between July 1821 and the beginning of 1823). In all these late works, however – neoclassic or Romantic, poetic or dramatic, factual or mythic, grave or comic – human action is sceptically reduced in a longer perspective, historical or cosmic, and individuals are portrayed as the victims of either retrospective reinterpretation or divine providence – or, as it may be, simply the luck of the draw.

Three neoclassical dramas

Byron was nothing if not a tourist, and soon after his arrival in Venice in November 1816, he visited the Ducal Palace, where the council chamber contains a frieze made up of portraits of the Venetian doges – except one, Marin Falier (1278–1355), whose position is covered with a painted black cloth bearing a sinister message: 'Here is the place of Marin Falier, beheaded for his crimes.' Almost immediately Byron wrote to John Murray asking for an extract from the standard English history of Venice. Falier's offence was unusual, he told his publisher. 'I mean to write a tragedy upon the subject which appears to me very dramatic – an old man – jealous – and conspiring against the state of which he was the actual reigning Chief – the last circumstance makes it the most remarkable – & only fact of the kind in all history of all nations' (*LJ* V. 174).

The Venetian present came to occupy Byron's attention more than its past in the months that followed, and it was not until the spring of 1820 that he returned to the story of Doge Falier, by which time he had left Venice and settled in Ravenna. More significantly, he had also written the fourth canto of *Childe Harold*, *Beppo*, *The Lament of Tasso*, *The Prophecy of Dante*, 'Venice. An Ode', and the first four cantos of *Don Juan* – which is to say that his attitude to his work and what he wanted to achieve with it had significantly changed. *Childe Harold* IV and its cognate works on Italian subjects had deepened Byron's historical sense, but the comic poems in *ottava rima* had also initiated a war to the knife with what in his 'Letter to John Murray' of 1821 Byron would call 'the grand "primum mobile" [motive force] of England': 'Cant political – Cant poetical – Cant religious – Cant moral – but always *Cant* – multiplied through all the varieties of life' (*CMP* 128). The main theatre in this war involved both the 'Lake School' of English poets (that 'provincial gang of scribblers' (*CPW* V. 85), Wordsworth, Coleridge, and Southey) and the 'Cockney' one (Leigh Hunt and Keats). *Don Juan* would become a moral tour de force in that campaign, while *Cain* would prove a theological one. *Marino Faliero* and its two neoclassical stablemates pursued a subtler line, taking issue with Romantic dramatic aesthetics and the movement's idolatry of Shakespeare. But they also recurred to the nature of history, and how it might be understood in imaginative literature.

Byron belongs to that (to modern eyes) strange group of intellectuals who profess to despise Shakespeare. 'Shakespeare's name,' Byron wrote in 1814, 'stands absurdly high and will go down. ... That he threw over whatever he did write some flashes of genius, nobody can deny: but this was all' (*LJ* IV. 84–5). By 1821, this act of provocation had transformed itself into an element in the cultural war described above. Now Shakespeare was 'the *worst* of models – though the most extraordinary of writers' (*LJ* VIII. 152). Italians think of Dante, Byron said, 'as Leigh Hunt and the Cockneys do of Shakespeare, that the language came to a standstill with the god of their idolatry, and want to go back to him'.[1]

Certainly Shakespeare had long since been a model and a god to Romantic literary theory, as Byron was aware. Though he had not read Lessing, Goethe, Schiller, or Herder, Byron had been exposed to the German school of thought on this matter through the writings of his acquaintance, Madame de Staël (particularly *De l'Allemagne* ['On Germany'], which he read in 1813), August Wilhelm Schlegel (*Lectures on Dramatic Art and Literature*, which de Staël lent him in Switzerland in 1816), and August's brother Friedrich (*Lectures on the History of Literature, Ancient and Modern*, which he read in January 1821). These critics followed a similar line: that Shakespeare and the ancient Greek playwrights were as different from one another as a Gothic cathedral and a Classical temple, and that the former, by virtue of his voracious humanism and his indifference to dramatic rules, was a model for modern, Northern European playwrights. The famous 'three unities' of Classical theatre – described in Aristotle's *Poetics* as dramatic action set in one location, in a twenty-four-hour time period, without any form of sub-plot – were particularly to be reprobated: 'confining and self-imposed fetters', Friedrich Schlegel called them, 'based on error and misconception … opposed to the fundamental principles of poetry'.[2]

The Germans made the running on such matters, but the British were not far behind, and Byron came across similar comments in several English sources. Coleridge's lectures on literature (some of which Byron attended) and his critical work, *Biographia Literaria* (which he read) echoed the German account, rejecting 'the iron bondage of space and time' in drama, and the neoclassical principle that 'binds us down to the meanest part of our nature'.[3] Hazlitt's *Lectures on the English Poets* (which Byron had in his library) continued the attack on the unities and praised Shakespeare for ignoring them. Hunt's preface to his collection of poems, *Foliage* (delivered to Byron by Shelley in Venice), went so far as to associate a taste for Shakespeare with one for Wordsworth and Coleridge.

Byron retaliated against such views with a firm belief that the Romantic aesthetic – himself, Lake and Cockney schools included – was, as he put it in 1818, 'on the wrong tack'. Then he changed metaphor:

> The next generation … will tumble and break their necks off our
> Pegasus, who runs away with us; but we keep the *saddle*, because we

broke the rascal and can ride. But though easy to mount, he is the devil to guide; and the next fellows must go back to the riding-school ... and learn to ride the 'great horse'. (*LJ* VI. 10)

By February 1821, with *Marino Faliero* written and *Sardanapalus* under way, Byron was much clearer on the aesthetic and cultural implications of his 'riding-school'. 'It appears to me', he wrote to Murray,

> that there is room for a different style of the drama – neither a servile following of the old [Shakespearean] drama – which is a grossly erronious one – nor yet *too French* [neoclassical] – like those who succeeded the older writers. – It appears to me that good English – and a severer approach to the rules – might combine something not dishonourable to our literature. (*LJ* VIII. 78)

'I want to make a *regular* English drama', he said; '& to make it more Doric and austere' (*LJ* VIII. 186–7, 223). For Byron, any source of regularity was better than the anarchy of the 'old drama', and it is clear that this decision was in part a result of his response to the Romantic image of Shakespeare. Byron's reference to the Doric – the simplest and most massive order of Classical Greek architecture – gives us a clue to the depth of his neoclassical pretensions on this issue. In the face of Germans and English alike, it was his intention to revive the Classical Aristotelian model and exploit the particular dramatic opportunities the three unities provided for concentration and lucidity – just as his Romantic peers valued Shakespeare for his diffusion and obscurity.

'You will find this very *un*like Shakespeare – and so much the better in one sense', Byron wrote; 'It has been my object to be as simple and severe as [the Italian neoclassical playwright] Alfieri – & I have broken down the *poetry* as nearly as I could to common language' (*LJ* VIII. 152). This comment brings us to the fertile paradox of these three plays: that though he fulminated against Shakespeare as a model, and dragged him willy-nilly into a personal conflict with Anglo-Germanic Romanticism, Byron managed to combine a neoclassical dramatic *structure* with a Shakespearean dramatic *idiom*. He proved to have a conspicuously Shakespearean appetite for 'common language', from which his programmatically neoclassical dramas benefit – in contrast to the sub-Shakespearean plays his poetic contemporaries produced, which suffer from a distinct lack of clarity in both structural and idiomatic terms.

Every one of Byron's major poetic peers dabbled in drama, from Wordsworth's *The Borderers* and Coleridge's *Remorse* to Shelley's *The Cenci* and Keats's *Otho the Great*. (Even Blake wrote a fragmentary 'Edward the Third'.) Each poet hoped, indeed expected, that success in the theatre would overcome his relative lack of success in the publishing field, and each of them conspicuously failed in that attempt. Byron, by contrast, distanced himself from the theatre almost completely, and wrote better plays as a direct result. In fact, he never intended them for performance at all – given what he knew of the London stage – and was irritated when *Marino Faliero* was produced at Drury Lane in April 1821 (it had a modestly successful run of seven performances). 'Success [on stage]', he wrote in his preface to the play, 'would give me no pleasure, and failure great pain' (*CPW* IV. 305).

So Byron's success as a playwright reminds us that he had another qualification for writing drama, apart from a pronounced literary-critical interest in the form: his membership of the management sub-committee at Drury Lane Theatre between June 1815 and his departure from England the following year. We saw from a journal extract quoted in Chapter 3 – 'Then the scenes I had to go through!' – that he took his dramaturgic duties with due seriousness. Drury Lane had a collection of 500 unused scripts, for example, and he 'in person & by proxy' went through them, looking for something producible: 'I do not think that of those which I saw', he wrote, 'there was one which could be conscientiously tolerated. – – There never were such things as most of them' (*LJ* IX. 35). He asked fellow-authors such as Coleridge and Walter Scott to write for the theatre, to no avail, and even began a gothic drama of his own, *Werner*, which was finally completed in 1822. He did manage to attract one genuine success, however: *Bertram; or, The Castle of St Aldobrand: A Tragedy, in Five Acts*, by Charles Maturin (known nowadays only as the author of the gothic novel, *Melmoth the Wanderer*), which had a decent run in 1816. But this was the only original drama Byron could find: in his time Drury Lane depended almost totally on Shakespearean and Restoration revivals, melodramas, and farces.

The dramas written by the likes of Maturin tended to have one thing in common: 'Although the vast majority of noncomic plays within European drama before the late nineteenth century at least pretended to have some historical basis', Herbert Lindenberger writes, 'only the smallest number display any serious concern for history.'[4] Each of Byron's neoclassical plays is historical: *Marino Faliero* is set in 1355, *The Two Foscari* in 1457, and *Sardanapalus* (more vaguely, to be sure) in the seventh century BC. But it is not fidelity to the historical record that mattered so much to Byron as the provision within the plays of historical consciousness among the protagonists: an awareness in them that the present they are living in will in time inevitably *become* the past, subject to some degree of historical reconstruction even as it is recorded. So eager was Byron to produce this effect that historical consciousness becomes in these plays a theme in its own right, rather than simply an aspect of their technique. Hence his time at Drury Lane remained a vital negative influence on the dramas he wrote five years later: whatever he did would *not* be like what he had read, seen, and endured in London.

Thus, Byron's neoclassical 'experiment' (*LJ* VIII. 144, 185) took up a complex position in his ongoing aesthetic interests and his relation to the European literary culture of his time. By contrast, the plays themselves are puritanically simple in terms of structure and development. Most acts contain only one scene, and events follow in smooth sequence within a limited time frame in one location, without any secondary interest, as Classical precept required – which makes them unexpectedly easy to read. This format is unfamiliar to an Anglophone readership, for which Shakespeare is the dramatic model. But because events in these plays are handled so directly, Byron has room for long passages of dialogue in which the protagonists' reactions to events outnumber the events themselves. Again, this style of presentation is highly un-Shakespearean, but it is a major source of Byron's achievement in the plays. Like the issue of characters' historical awareness, this preponderance of discourse itself becomes an issue in the neoclassical dramas, which are highly self-conscious where rhetoric and the relation of speech to action are concerned.

Each of these plays engages with the politics of leadership, the nature of the state, and the justification or otherwise of insurrection. In *Marino Faliero*, the head of state leads a rebellion against the state itself; in *Sardanapalus*, a benevolent despot is the victim of just such an uprising; in *The Two Foscari*, a police state exterminates any prospect of protest or disobedience – going so far as to dethrone a doge who has just sentenced his own son to exile. The relation of all this to Byron's own position vis-à-vis the politics of his native Britain and post-Napoleonic Italy is complicated by the author's political ambivalence as both rebel and aristocrat. Political though these plays are, for example, the multitude hardly exists in any of them. 'There's no people', Doge Foscari tells the senator sent to evict him; 'There is a *populace*, perhaps, whose looks / May shame you' (*TF* V. I. 257–8). Sardanapalus refers to the Assyrians only in the vaguest terms, and only in the final (fascinating) scene of *Marino Faliero* are Venetian citizens allowed on stage, at a distance, to witness the death of 'him who would have freed us' (*MF* V. IV. 21). These are refracted images of the politics without democracy of Byron's time.

The plays also, and accordingly, share an all-pervading sense of crisis and constraint, which the three unities intensify. No subplot provides relief or gives central characters time off stage, and time and space are manipulated with brutal efficiency. *Marino Faliero* heads towards the dawn of a thwarted revolution ('on the dial … of to-morrow's sun'; *MF* II. II. 39–40), just as *Sardanapalus* heads towards the twilight of a broken dynasty ('The sun goes down … / Taking his last look of Assyria's empire'; *Sard.* II. I. 1–2), and the protagonists of both plays frequently remind us of the passage of time in both realist and symbolic terms. *Marino Faliero* and *Sardanapalus* are about rebellions and it follows that time is of the essence in them. *The Two Foscari* is, after *The Prisoner of Chillon* and *The Lament of Tasso*, Byron's third great treatment of incarceration, and the exploitation of space (or the lack of it) in the scene is correspondingly profound. Venice is famously a place with 'A palace and a prison on each hand' (*CHP* IV. 2), but in this play the doge's office and his son's cell seem almost above and below the torture-cum-judgement chamber of the city's sinister administrators: 'the Ten'. The Duke's palace is his son's prison, and vice versa (*TF* I. I. 206–7). Both Foscari, attached to Venice by fanatical patriotism, are ultimately squeezed out of the palace to which they cling, and both die at the threshold to freedom that they cannot cross. At the beginning of the fourth act of *Marino Faliero*, the aristocrat Lioni, whose life (unbeknownst to him) is threatened by an insurrection timed to take place within hours, looks out with supreme dramatic irony on the quiet canals of Venice, and congratulates himself on the permanence and longevity of what he sees, when we have just witnessed the meeting of a revolutionary cell. At the end of the play, Faliero will be beheaded on the 'self-same spot' where he was crowned (*MF* V. I. 573). Sardanapalus is a ruler wholly associated with his palace, which he never leaves. He is trapped in it, and finally destroys it to keep it from his enemies – transparently the building represents him, as feminine pleasure dome and masculine castle combined. All these effects are the direct outcome of neoclassical dramatic practice: the 'fetters' Friedrich Schlegel derided have become a dramatic impetus.

Another element these plays share is the presence in each of a similar heroine: Faliero's young wife Angiolina (a slur on whose honour is the catalyst for the doge's treason); Sardanapalus's mistress Myrrha (who as a woman and a slave is capable of rousing the King's masculinity and power of command when no one else can); and Jacopo Foscari's wife Marina (whose unremitting antipathy to Venetian injustice counterpoints her husband's blind patriotism). These women have a far more assured sense of themselves than do their menfolk. Marino Faliero is obsessed with his name and status, whereas Angiolina disregards the judgement of society, insisting that the fact of honour is more important than the appearance of it (*MF* II. I. 57–74). As a Greek, 'born a foe to monarchs' (*Sard.* I. II. 499), Myrrha is perfectly sure she has lowered herself by becoming a king's lover, and moves effortlessly between the values of love and war that Sardanapalus cannot reconcile. As her very name implies, Marina embodies both the state and nature of Venice, travestied by the secrecy, treachery, and violence of its oligarchic rulers: 'your midnight carryings off and drownings, / Your dungeons next the palace roofs, or under / The water's level' (*TF* II. I. 305–7). 'Feminine reasonableness is indeed the only counterbalance, in these later plays, to masculine manias'[5] – but there is no point looking in these three women for the fluid human interest we find in the heroines of *Don Juan* or Shakespearean drama. That is not their function. Neoclassical drama draws its strength from the graphic presentation of rival forces (reason and mania, for example), not from subtleties of dramatic interrelation.

The heroines' reliance on nature and reason is contrasted with the stoicism exhibited in the historical plays, and (*TF* II. I. 332–66) Doge Foscari voices one of Byron's most extended treatments of the theme when he describes humanity as 'clay from first to last, / The prince's urn no less than potter's vessel'. The three heroes make identical claims to personal-cum-political integrity, which only shows how elusive that quality actually is: 'I will be what I should be, or be nothing' (*MF* II. I. 453), 'I am not what I should be' (*Sard.* IV. I. 334), and 'I shall be found / *Where* I should be, and *what* I have been ever' (*TF* II. I. 42–3). The two Venetian rulers dread any departure from the established norm, and their thoughts rotate obsessively around 'desperate firmness' (*TF* IV. I. 344), whether they uphold the state or attempt to bring it down. Sardanapalus occupies a more complicated position. At the beginning of the play his stoicism is a self-indulgent and theatrical gesture: 'So let me fall like the pluck'd rose! – far better / Thus than be wither'd' (*Sard.* I. II. 605–6). At the end he rejects despair from a more considered position:

> When we know
> All that can come, and how to meet it, our
> Resolves, if firm, may merit a more noble
> Word than this is to give it utterance.
> But what are words to us? we have well nigh done
> With them and all things.   (*Sard.* V. I. 223–8)

The firmness and value of 'resolves', entered into in the past or in the present, are key issues in these dramas, because they exist in political and personal contexts of small concern to Childe Harold or Napoleon. Stoicism in the plays is a value the heroes must positively live up to and justify, rather than use as a screen against the world.

Nothing is less Romantic than neoclassicism, and in stylistic terms these three dramas must surely be placed on the anti-Romantic side of Byron's ledger. But (as the discussion of Romanticism suggested in Chapter 2) it is important to look deeper than style in making such decisions. In these unusual plays it is a far-reaching idea of history that the playwright is seeking to convey – one fundamentally out of tune with neoclassical thought.

'Know then thyself,' Alexander Pope wrote in 1733, 'presume not God to scan; / The proper study of mankind is man.' Enlightenment writers such as Voltaire, Diderot, Montesquieu, and Pope knew that humanity was a diverse species, and that Persians and Parisians did not see things the same way. But they felt that such differences could be overcome by the spread of reason, and that history (a science they renovated, even if they did not invent it) would be at once the record of human variety and a means of reducing it. If you want to know about Greeks and Romans, the philosopher and historian David Hume said, study the French and the English:

> Mankind are so much the same, in all times and places, that history informs us of nothing new or strange in this particular. Its chief use is only to discover the constant and universal principles of human nature, by showing men in all varieties of circumstances and situations, and furnishing us with materials, from which we may form our observations, and become acquainted with the regular springs of human action and behaviour.[6]

Byron's plays may be neoclassical in style, but they are Romantic in intellectual interest. They do not, for example, share Hume's faith in 'the constant and universal principles of human nature'. For Byron, history is something less like the passive acquisition of moral materials, and more like Napoleon's famous definition: 'a fairy tale told by the victors'. In *Childe Harold* IV, history is a jumble bequeathed by the past ('we but feel our way to err'). The neoclassical dramas see the same process from the other end of the telescope: through the eyes of historical protagonists, rather than students of history like Harold. Each of Byron's protagonists knows that he is acting in *history*: not just the passage of time, but the recording of action. Knowing this, each individual becomes acutely conscious of what futurity will make of what he or she has done or failed to do in his or her own present. 'Such a present', the French philosopher Paul Ricoeur writes, 'has a future made up of the expectations, the ignorance, the forecasts and fears of men of that time, and not of the things which we know happened'.[7] For a revolutionary like Faliero, this set of expectations takes a highly dramatic form. 'If this / Attempt succeeds,' he tells a fellow conspirator,

> and Venice, render'd free
> And flourishing, when we are in our graves,
> Conducts her generations to our tombs,
> And makes her children with their little hands
> Strew flowers o'er her deliverers' ashes, then
> The consequence will sanctify the deed,

And we shall be like the two Bruti in
The annals of hereafter; but if not,
If we should fail, employing bloody means
And secret plot, although to a good end,
Still we are traitors, honest Israel.   (*MF* III. I. 67–78)

The conspirators agonize constantly, therefore, about how posterity will treat their 'memory', and how 'Freedom's fountain' and the 'bright millennium' will justify the means they employed – provided they are successful. 'I know the penalty of failure / Is present infamy and death', Faliero says; 'the future / Will judge, when Venice is no more, or free; / Till then, the truth is in abeyance' (*MF* V. I. 254–7).

Sardanapalus, too, feels hemmed in by the 'annals' of the Assyrian past, and the future plotted out in the stars his priests study. His and Myrrha's romantic suicide will be, he says, 'a light / To lesson ages, rebel nations, and / Voluptuous princes … / A problem few dare imitate, and none / Despise' (*Sard.* V. I. 440–2, 447–8). In fact, in *The Two Foscari*, set 100 years after *Marino Faliero*, we can already see the earlier doge's history being adjusted by his successor (*TF* V. I. 228–34). Jacopo Foscari's cell walls are, he says, 'More faithful pictures of Venetian story, / With all their blank, or dismal stains', than the frieze of ducal portraits in the Council Chamber above his head (*TF* III. I. 118–21). For the son, 'This stone page' of confinement 'Holds like an epitaph' the history of those confined (*TF* III. I. 19–20); for the father, the palace walls from which the Ten seek to evict him 'Could tell a tale' of the oligarchy's injustice and inhumanity (*TF* V. I. 217), which even routinely slays people's memory (*TF* I. I. 351) to preserve law and order.

Byron's realization in the neoclassical plays builds firmly on what he discovered, intellectually speaking, in *Childe Harold*, the Eastern tales, and the four 'philosophical' poems studied in Chapter 6: that history never leaves the hands of interested parties to be adjudicated with Hume's philosophical serenity. Humanity never attains a position above the melee, where reason can settle the differences and provide a consensual account of the past. The past is always fought over – and it was fought over in prospect even when it was the present. No matter how regular these plays may be in aesthetic terms, the moral and psychological interest they take in how it *feels* to be one of the protagonists in the dramas concerned is too Shakespearean – and too Romantic – for them to provide a smoothly neoclassical account of what Hume called 'the regular springs of human action and behaviour'. Their aesthetic 'regularity' does not coincide with a historiographical one, and the coexistence of these neoclassical dramas alongside the Shakespearean efforts of his English contemporaries is evidence for the fundamental diversity of Romantic thought and creativity.

Three mysteries

In his neoclassical plays Byron posed the question: what would time feel like to those caught up in it, if they felt that the future controls that account of time we call history? The second group of texts considered here exchange that perspective for a related one: eternity seen from a temporal (that is, human) point of view. There are four texts here – *Cain, Heaven and Earth, The Vision of Judgment*, and *The Deformed Transformed* – of which two are fragmentary, and none is the least bit neoclassical in its handling of these radically abstract themes. *Cain* and *The Deformed Transformed* are also markedly 'Mephistophelian', in the sense that in them a suicidal man (like Marlowe's and Goethe's Faust) is chosen for intellectual education at the hands of a diabolical spirit.

But the two mysteries, *Cain* and *Heaven and Earth* (named 'in conformity with the ancient title annexed to dramas upon similar subjects' in the medieval Mystery Play tradition; *CPW* VI. 228), face more challenging dramatic issues than do the three historical plays. The depiction of good and evil in absolute terms, as God and Satan, had caused problems even for Milton in *Paradise Lost*. But whereas Milton had solved his problem (as far as Satan was concerned, at least) by importing into his epic the dramatic soliloquies of Shakespearean anti-heroes, Byron did not do the same for Lucifer in *Cain*. This left him with a satanic tempter who promises a knowledge of the world he can never deliver – a sham present in all forms of the Faust myth, to be sure. But it also left him with (on the one hand) a dark angel who, by definition, knows more about the world than the dramatist does, and (on the other) an innocent human who knows nothing about the world whatsoever. Generating human interest out of this conflict is a challenge. Furthermore, Satan's soliloquies in *Paradise Lost* give us a sense that we can believe some of what he is saying, since he says it to himself. It was hard for Byron to make drama from one protagonist who is a model of cynicism, and another who is a model of naivety, especially when we are given comparatively little access to their inner thoughts.

Many of Byron's readers were genuinely scandalized by what they found in *Cain*, whereas the play is at heart scrupulously orthodox. 'Byron seems to have assumed what most readers have not,' Robert Ryan writes:

> that Lucifer and Cain have to behave and speak like rebels against
> the sovereignty of Jehovah; that Lucifer's indictment of God and the
> divine order must be plausible enough to impress the skeptical young

man who is to be seduced from his proper allegiance; that, despite some humanistic rhetoric, Lucifer's moral position in the play is that of an accessory to murder; and that Cain, ill-natured from the start, continually demonstrates the inherited corruption he continually denies until finally it drives him to commit the deadliest of sins.[8]

As was the case with the neoclassical plays, the drama lies not with personalities but with positions: deism versus fundamentalism, for example, or humanistic rhetoric versus the mystery of being (*Cain* I. I. 322).

Byron hoped that *Cain* and *Heaven and Earth* would be published together, and it is easy to see why. The first concerns the aftermath of one biblical disaster (the Fall), the second the prelude to another (the Flood). In one we witness the origins of 'Cain's race' (*HE* III. 386), in the other we witness its destruction. But in both dramas human values (of the kind we assert in history) are contrasted with larger, 'cosmic', or 'creational' values (of the kind which govern the universe, not the world, and eternity, not history). 'Peace, child of passion, peace!', Noah tells his son Japhet in *Heaven and Earth*; 'If not within thy heart, yet with thy tongue / Do God no wrong! / Live as he wills it – die, when he ordains' (*HE* III. 684–7). From the perspective of divine providence and ordinance, men and women are only the children of passion, and must submit to providence – right down to the hour of their death. These dramas are as haunted by Milton, therefore, as the earlier group had been by Shakespeare.

These two sets of values (human and 'creational') are difficult to reconcile, and Lucifer's procedure in *Cain* is to prompt and exacerbate human ideals, and contrast them with the severity of God in a way that hurls the hero into murderous isolation from both his family and providence. 'I know the thoughts / Of dust, and feel for it, and with you', Lucifer pretends (*Cain* I. I. 100–1). Cain yearns (anachronously, of course) for Enlightenment values like equality, sympathy, and happiness in a theocratic context to which they are marginal, and attempts a commensuration of life and knowledge that Lucifer easily converts into a sophistical opposition. 'Choose betwixt love and knowledge', Lucifer tells him, 'since there is / No other choice' (I. I. 429–30) – and Cain is both too browbeaten and too surly to ask why that choice is a necessary one. Happiness is not a right conferred by authority, neither does knowledge lead to it, but in his innocence and confusion Cain assumes both these things are true. Lucifer meanwhile is content to have him believe that God's solitude must amount to selfish and despotic anti-humanism, the only reasonable response to which is mental rebellion, Childe Harold-style: 'Nothing can / Quench the mind, if the mind will be itself / And centre of surrounding things' (I. I. 213–15). Anything else would be 'grov'ling' (I. I. 292). But Lucifer also reduces intellectual self-reliance to nothing, by 'showing' Cain a catastrophist history of the previous incarnations of the earth. So he isolates and humiliates him at the same time, like a brainwasher from a religious cult.

To anyone not as unhappy as Cain, Lucifer's arguments would appear the web of sophistries that they are, and Cain's wife Adah sees through them instinctively. One human value *is* common with the divine, and that is love, the existence of which Lucifer represses as best he can. ('Delusion', he calls it; II. II. 272.) 'Who / Art thou', Adah says to him, 'that steppest between heart and heart?' (I. I. 348–9). 'Love us, then, my Cain!' she says of herself and their child; 'And love thyself for our sakes, for we love thee' (III. I. 147–8). 'The object of the demon', Byron wrote,

> is to *depress* him [Cain] still further in his own estimation than he was
> before – by showing him infinite things – & his own abasement – till he
> falls into the frame of mind – that leads to the Catastrophe – from mere
> *internal* irritation – *not* premeditation or envy – of *Abel* … but from
> rage and fury against the inadequacy of his state to his Conceptions – &
> which discharges itself rather against Life – and the author of Life – than
> the mere living.   (*LJ* IX. 53–4)

Certainly, Cain's humanistic 'Conceptions' can serve only as an intellectual irritant in the world of infinite things, but it is also love – 'mortal converse' (III. I. 184) – that his rationally induced bewilderment has stripped away. Whether this will result in suicide or murder, Lucifer does not care: death is the gift to the universe that he says comes from God but that he delivers himself, and he uses a man 'who abhor[s] / The name of Death so deeply, that the thought / Empoison'd all my life' (III. I. 371–3) to bring it about. Perhaps it was the drama's profound pessimism, rather than its nonconformity, which really upset readers in Byron's own day – certainly its pessimism proved enormously influential in the remainder of the nineteenth century, among Continental thinkers in general and Russian ones in particular.

Human values, however frail, are more resilient in Byron's second 'mystery' because 'the focal problem in *Cain* is the limits of human knowledge just as the focal problem in *Heaven and Earth* is the limits of love'.[9] 'Methinks a being that is beautiful / Becometh more so as it looks on beauty', Japhet says (*HE* II. 6–7), whereas the women's angelic lovers ('passionless and pure'; III. 715) are beyond any such improvement. The play is more dramatic, too, as Japhet is able to resist the visions of cyclical destruction offered by the mocking spirits that live at the foot of Mount Ararat. Jehovah inhabits eternity, and man lives in time, Japhet realizes. 'Without man, Time, as made for man, / Dies with man, and is swallow'd in that Deep / Which has no fountain' (III. 306–8); but Japhet is more philosophical than Cain about such possibilities. When Aholibamah, the more worldly of the two Cainite women, resumes her forefather's ideological line, demanding 'a God of love, not sorrow', Japhet brings her down to earth with a genuinely humanistic thump: 'Alas! What else is Love but Sorrow?' (III. 460–1). Japhet's love may be doubly hopeless, as Anah prefers her angel lover and is doomed to drown anyway, but at least he shares the selflessness she demonstrates in her rebellious passion for her seraph. 'Why', he says at the fragment's conclusion, 'when all perish, why must I remain?'

The Vision of Judgment is a comic poem more frequently associated with *Beppo* and *Don Juan*, sharing the *ottava rima* form as it does. But it, too, dramatizes a contrast between humane and cosmic values, illustrated when the deceased George III is brought up to the Heavenly Gates by Satan to contest ownership of the king's soul with the Archangel Michael.

As counsel for the prosecution, Satan rhetorically overstates his case, as Byron and his fellow Whigs habitually did: 'from the Caesar's school,' he suggests, 'Take the worst pupil; and produce a reign / More drench'd with gore, more cumber'd with the slain!' (350–2; Napoleon's reign springs to mind). Then Satan produces witnesses:

> In short, an universal shoal of shades
> From Otaheite's Isle [Tahiti] to Salisbury Plain,
> Of all climes and professions, years and trades,
> Ready to swear against the good king's reign,
> Bitter as clubs in cards are against spades:
> All summon'd by this grand 'subpoena,' to
> Try if kings mayn't be damned, like me or you.   (474–80)

From this crowd two figures from the early years of George's reign are chosen to testify: the radical MP John Wilkes and the anonymous journalist 'Junius'. But both refuse to repeat the accusations they made *in propria persona* back on Earth, and prefer to let bygones be bygones, at which point another devil arrives bearing the still living poet laureate, Robert Southey, whose own memorial ode, *A Vision of Judgement* (1820) had inspired Byron in the first place.

It is apparent that Byron found Southey both more objectionable and more amusing than the king who 'left a realm undone' (62), and in the rumpus caused by the Laureate's starting an impromptu poetry reading, George 'slipp'd into heaven', where the narrator leaves him, 'practising the hundredth psalm' (846–8): 'Enter into his gates with thanksgiving, and into his courts with praise: be thankful unto him, and bless his name. For the Lord is good; his mercy is everlasting; and his truth endureth to all generations.' Like the British Isles over which he ruled, George has 'floated on the abyss of Time' (335), beyond history, beyond detraction, out of the vortex of posterity, and into the shelter of the everlasting mercy praised in the Book of Psalms. The only person who demands his punishment is the Devil, and justice is thwarted by a Tory poetaster who confounds 'Times present, past, to come, heaven, hell, and all' into chaos (806).

But *The Vision of Judgment* is an unusual poem: a strange blend of the cosmic and the comic, and a striking achievement in terms of tone, for whereas it shares an overall sense of irony with the other *ottava rima* poems, it is also darkly earnest in its hatred of war. (Byron 'was the first great Englishman', Ruskin said, 'who felt the cruelty of war, and, in its cruelty, the shame.')[10] So it manages to be a parody of Milton, and Miltonic all the same. There are jokes about whether or not George is wearing his head, since the last monarch who came this way (Louis XVI of France) had been guillotined (141–68); but Lucifer is every inch the grave and impressive Prince of Darkness:

> bringing up the rear of this bright host
> A Spirit of a different aspect waved
> His wings, like thunder-clouds above some coast
> Whose barren beach with frequent wrecks is paved;
> His brow was like the deep when tempest-tost;
> Fierce and unfathomable thoughts engraved
> Eternal wrath on his immortal face,
> And *where* he gazed a gloom pervaded space.   (185–92)

And Michael is dazzling in proportion to this gigantic Byronic hero: 'A beautiful and mighty Thing of Light, / Radiant with glory, like a banner streaming / Victorious from some world-o'erthrowing fight' (218–20). 'Between his Darkness and his Brightness', Byron notes, 'There passed a mutual glance of great politeness' (279–80), as if all wars, even those in heaven, eventually lose the bitterness that marked their origins. In a context of that degree of sublimity, it is hard for Byron to maintain his sense of outrage, even at an individual who had accused him of belonging to a 'satanic school' of poets, let alone an ancient and enfeebled monarch, a human like the rest of us, who practised, furthermore (95–6), 'that household virtue, most uncommon, / Of constancy to an unhandsome woman.' Once again the poet proves too humane to be an undeviating satirist.

The Deformed Transformed

Of all these 'mystical' works *The Deformed Transformed* is the most interesting. It was begun in January 1822, but abandoned as a fragment in May 1823. In a fascinating essay, the critic Anne Barton has traced the play's coexistence with *Don Juan* in this period (especially with the Siege of Ismail in Canto VI, which is paralleled by the sack of Rome in *The Deformed Transformed*, itself paralleled in the Eastern Tale, *The Siege of Corinth*, from 1815), and the drama's origins in central Romantic works like Goethe's *Faust* (Part One, 1808) and Mary Shelley's *Frankenstein* (1818). Furthermore, as Barton says, 'the play fuse[s] the two distinct types of drama between which Byron had previously alternated – the "metaphysical" and the historical.'[11] It also adds the Mephistophelian element from Marlowe, Goethe, and *Manfred* to the historical one of *Childe Harold* IV and the neoclassical plays. Perhaps for these very reasons, and because it was in time outgrown by *Don Juan*, the play ground to a halt. ('I can't *furbish*', Byron told Murray in 1820: 'I am like the tyger (in poesy) if I miss my first Spring – I go growling back to my Jungle'; *LJ* VII. 229). But the drama offers tantalizing hints of what Byron might have done had he brought it to a conclusion.

The Deformed Transformed is clearly Faustian, but leaves traditional versions of the myth behind. There is no satanic agreement regarding Arnold's soul, for example; the diabolical escort requires 'no contract save your deeds' (I. I. 151), and everything is left subject to Arnold's will. The Faustian (and Cainite) demand for knowledge is replaced by a desire for *experience*, and Byron turns Mephistopheles from tempter to witness. As *Don Juan* does, the play allows Byron to split himself into a beautiful, passionate hero, and a sceptically intellectual commentator. The Northern Arnold is transformed into the Homeric hero Achilles and – irony of ironies – finds himself rivalled for the love of Olimpia (that is, Olympia, the embodiment of classical Greece, origin of both love and learning) by his own cast-off body, now inhabited by the diabolical spirit who had effected his transformation in the first place ('Caesar'). Of all Greek heroes Arnold chooses the one who is crippled in the foot – the 'Achilles' heel' – just as Byron himself was. Valour and beauty are no match for ugliness and intellect, and when we note that the play starts with Arnold's mother saying, 'Out, hunchback!', and him replying, 'I was born so, mother!', we can see the autobiographical forces at work in that idea.

But the forces at work are by no means only autobiographical. Arnold is a 'sample of humanity' (II. II. 27), like Cain: a suicidal orphan with nothing to live for, and every inch a rebel without a cause. Being deformed, his urge is an over-compensatory one: 'to o'ertake mankind / By heart and soul' (I. I. 314–15). Being transformed into a warrior and a beauty he should take the world by storm – but, as Caesar says, 'you shall see / Yourself for ever by you, as your shadow' (I. I. 447–8). The vision is not paranoid, as in Marlowe's and Goethe's *Faust*, but schizoid, as in Thomas Mann's fable, 'The Transposed Heads' (1940): the hero is transformed but cannot leave his old self behind.

Off the schizoid couple go, to 'Where the world is thickest', as Arnold asks – that is, 'where there is War / And Woman in activity' (I. I. 493–6). War they see in abundance at the sack of Rome, while Caesar comments ironically – Byronically – on the incorrigibility of mankind. But Olimpia, whom Arnold saves from rape, is attracted to his alter ego: 'thus Arnold [becomes] jealous of himself under his former figure, owing to the Power of Intellect &c', as Byron noted to himself in the fragmentary third part of the drama (*CPW* VI. 574). This is a strikingly cool treatment of his own position as a cripple among the able-bodied and a celebrity among the mediocre, unable to transform himself by either diabolical or artistic means into anything other than himself: a self eternally split between mind and body. The implicit suggestion is that physical deformity breeds cynicism, or accompanies it, to say the least. As an attempt to bring the metaphysical and historical perspectives under a single lens the drama founders. As an attempt to see himself, like his fellow human beings, as an intersection of the unique and the recurrent, and a conflict of the idealistic and the sceptical, it is one of Byron's most remarkable experiments.

Chapter 8

Don Juan

Don Juan is one of the five great long poems in English, alongside Chaucer's *Canterbury Tales* (1387–1400), Spenser's *The Faerie Queene* (1596), Milton's *Paradise Lost* (1667), and Wordsworth's *The Prelude* (1850). But it rarely receives the degree of recognition which that status should imply. One of the reasons for this is that Byron's poem does not wear its ambitions on its sleeve as these other works do. The *Canterbury Tales* clearly constitutes a synoptic account of English medieval life, and Spenser went so far as to write a letter to Sir Walter Raleigh in 1589, explaining that his unfinished epic would dramatize the 'twelve private moral virtues' of the Christian gentleman. Milton said that *Paradise Lost* would do nothing less than 'justify the ways of God to men' (a thing 'unattempted yet in prose or rhyme', according to him), and even when Wordsworth referred to *The Prelude* modestly as 'the poem on the growth of my own mind' it was something more than his own personal development he was thinking of – the growth of his mind would in his view be a norm and standard for the rest of humanity.

By comparison, Byron was diffident where the aims of *Don Juan* were concerned. Some comments are typical: 'meant to be a little quietly facetious upon every thing' (*LJ* VI. 67); 'merely some situations – which are taken from life'; 'a work never intended to be serious', with no 'intention but to giggle and make giggle' (*LJ* VI. 77, 208); 'a poetical Tristram Shandy – or Montaigne's Essays with a story for a hinge' (*LJ* X. 150). True, he also referred to it as 'the most moral of poems' (*LJ* VI. 99), but in only the vaguest of terms.

Nor did Byron's early critics help establish the poem's serious purpose. Goethe spoke of *Don Juan* 'manifesting the bitterest and most savage hatred of humanity, and then again penetrated with the deepest and tenderest love for mankind', and Shelley told Byron that the poem 'present[s] in its true deformity what is worst in human nature'. If minds like these could see Byron's poem in such pious, lurid, and misleading terms, an anonymous critic at the *Edinburgh Review* can be forgiven for describing *Don Juan* as no more than 'measured prose, replete with bad puns, stale jests, small wit, indecency, and irreligion'.[1]

If Byron's poem does belong with the four listed here, it must have originated in, or at least discovered within itself, an ambitious purpose of the kind they demonstrate. This is a 16,000-line poem, twice the length of *The Prelude*, and such projects cannot be sustained on a whim. Byron's purpose will be addressed directly in the second part of this chapter; the first considers some technical and generic matters that constitute an important background to that discussion.

Style and origins

Don Juan grew out of *Beppo*, and like that poem was an experiment (*LJ* VI. 24, 68) in Anglicizing a comic tradition carried on by three Italian poets in particular: Luigi Pulci (1432–84), Francesco Berni (1497–1535), and Giovanni Battista Casti (1724–1803). Of these, Casti's 'materialistic and hedonistic'[2] *Novelle Galanti* ('ritzy stories' might be an English equivalent of the title) made a deep impression when a friend gave them to Byron in Geneva in 1816: 'I have almost got him by heart … I long to go to Venice to see the manners so admirably described' (*LJ* V. 80).

Casti's *Novelle* were written in *ottava rima*, or 'eighth rhyme': a verse form 'as old as the hills in Italy' (*LJ* VIII. 229), and much simpler than the intricate Spenserian stanza of *Childe Harold*. *Ottava rima* is made up of a sestet (*ababab*) and a concluding couplet (*cc*). The form is not inherently comic, and has been used for non-comic poems in both Italian (Ariosto's *Orlando Furioso*, for example) and English (Keats's 'Isabella', Shelley's *The Witch of Atlas*, and W. B. Yeats's 'Sailing to Byzantium', for example – not to forget Byron's own 'Epistle to Augusta' of 1816). Yet for two reasons it does lend itself to comedy. First, two sounds must be rhymed three times in the stanza, which can easily be put to comic purpose in a rhyme-poor language like English, given 'the stubborn, unaccommodating resistance which the consonant endings of the northern languages make to this sort of endless sing-song', as Hazlitt put it.[3] So a verse which begins, 'Oh, ye immortal Gods! what is Theogony? / Oh, thou too mortal Man! what is Philanthropy?' is clearly setting the reader up for a ride – in this case one that involves mahogany and lycanthropy (IX. 153–60). Second, the couplet in *ottava rima* is (as it was not in the Spenserian stanza) 'alienated': un-anticipated by earlier rhyme sounds – 'the encased bombshell of the stanza' as Catherine Addison puts it, 'whose disjunctive structure asks for an interplay of at least two voices in each unit', above all a comic or ironic deflation in the couplet of the opening sestet.[4] In Canto I, Byron describes the evening on which Juan and Julia will be caught 'in the fact' by her husband:

> 'Twas, as the watchmen say, a cloudy night;
>   No moon, no stars, the wind was low or loud
> By gusts, and many a sparkling hearth was bright
>   With the piled wood, round which the family crowd;
> There's something cheerful in that sort of light,
>   Even as a summer sky's without a cloud:
> I'm fond of fire, and crickets, and all that,
> A lobster-salad, and champagne, and chat.   (I. 1,073–80)

The mood so carefully evoked in the narrative voice is dashed by the commentary. But *ottava rima* is extremely flexible: the encased bombshell need never explode, and the stanza can carry narrative with ease, as *Don Juan* demonstrates throughout its length. The poem's supremely careless and carefree appearance depended on a great deal of revision, as Byron worked to evoke and balance the various 'voices' the format encouraged: humorous, reflective, or dramatic (see Fig. 1).

Byron was familiar with *ottava rima* before he arrived in Italy, but it was not until the English translator William Stewart Rose visited him in Venice in September 1817 that the idea of creating an English equivalent of the *Novelle* occurred to him. Rose was himself the translator of another of Casti's comic poems, the *Talking Animals*, and would eventually translate *Orlando Furioso*. But he brought with him to Venice a newly published pseudonymous mock epic in *ottava rima* by the English poet John Hookham Frere: *Prospectus and Specimen of an Intended National Work ... by William and Robert Whistlecraft ... Relating to King Arthur and His Round Table*. With Rose's encouragement and Frere's ponderous example, Byron's *Beppo* – written in two nights, 9–10 October 1817 – came to pass, and when it was published successfully in February the following year it took only four months before Byron tried his hand at another such tale: the first canto of *Don Juan*.

But a great poet does not step into the same river twice, and the new poem was no mere continuation of its predecessor. Another visitor to Venice in September 1817, Byron's friend Douglas Kinnaird, brought a less welcome gift than *Whistlecraft*: a copy of Coleridge's *Biographia Literaria*. This was never a book that Byron was going to appreciate – attempting, as in effect it did, to justify the ways of Wordsworth to man. But its twenty-third chapter

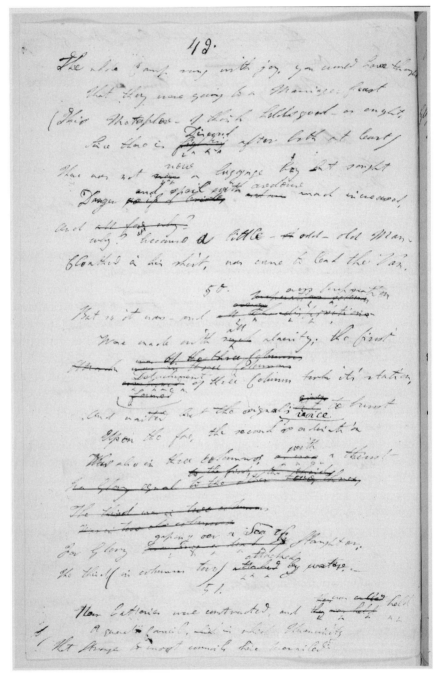

Figure 1. Byron's manuscript of *Don Juan*, Canto VII, 385–403.
MS Ashley 5163. By permission of the British Library.

included an attack on, of all things, the one serious play that Byron had managed to produce at Drury Lane theatre during his period of management there: Charles Maturin's *Bertram*, which 'Jacobinical [French-revolutionary] drama' Coleridge contrasted, as 'an insult to common decency', with the long European tradition of *Don Juan* plays, in which the guilty adulterer (unlike Maturin's hero) always met an appropriately sticky end. Coleridge's laborious and otiose critique – neither 'grateful nor graceful' in a writer Byron had supported and sought to involve at Drury Lane (*LJ* V. 267) – put Byron's Italian experiment on a new footing by giving him a hero (Don Juan) and a cause (opposition to British moralistic cant) at one and the same time.

The case has often been made that Byron wrote the first canto of *Don Juan* in the same spirit that he wrote *Beppo*, 'with little forethought and no plans for a poem of length', as Peter Graham suggests.[5] We saw in Chapter 4 that Byron said of *Don Juan* 'I *have* no plan – I *had* no plan – but I had or have materials' (*LJ* VI. 207), and that is a comment repeated within the poem itself: 'the fact is that I have nothing plann'd, / Unless it were to be a moment merry, / A novel word in my vocabulary' (IV. 38–40).

But even with the support of the author, this proposition should be taken with a pinch of salt. Byron's first specific reference to *Don Juan* in his correspondence (19 September 1818) was to 'the First Canto … of a poem in the style and manner of "Beppo"' (*LJ* VI. 67), which hardly suggests a short production. We have seen that Byron hedged his bets in 1811 where *Childe Harold* and *Hints from Horace* were concerned, and that *Beppo* was a triumph of intellectual subterfuge, luring readers to the conclusion that it was nothing more than 'gay and desultory babbling'. *Don Juan* was surrounded by similar acts of prevarication, whereas the first stanza of the poem in fact commits its author to something genuinely ambitious:

> I want a hero: an uncommon want,
>   When every year and month sends forth a new one,
> Till, after cloying the gazettes with cant,
>   The age discovers he is not the true one;
> Of such as these I should not care to vaunt,
>   I'll therefore take our ancient friend Don Juan,
> We all have seen him in the pantomime
> Sent to the devil, somewhat ere his time.   (I. 1–8)

This indicates a more substantial production than *Beppo* – and a more literary one, too. *Beppo* was a hero taken from life; Don Juan was a fictional object nearly 200 years old in 1818, and *Don Juan* flirts with European epic from its very first line, indicating both Byron's need for and lack of a hero to put alongside Homer's and Virgil's. Moreover, Don Juan is famed above all for the serial nature of his sexual adventures, whereas *Beppo* is wholeheartedly anecdotal and self-contained. *Beppo* ends with narrative closure, as the expected climax fails to eventuate and the protagonists come to a harmonious and expeditious domestic arrangement. Juan's affair with Julia, by contrast, leaves her in a convent at the end of the first canto, but him exiled and available for further adventures.

'Our ancient friend Don Juan' was an aristocratic serial seducer of women from all stations in life who, the story goes, invited the statue of the father of one of his victims to dinner, having killed the man himself in the first place. The statue keeps the appointment and drags the unfortunate Don to Hell. The Spanish monastic playwright Tirso de Molina invented this mythic ne'er-do-well in his *Trickster of Seville and the Stone Guest* (*c*.1630), and his formula was repeated by dozens of playwrights, most famously Molière (1665), Goldoni (1736), and Pushkin (1830) – not to mention Mozart's opera, *Don Giovanni* (1787), containing the famous 'Catalogue Aria' sung by the Don's servant, Leporello (Act I, Scene ii), listing his master's sexual conquests:

> In Italy, six hundred and forty;
> In Germany, two hundred and thirty-one;
> A hundred in France; in Turkey, ninety-one;
> In Spain already one thousand and three …

Whether Byron saw *Don Giovanni* we do not know – though there is every chance that he did, as it was regularly performed in Venetian theatres. But though he could sing a catalogue aria of his own when the mood took him (see *LJ* VI. 92: 'since last year I have run the Gauntlet'), his Juan is a deliberate inversion of the tradition. A teenaged neophyte and no middle-aged rake, he is as much the victim as the perpetrator of the 'seductions' the poem contains (which are nothing like the coldly mechanical transactions of the de Molina tradition in any event). Moreover, the women in Juan's life by no means constitute an endless stream of indifferent sex objects, dark or fair ('In Italy, six hundred and forty … ', and so forth), but the reverse. In Byron, Juan is the *ingénu*, and the women exercise sexual selection over him.

Byron's choice of hero was portentous and prodigious, with immediate implications for both the poem's length and its sphere of moral interest. Accordingly, we can see him in the first verse of his experiment homing in on 'the grand "primum mobile" of England': cant – abundantly on display in Coleridge's reactionary critique of *Bertram*. By stanza six, Byron had already explicitly associated his new tale with epic practice ('Most epic poets plunge in "medias res"'); in stanza 200, he committed himself further, though humorously ('My poem's epic ... '). The poem shuffles unceasingly thereafter as regards its own status as mock-performance or epic in earnest, but by the end of Canto I the plan is clear, though flexible. After the scandal of Juan's first affair, his mother 'had resolved that he should travel through / All European climes, by land or sea, / To mend his former morals and get new, / Especially in France and Italy' (I. 1521–4): an *Odyssey* or *Aeneid* for a post-heroic world.

Don Juan is, therefore, not only a sexual inversion of the heartlessly scientific chauvinist of the dramatic legend, and a playful inversion of epic sententious-ness – it is also an inversion of *Childe Harold's Pilgrimage*. 'Don Juan's pilgrim-age is Childe Harold's in reverse,' as Bernard Blackstone puts it: 'the direction is from sunshine to snow, from freedom to confinement, from the Alhambra to Newstead.'[6] Where *Childe Harold* was centrifugal, tracking the outward jour-neys of its hero (the first of which, from Spain through the Mediterranean to the isles of Greece and Constantinople, Juan reprises in Cantos I–VI), *Don Juan* is centripetal, inexorably drawing its hero back to 'the state of mind Byron was in when he returned to England in 1811'[7] (a state of mind anatomized in the poem's final section, the 'English Cantos', XI–XVI). The two poems are the meditative and comic sides of the same coin.

Any very long poem is likely to get called an epic, but Byron's poem has constituted a generic puzzle in other respects, too. 'If *Don Juan* then be not a satire – what is it?', a critic wrote in 1819; 'A more perplexing question could not be put to the critical squad.'[8] Byron repeatedly described his poem as a satire, especially as it lengthened. At first it was 'a playful satire' (VI. 208); then the first four cantos involved 'much philosophy – and satire upon heroes and despots and the present false state of politics and society' (*LJ* IX. 196); it was also, apparently, 'a satire on affectations of all kinds' (*LJ* X. 116). Within *Don Juan* Byron referred to it as 'this Epic Satire' (*DJ* XIV. 790), though he also repeated the sentiment we saw voiced at the beginning of his career (in 'Childish Recollections') that 'I've not the necessary bile [for satire]; / My nat-ural temper's really aught but stern' (*DJ* XI. 500–1).

But satire requires more than the capacity to be stern: something missing in Byron that marks him as a Romantic writer. If we are reluctant to use the word 'tragedy' of Byron's plays, it is for much the same reason that we are reluctant to use the word 'satire' of *Don Juan* – though there are tragic elem-ents in the former, and satiric elements in the latter. It is not enough for satire to urge the moral improvement of humanity, for example (any more than it is enough for tragedy that an 'innocent' should die). Almost all literature wants to benefit the human race in some way or another, by improving the ways we think or feel, and innocent people die every day in circumstances we can call 'tragic' only in a loose sense. To be convincing, both forms require a set of shared beliefs (ultimately religious where tragedy is concerned, social where satire is concerned) at large in the culture producing them. Classic eighteenth-century satire like Pope's is built on an implicit consensus between writer and reader that the satirized object, whoever or whatever it may be, is demonstrably anomalous and undesirable, just as Shakespearean tragedy is built on the shared belief that its heroes and heroines, however culpable, are nobler than ourselves. But as we saw in Chapter 2, such shared beliefs (of the kind in circulation during the Enlightenment) were the very things that the Romantic movement questioned, so its difficulties with both tragedy and satire are to that extent predictable.

'Byron's genius was essentially a comic one,' the twentieth-century poet W. H. Auden argued, 'and his poetic history is a quest, finally successful, to discover the right verse vehicle for the comic poet of his time.' 'The goal of satire,' Auden went on,

> is reform; the goal of comedy, acceptance … Satire is angry and optimistic – it believes that the evil it attacks can be abolished; Comedy is good-tempered and pessimistic – it believes that however much we may wish we could, we cannot change human nature and must make the best of a bad job.[9]

Byron wrote satirical poems throughout his career, from *English Bards and Scotch Reviewers*, *Hints from Horace*, *The Curse of Minerva*, and *Waltz*, to *The Blues*, *The Vision of Judgment*, and *The Age of Bronze*. Everything he wrote is interesting, but his satires do illustrate Auden's point: Byron's disbelief in the idea that evil can be abolished, and an inner conviction (visible in his letters as well as *Don Juan*) not only that humanity must 'make the best of a bad job', but that it was most human when it did so. Byron's quest, then, was for a Romantic, post-Enlightenment, comic idiom, good-tempered and pessimistic, rather than angry and optimistic like Pope or Voltaire. 'For my part,' he confessed in *Don Juan*, 'I am but a mere spectator, / And gaze where'er the palace or the hovel is, / Much in the mode of Goethe's Mephistopheles' (XIII. 54–6). This is not the moral posture of a satirist; rather, it suggests that *Don Juan* is 'comic' in an older and deeper sense even than Auden had in mind, much as Dante's epic is called the *Divina commedia*, and Balzac's cycle of novels is entitled the *Comédie humaine*. That sort of comedy is a depiction of the world – from *Inferno* to *Paradiso* and hovel to palace – that does more than *rival* the tragic vision of experience; it *encompasses* that vision, and sees even tragedy as something part of a larger pattern, beyond our intellectual grasp.

Vision and attitude

'*Don Juan* could not have been written', Bernard Beatty suggests, 'without the eighteenth-century alliance between British and French sceptical philosophizing and liberal political sentiment ... but the poem also does things which that tradition does not allow.'[10] In surveying the poem's origins and its generic qualities we gain a sense of both its originality and its traditionary indebtedness. But the poem also manifests that 'true progress' Peter Porter spoke of in Chapter 3: a progress which did not involve the rejection or transcendence of Byron's earlier achievements but the conversion of them into Auden's 'right verse vehicle' for what he had to say. Sceptical philosophy and liberal politics contributed to that progress, but they were not enough to satisfy the questions to which he ultimately sought answers in his work. A passing remark Byron made to a pious friend after his return to England in 1811 reveals the extent of his intellectual curiosity, and the places where he looked to satisfy it. 'I am where I was,' he wrote; 'verging towards [the seventeenth-century rationalist philosopher] Spinoza; and yet it is a gloomy Creed, and I want a better, *but there is something Pagan in me that I cannot shake off* ... I deny nothing, but doubt everything' (*LJ* II. 136; italics added).

Byron's paganism is hard to define, but we have noted three important ingredients of it in earlier chapters. Byron's letters, for example (and a good deal of his poetry, too), demonstrate a strikingly *materialistic* view of the world, in which physical objects, including people and places, are the most important things with which humans have to deal. (Indeed, the only abstraction powerful enough to compete with materialism is liberty, as we saw in Chapter 6.) 'The great object of life is Sensation', Byron argued (*LJ* III. 109), and a major source of his distrust of the Lake School of English poets was that 'They know nothing of the world; and what is poetry, but the reflection of the world?' (*LJ* IV. 85). 'Is it not *life*, is it not *the thing*?' Byron had asked where *Don Juan* was concerned; but then 'what a strange thing is the propagation of life! – A bubble of Seed which may be spilt in a whore's lap ... might (for aught we know) have formed a Caesar or a Buonaparte' (*LJ* IX. 47). Materialism is mysterious, then; but it also resolves mysteries. In a materialist universe, as the Greek philosopher Epicurus put it, 'Death is nothing to us; for the body, when it has been resolved into its elements, has no feeling, and that which has no feeling is nothing to us.'[11] The greatest fruit of Epicurean self-sufficiency is freedom from the fear of death: 'In the midst of myriads of the living & the dead worlds – stars – systems – infinity', as Byron put it, 'why should I be anxious about an atom?' (*LJ* IV. 78).

The second 'pagan' element in Byron's thinking about what he called the 'fiery dust' of humanity (*DJ* II. 1,696) is one we have seen at work in his Eastern Tales (where space and culture were concerned) but also in his neoclassical plays (where time and history were concerned): *relativism*. 'Man is the measure of all things', another Greek philosopher, Protagoras, had said: there is no higher authority on the basis of which to award preferences where human conduct is concerned. The cross descends in the Eastern Mediterranean, and the minarets arise; the reputations of Venetian doges are in the hands of posterity; the Baroque churches of Rome are built on unclassical principles above classical ruins. 'Great names are nothing more than nominal, / And love of glory's but an airy lust' (*DJ* IV. 801–2). No one can say whether these things are right or wrong, only that different human practices arise as circumstances dictate.

If material sufficiency, rather than principle, is an individual's best measure of satisfaction with the world, and if the individual concerned is honest enough to see that what counts as sufficiency is not an absolute but is culturally conditioned, then some form of *stoicism* is likely to follow. Material satisfaction is good, but it may be taken from you; happiness is only a social construction; therefore a stalwart indifference to both pleasure and pain is the most reliable source of contentment in a changing world. The stoic ideal, as Roman Emperor Marcus Aurelius put it in his classic exposition of the attitude, the *Meditations* (second century AD), was an individual 'unsullied by pleasures, proof against pain, untouched by insult, and impervious to evil', who 'will strike no poses, utter no complaints, and crave neither for solitude nor yet for a crowd'.[12] As we have seen, this is a point of view repeatedly dramatized by Byron, in Conrad's 'self-collected mien' (*Corsair* II. 300), Napoleon's 'innate philosophy' (*CHP* III. 349), and in Doge Foscari as 'the stoic of the state' (*TF* IV. I. 214). 'Ambition, glory, love, the common aim / That some can conquer, and that all would claim', Byron said of Lara – perhaps the consummate Byronic hero – 'Within his breast appear'd no more to strive' (*Lara* I. 79–81). Childe Harold comes to the same conclusion:

> Love, fame, ambition, avarice – 'tis the same,
> Each idle – and all ill – and none the worst –
> For all are meteors with a different name,
> And Death the sable smoke where vanishes the flame.
>
> (*CHP* IV. 1,113–16)

The four great English poems with which *Don Juan* was compared at the beginning of this chapter each offer something profounder than a mere view of the world – something better described, perhaps, as a theodicy: a vindication of the appropriateness of earthly arrangements. And this 'pagan' set of attitudes in combination is *Don Juan*'s theodicy. Ancient and timeless, pre- and post-Christian, pre- and post-rational, it assumes that we live in a material world, and that the chief moral problems we confront are material ones; that there is no higher authority than humanity adjudicating our solutions to such problems, or that if there is the gods keep such judgments to themselves; and that a stoical self-reliance is the best protection we can cultivate against the ineluctable disappointments natural to the world in which we find ourselves.

The narrator embodies this set of attitudes continually as he comments on Juan's career – from bedclothes to shipwrecks (and beyond): see *DJ* I. 977–1,016, 1,705–60; II. 1,409–40, 1,705–20; III. 1–88; VIII. 481–536; IX. 81–168; XI. 1–48; XIII. 1–88. But it is made explicit in two parts of the poem in particular. The slave market at Constantinople, to which Juan is taken in Canto V, is clearly the slave market of life itself: a materialistic and multicultural arena where men and women are bought and sold with cosmic indifference. 'All, when life is new, / Commence with feelings warm and prospects high', Juan's English fellow-prisoner tells him:

> But time strips our illusions of their hue,
> And one by one in turn, some grand mistake
> Casts off its bright skin yearly like the snake.   (V. 166–8)

'Love's the first net which spreads its deadly mesh', John Johnson goes on, reprising the attitudes voiced in *Lara* and *Childe Harold*; 'Ambition, Avarice, Vengeance, Glory, glue / The glittering lime-twigs of our latter days, / Where still we flutter on for pence or praise' (V. 173–6). In short, 'Men are the sport of circumstances, when / The circumstances seem the sport of men' (V. 135–6). Struggle is futile and demeaning, Johnson advises; patience and forbearance are all. Byron's use of humour and irony in *Don Juan* is itself a continuously present form of comic resilience in the face of fortune. Good-tempered but pessimistic, humour and irony tell us that there is nothing to fear – but also nothing to expect – in the situations humanity has faced and survived many times before.

The opening of Canto XIV is a more complete statement of Byron's position. Philosophical systems contradict each other, he says, and offer no guidance. Life and death are impenetrable mysteries. Suicide is intellectually attractive but too dreadful to contemplate physically. The poet makes no claim to authority on such matters ('mine's a bubble not blown up for praise, / But just to play with, as an infant plays'; XIV. 63–4). His fame gives him no pleasure, and he has lost it anyway because of his refusal to subscribe to the illusions peddled by society. The female sex ('Poor Thing of Usages! Coerc'd, compell'd, / Victim when wrong, and martyr oft when right'; XIV. 181–2) suffers egregiously in this system, but, 'By various joltings of life's hackney coach' (XIV. 205), continues to re-stock it. Sexual attraction, therefore, is the only lure that makes life bearable, even as it is the mechanism that keeps the entire charade in play:

> And when upon a silent, sullen day,
>   With a Sirocco, for example, blowing,
> When even the sea looks dim with all its spray,
>   And sulkily the river's ripple's flowing,
> And the sky shows that very ancient gray,
>   The sober, sad antithesis to glowing, –
> 'Tis pleasant, if *then* any thing is pleasant,
> To catch a glimpse even of a pretty peasant.   (XIV. 217–24)

Given this state of affairs, a stoical and materialist reliance on the pleasures the world has to offer – and *Don Juan* is nearly as taken up with food, clothing, and domestic furniture as it is with sex – is a human necessity.

Despite appearances, Byron's theodicy is not a misogynist one, and Caroline Franklin is right to note that the 'subtle and complex representation of women in *Don Juan* is unrivalled in male-authored art of the period'.[13] But male-authored is what the poem is, even though its subversion of its patriarchalist parent-myth is active and significant. For the *narrator*, women and sex are sources of pleasure in an unsatisfactory world – though his attitude to this 'Poor Thing of Usages' remains a charitable one (see II. 1,585–600). So women play their (supporting) role in the pagan conspectus. In the *narrative*, on the other hand, the situation is genuinely 'subtle and complex'. The heroines exercise the stoic's right to maximize pleasure and minimize pain, just as the hero does. In almost every case, the women in the poem gravitate towards Juan as he does towards them, in a way that the poem clearly regards as being consistent with the teachings of 'nature's good old college' (II. 1,088): the healthily egoistic desires of a normal human being. 'My blood still rushes where my spirit's set', Julia tells Juan (I. 1,555), and, in an unexpected way (for which, it seems, we owe a debt of gratitude to Coleridge and his conservative reading of the Don Juan myth, which inspired Byron both to invoke and subvert it), it is the women in the poem who serve as an index of the human desire for 'A something all-sufficient for the *heart*' (XIV. 585). (Julia is married to a much older man, Haidee is spellbound in the Cyclades, and Gulbeyaz is immured in a harem.) It is women, not men, who turn out to be central to the vindication of existence that Byron has to offer, and the sexual desire they feel for Juan is symbolic of those desires we all feel (sexual or otherwise) for human sufficiency.

But, as I say, that vindication remains a male-authored one, and the women of *Don Juan* do not constitute a statistically representative random sample by any means. Rather, the poem exhibits two groups (one in the Mediterranean, the other in England) of three women, the members of which conform to an utterly male set of sexual stereotypes: maiden (Haidee and Aurora), wife (Julia and Adeline), and – for want of a better word – vamp (Gulbeyaz and 'her frolic Grace', the Duchess of Fitz-Fulke). The poem repeats itself in its Mediterranean and English phases, and re-presents Juan with the sexual choices men imagine for themselves – Byron included, as a bachelor back from the Grand Tour in 1811, choosing between Annabella Milbanke, Frances Wedderburn Webster, and Caroline Lamb.

Though these women conform to a narrow group of patriarchal stereotypes, they are not fixed quantities. Their changeableness – which Byron referred to in ungendered terms as 'mobility' (XVI. 820) – is more significant than the privilege traditionally accorded to women by chauvinistic men. It is normal among humanity at large, being part of our moral pursuit of happiness. So Julia transits from a guilt-ridden wife, to a deceitful shrew with a lover hidden under her bedclothes, to that chastened but dignified spirit whose last letter to Juan hangs like an irresolvable and irreducible cloud over the rest of the poem: 'Man's love is of his life a thing apart, / 'Tis woman's whole existence' (I. 1,545–6). Haidee starts out feeding her lover picnics in a beachside cave; by Canto III the couple has moved in to her absent father's palace and all sense of romantic ingenuousness has been forgotten. Her clothes and jewellery (which Byron describes with erotically fixated exactitude) begin to confine her even as they make her more desirable (III. 553–608). But after Juan is dragged away at her father's order Haidee dies insane, pregnant with his child, and is buried on her island, 'now all desolate and bare' (IV. 569). The sultana Gulbeyaz is a creature of almost overwhelming sexual magnetism and splendour: 'There was a self-will even in her small feet, / As though they were quite conscious of her station – / They trod as upon necks' (V. 883–5). But she is dragged into the dust by Juan's rejection of her, and suffers terrible pangs of unrequited love:

> With the first ray, or rather grey of morn,
>   Gulbeyaz rose from restlessness; and pale
> As Passion rises, with its bosom worn,
>   Arrayed herself with mantle, gem, and veil.
> The nightingale that sings with the deep thorn,
>   Which Fable places in her breast of Wail,
> Is lighter far of heart and voice than those
> Whose headlong passions form their proper woes.   (VI. 689–96)

Of the four poets mentioned at the beginning of this chapter, only Chaucer could rival, in dramatic terms, the narrative in which these three Mediterranean women appear, from Cantos I to VI of *Don Juan*, and only he presents, in the *Canterbury Tales*, a similarly 'subtle and complex' gallery of female figures. Byron's 'English Cantos' are no less remarkable, but forgo the episodic picaresque in favour of style that owes little to narrative *verse* at all, and often seems to anticipate rather the novels of Charles Dickens and George Eliot, which appeared a generation or two after *Don Juan*. This part of the poem is incomplete, and only Adeline Amundeville – 'Her heart was vacant, though a splendid mansion' (XIV. 674) – is fully drawn, but the political house party Adeline and her husband convene anticipates in ethos and in detail the depiction of country house life we find in novels like Dickens's *Bleak House* (1853) and Eliot's *Felix Holt* (1866), to name but two. Like those novels, *Don Juan* presents a devastating critique of modern English aristocratic life and its 'pagan' discontents:

> The elderly walked through the library,
>   And tumbled books, or criticised the pictures,
> Or sauntered through the gardens piteously,
>   And made upon the hot-house several strictures,
> Or rode a nag, which trotted not too high,
>   Or on the morning papers read their lectures,
> Or on the watch their longing eyes would fix,
> Longing at sixty for the hour of six.   (XIII. 809–16)

From youth to old age men and women need a meaningful reason to exist. 'All present life is but an Interjection', Byron insists:

> An 'Oh!' or 'Ah!' of joy or misery,
> Or a 'Ha! ha!' or 'Bah!' – a yawn, or 'Pooh!'
> Of which perhaps the latter is most true.   (XV. 6–8)

But all these 'are better', he goes on (with Adeline in mind),

>   than the sigh supprest,
> Corroding in the cavern of the heart,
> Making the countenance a masque of rest,
> *And turning human nature to an art.*   (XV. 17–20; italics added)

The women in the poem instinctively reject that fate by finding someone to love – and we are sure Adeline will do the same, trapped in a loveless marriage as she is, though English manners might delay her decision.

So Byron's pagan attitudes are healthy, sane, and normal – a positive and time-honoured way of making life bearable and rewarding in all its panoramic variety. What a critic has said of another post-Homeric epic, James Joyce's *Ulysses*, could be said of *Don Juan* with equal justice: 'What is most important in the book is the vivid, ranging, deeply-felt and yet precisely controlled vitality it reveals and embodies *within* the apparent chaos.'[14] And the poem makes us recognize that vitality, in its many different forms, is something Byron pursued from his very earliest poems to his last. But the pagan theodicy of *Don Juan*, which does so much to discover human resilience, can also constitute 'a philosophy of negation and of flight from the world', as the Spanish-American philosopher George Santayana put it.[15] 'The materialist', he argued in an essay on the greatest Epicurean poet, the Roman Lucretius, 'is primarily an observer'

> and he will probably be such in ethics also; that is, he will have no ethics, except the emotion produced upon him by the march of the world. If he is an *esprit fort* [a 'strong spirit'; a freethinker] and really disinterested, he will love life; as we all love perfect vitality, or what strikes us as such, in gulls and porpoises. This, I think, is the ethical sentiment psychologically consonant with a vigorous materialism: sympathy with the movement of things, interest in the rising wave, delight at the foam it bursts into, before it sinks again.[16]

This is the existential ideal *Don Juan* holds out to its readers: a passion for 'perfect vitality', sympathy, interest, and delight, controlled by a stoical asceticism and an awareness of mortality.

But asceticism and irony can go too far; the tree of knowledge, as Cain discovered, is not the tree of life. Santayana went on:

> To introduce ascetic discipline, to bring out the irony of experience, to expose the self-contradictions of the will, would be the true means of mitigating the love of life; and if the love of life were extinguished, the fear of death, like smoke rising from that fire, would have vanished also.[17]

To abolish the fear of death is, *ipso facto*, to abolish the love of life, and so Byron's pagan theodicy is repeatedly punctuated, inside and outside *Don Juan*, by profound but agnostic doubts about the integrity and truth of that view of the world – particularly when the absolutes of life and death were concerned. 'A *Creator* is a more natural imagination than a fortuitous concourse of atoms', he remarked (*LJ* IX. 47); and even if 'the immortality of the soul is a "grand peut-être" ['big maybe': the French writer Rabelais's dying comment on life after death] … still it is a *grand* one' (*LJ* VIII. 35). The stoical advice issued to Juan in the slave market at Constantinople is interrupted by an awestruck account of the death of Commandant del Pinto (V. 257–312) – a prose version of which we read in Chapter 3. And *Don Juan* as a whole reminds us that the voice of stoical sweet reason is that of a narrator, a commentator, and an observer. That voice is a luxury unavailable either to Juan or to those poor things of usage, the women he meets. In April 1819, Byron sent Teresa Guiccioli his equivalent of Julia's parting letter to Juan – filled with the same recognition that 'the ethical sentiment psychologically consistent with a vigorous materialism' was not enough, in the end, to live by. 'For some years', he said,

> I have been trying systematically to avoid strong passions, having suffered too much from the tyranny of Love. *Never to feel admiration* – and to enjoy myself without giving too much importance to the enjoyment in itself – to feel indifference toward human affairs – contempt for many, but hatred for none, – this was the basis of my philosophy. I did not mean to love any more, nor did I hope to receive Love. You have put to flight all my resolutions – now I am all yours – I will become what you wish – perhaps happy in your love, but never at peace again.   (*LJ* VI. 118)

'Man is born *passionate* of body – but with an innate though secret tendency to the love of Good in his Main-spring of Mind. – – But God help us all! – It is at present a sad jar [a container, but also a clash] of atoms' (*LJ* IX. 46). There are many epigraphs to *Don Juan*, but this will do as well as any.

An alternative vision

What is offered above is an account of what *Don Juan* has to say, in existential terms, about 'the controlless core / Of human hearts' (I. 924–5). A recently offered alternative account of the poem is not only important in itself; it also allows me to discuss a part of *Don Juan* not considered thus far. In a series of critical works and editorial commentaries, Jerome McGann has made the case for a different theodicy in *Don Juan*: a historical one.

There are two important elements in McGann's argument. The first is that after a long intermission, from the end of 1820 to the beginning of 1822, Byron returned to *Don Juan* and swiftly moved his hero from the harem at Constantinople to the Siege of Ismail – the only authentic historical event in the poem, which took place in late 1790. At the beginning of 1821, Byron had also written to John Murray about his plans for the poem after Canto V:

> I meant to take him the tour of Europe – with a proper mixture of siege – battle – and adventure – and to make him finish … in the French Revolution … I meant to have made him a Cavalier Servente in Italy and a cause for a divorce in England – and a Sentimental 'Werther-faced man' in Germany – so as to show the different ridicules of the society in each of those countries.   (*LJ* VIII. 78)

(The Count in *Beppo*, like Byron himself, was a 'cavalier servente' or married woman's male companion; and Goethe's *The Sorrows of Young Werther* (1774) is a German Romantic novel about a lovelorn suicide.) So the Siege of Ismail and 'the Terror' of 1794 provide a pair of dates for Juan's travels and their conclusion, and from these McGann concludes that in 1822 Byron decided to 'go on with his poem in a serious and continuous way' (*CPW* V. 717) by committing himself to a historical vision of his own lifetime – albeit a three-tiered one:

> *Don Juan* examines the period 1789–1824 in terms of its three dominant phases: the early years of the French Revolution (the poem's displaced fiction [i.e., Juan's career]); the epoch of the Napoleonic Wars (viewed through Byron's analogous and contemporary experience of those years); and the epoch of the European restoration (dramatically fashioned and presented at the poem's immediate narrative level).[18]

So *Don Juan* is 'fundamentally an autobiographical poem which comments upon and interprets the course of history between 1787 and 1824'[19] – that momentous period discussed in Chapter 2.

McGann's account is ambitious, and holes can be picked in it. Byron entertained other plans for *Don Juan*, for example, which did not amount to much: in Canto I the narrator is a friend of Juan's family (I. 185–92, 401–3), and Byron wrote a preface to the poem (*CPW* V. 81–5) that presents it as being narrated by a Spanish gentleman during the Peninsular War. The plans he discussed with Murray for episodes in Germany and France are attractive and plausible – and certainly adulterous love in Italy, illicit love in England, and unrequited love in Germany would continue Juan's sentimental education, Childe Harold-style. But Byron was rarely comfortable writing outside the two worlds he knew well – England and the Mediterranean – and he knew next to nothing about Germany or France. (He certainly took Juan out of Russia quickly enough, nor did he use Juan's trip across Europe from St Petersburg to London as an opportunity to make a Young Werther of him.) So laying stress on a mercurial poet's plans may be unreliable.

Furthermore, if what McGann calls 'precise chronology'[20] is Byron's aim, he is slack in maintaining it. Adeline is 21 years old (XIV. 431–2) when Juan meets her, and he should be seventeen, but Byron says he is 'her junior by six weeks' (XIV. 407). If Juan is meant to reside in London in 1791, Byron only occasionally reminds himself of historical events of that time (XI. 176, XII. 655–6, 665–72), before forgetting it altogether, and returning to a metaphorical dramatization of his own return to England in 1811.

McGann's account also places emphasis on what I take to be the poem's weakest section: the Siege of Ismail and the court of Catherine the Great (Cantos

VII–X, inclusive). In that section, dubiously satirical elements are to the fore: the Preface to Cantos VI–VIII includes a hysterical attack on Castlereagh ('the most despotic [minister] in intention and the weakest in intellect that ever tyrannized over a country'; *CPW* V. 295) and Canto IX contains one on Wellington as 'the best of cut-throats' (IX. 25) – as if Napoleon had never shed a drop of human blood, nor populated the thrones of Europe with his own brothers and sisters. Byron spoke about 'throw[ing] away the scabbard' in such passages, and the 'fearful odds' of doing so (*LJ* IX. 191), but he was more effective as a subtle critic than an obstreperous one, just as McGann's histor- ical reading is most successful as regards the hyper-reflexive song, 'The Isles of Greece',[21] interpolated in Canto III, long before what he calls Byron's 'aggres- sive and engagé [committed] resolution' to nail his narrative to historical fact (*CPW* V. 717). Byron's belief that 'The drying up a single tear has more / Of honest fame, than shedding seas of gore' (VIII. 23–4) is a beautiful and venerable sentiment, but his expectation that clear distinctions can be drawn between 'freedom's battles' and those fought by 'over-pensioned Homicides' (*CPW* V. 297) carries more hope than conviction. Perhaps we have let Byron's anti-war message in the Ismail section blind us to its dramatic and narrative shortcomings – certainly, 'aggressive and engagé resolutions' are rarely the strong suits of poets, even satirical ones.

In the Ismail and Russian cantos, too, the subtle interplay between the sexes that characterizes the poem until that point deteriorates, as Juan becomes an unlikely mercenary, and Catherine the Great is depicted as 'the grand Epitome / Of that great Cause of War' (IX. 449–50), namely 'Thou gate of Life and Death' (IX. 434), the vagina. The jokes are coarse, too: about middle-aged women eagerly awaiting ravishment after Ismail falls to the Russians, for example. People and places are less brilliantly evoked. Bleakly, Byron speaks of 'holding up the Nothingness of life' (VII. 48), which was certainly neither his aim nor his achievement in earlier cantos. Juan's arrival in London, on 'that glittering sea / Of gems and plumes, and pearls and silks' (XI. 555–6) marks Byron's return to a world he knew and to the realm of emotional and moral complex- ities his novelistic genius could really come to grips with. No other poem, and few other narratives, can compare with the leisurely but brilliant exposure of London streets, English high life, and country pursuits that Byron launched into once he was back on home ground. There he stayed until he called a halt to the poem in May 1823 before sailing to Greece two months later, carrying fourteen stanzas of Canto XVII with him. Once there, he was too 'much occu- pied with business' (*LJ* XI. 125) to do more.

Don Juan fully deserves its place alongside the great long poems listed at the beginning of this chapter. The fact that it can provoke and sustain such widely differing accounts as those offered by Jerome McGann and by myself is as good an indicator of that fact as any other. Less solipsistic than *Childe Harold* and less frantic than the Eastern Tales, more vivid than Byron's neoclassical plays and more humane than his biblical ones, more robust than his lyrics and more profound than his satires, the comic epic is his triumph and his greatest legacy.

Chapter 9

Afterword

Many British writers have had an influence beyond the English-speaking world. Shakespeare and Dickens are particularly noteworthy in this regard. But Byron's impact on nineteenth-century Europe was historical, and not just literary. 'Before he came,' the Italian nationalist Giuseppe Mazzini wrote,

> all that was known of English literature was the French translation of Shakespeare, and the anathema hurled by Voltaire against the 'intoxicated barbarian.' It is since Byron that we Continentalists have learned to study Shakespeare and other English writers. From him dates the sympathy of all the true-hearted amongst us for this land of liberty, whose true vocation he so worthily represented among the oppressed. He led the genius of Britain on a pilgrimage throughout all Europe.[1]

Mazzini was writing in 1839. In the twentieth century, Byron's posthumous pilgrimage through intellectual Europe came to an end, and two key elements in his myth – the gloomy hero and the freedom fighter – withered away with the passage of time and the march of events. Philosophical existentialism and modern political ideology made both those figures look outdated, and what chiefly remained of Byron's influence, apart from his status as a literary celebrity, was the appeal of his later, comic verse. His improvisational, conversational, but also novelistic style continued to inspire poets: the Englishman W. H. Auden in his 'Letter to Lord Byron' (1937), the American Kenneth Koch in *The Duplications* (1977), and the Indian Vikram Seth in *The Golden Gate* (1986).

Mazzini's comment suggests that to concentrate on a small number of particular cases of Byron's influence would leave a false impression, so this section must proceed by painting some broad pictures involving many individuals.

Art and music

Byron's poetry is vigorously iconographic, and was illustrated almost as soon as it appeared. But he influenced two colossal figures of European Romantic art in a deeper way: the Englishman Joseph William Mallord Turner (1775–1851) and the Frenchman Eugène Delacroix (1798–1863). (Not every great Romantic painter was similarly attracted: 'The world is rid of Lord Byron,' the morally conventional John Constable wrote in May 1824, 'but the deadly slime of his touch still remains.')[2]

Turner exhibited only six works on Byronic themes – indicated in each case by the artist exhibiting lines from *Childe Harold* alongside his pictures. These are 'The Field of Waterloo' (1818), 'Childe Harold's Pilgrimage – Italy' (1832), 'The Bright Stone of Honour and the Tomb of Marceau, from Byron's "Childe Harold"' (1835), 'Modern Rome – Campo Vaccino' (1839), 'Venice, the Bridge of Sighs' (1840), and 'The Approach to Venice' (1844). But he also provided dozens of drawings and watercolours for engraved illustrations of Byron's works, and painted in the footsteps of the poet constantly. The affinity between *Childe Harold* and Turner's peripatetic urge to encompass continental Europe is clear. Turner even pursued an unfinished quasi-epic poem, 'The Fallacies of Hope', which demonstrates a good deal of Byron's sardonic attitude to empire and history.[3] And he returned the favour, by providing what has been called 'a definitive panorama of the Byronic world'.[4]

Turner's Byronic panoramas were physical; they depicted landscape and history. Delacroix, on the other hand, provided a panorama of introspection, violence, and exoticism that interpreted Byron in more emphatic terms. He was assisted in this enterprise by his own Eastern pilgrimage to Morocco and Algeria in 1832, which he drew upon for the rest of his life. 'Painting', he reminded himself in his journal in 1824, 'has advantages which no other art possesses':

> Poetry is full of riches; always remember certain passages from Byron, they are an unfailing spur to your imagination; they are right for you. The end of *The Bride of Abydos*; *The Death of Selim*, his body tossed about by the waves and that hand – especially that hand – held up by the waves as they break and spend themselves upon the shore. This is sublime, and it is his alone. I feel these things as they can be rendered in painting.[5]

And render those things Delacroix did, in a manner that no other artist has responded to a poet. *Childe Harold* he ignored, just as Turner specialized in it. But otherwise Delacroix painted five versions of *The Giaour* (1824, 1827, 1827,

1835, and 1856), four versions of *The Bride of Abydos* (1849, 1851, 1853, and 1857), two versions of *Lara* (1847 and 1858), one *Prisoner of Chillon* (1834), one *Mazeppa* (1828), two versions of *The Lament of Tasso* (1824 and 1830), a *Marino Faliero* (1826), a *Two Foscari* (1855), and a *Sardanapalus* (1828); as well as a shipwreck of Don Juan and a Don Juan with Haidee (1840 and 1856) – not to mention other pictures from the Greek War of Independence. Many of these paintings are masterpieces. As his journal entry suggests, Delacroix had a particular ability to concentrate on climactic moments in Byron's work, and that is why his paintings – even more than Turner's – constitute acts of interpretation rather than illustration.

Byron's influence was even broader in nineteenth-century music than it was in the visual arts. In Germany, Robert Schumann (1810–56) wrote incidental music for *Manfred*, planned an opera based on *The Corsair*, and set six songs by Byron; Felix Mendelssohn (1809–47) set two further songs; and the Hungarian Franz Liszt (1811–86) based his symphonic poem, 'Tasso: Lament and Triumph', on Byron's *Lament of Tasso*. Russian musicians were particularly responsive to the Byronic lure. Modest Mussorgsky (1839–81) set Byron's 'Destruction of Sennacharib', Nikolai Rimsky-Korsakov (1844–1908) set another two of Byron's lyrics, and Pyotr Tchaikovsky (1840–93) – an unhappily married, repressed homosexual – wrote a *Manfred* symphony in 1885. In Italy, three great composers of opera became involved in the Byronic legacy: Giacomo Rossini (1792–1868) composed a funeral cantata, 'The Weeping of the Muses at the Death of Lord Byron', in 1824; Gaetano Donizetti (1797–1848) wrote *Parisina* (1833) and *Marin Falier* (1835); and Giuseppe Verdi produced *The Corsair* (1840) and *The Two Foscari* (1844). Perhaps the most Byronic of the great nineteenth-century composers was the Frenchman Hector Berlioz (1803–69), whose *Memoirs* stand alongside Delacroix's *Journals* as pre-eminent records of Romantic creativity. Exiled to Rome under the terms of a scholarship as a young man, Berlioz read Byron in the confessionals at St Peter's to escape the summer heat, and experienced a pronounced sense of specular possession:

> His feet trod this marble, his hands explored that bronze. He breathed this air, his words vibrated in this stillness – words, perhaps, of tenderness and love … Yes, loved, a poet, free, rich – he was all these things. And in the silence of the confessional I ground my teeth till the damned must have heard and trembled.[6]

It is hardly surprising that Berlioz composed the most successful musical tribute to Byron, a concertante symphony, *Harold in Italy* (1834), in which the viola takes the part of the lonely pilgrim.

In the twentieth century, Byron's influence in classical music faded alongside his impact on the visual arts and literature, but the German composer Arnold Schoenberg (1874–1951) did write a remarkable setting of Byron's 'Ode to Napoleon Buonaparte' in 1942, aimed directly at Adolf Hitler from the composer's exile in the United States.

Literature

For many years in the twentieth century it was argued that Byron's impact on European literature was a sign of his mediocrity. His slapdash and meretricious poetry, it was said, 'translated well'. Certainly he was read with eagerness by the Continental poets of the nineteenth century. One recent collection of European Romantic poetry reprints 'Lord Byron's Last Love', by Adalbert von Chamisso (1781–1838), 'Childe Harold', by Heinrich Heine (1797–1856), 'To Lord Byron', by Alphonse de Lamartine (1790–1869), 'Address to Europe on the Death of Lord Byron', by Alfred de Vigny (1797–1863), 'Thought from Byron', by Gérard de Nerval (1808–55), 'To the Sea' ('Byron vanished, mourned by freedom ...'), by Alexander Pushkin (1799–1837), and 'I am No Byron', by Mikhail Lermontov (1814–41) – and this would be the tip of the iceberg in terms of lyric verse written in his name and under his influence.[7]

As were its musicians, Russian writers were particularly receptive to Byron. In fiction, Pushkin and Lermontov laid the foundation stones of Russian realism on a Byronic substrate. Pushkin's verse novel, *Eugene Onegin* (1833), is modern and realistic in terms of content, but in terms of narrative style and attitude it owes a great deal to *Don Juan*. Lermontov's *A Hero of Our Time* (1841), on the other hand, reinvents the Byronic hero as a tormented cavalry officer in Russia's war against the Muslim peoples in the Caucasus. The novelist Ivan Turgenev (1818–83) started out as a Byronic poet in works like 'Steno' (1834) and 'Parasha' (1843), but he also worked Byronic elements into a more significant literary archetype: the rootless young male intellectual confronting the meaninglessness of Russian life in works like 'The Diary of a Superfluous Man' (1850) and his masterpiece, *Fathers and Sons* (1862). The Byronic hero continued to stalk Russian fiction in the person of Stavrogin, the amoral protagonist of *Devils* (1872), by Fyodor Dostoevsky (1821–81), about a nest of self-destructive radicals in a provincial town.

Two great French realists were also affected by Byron. Gustave Flaubert (1821–80) visited the Castle of Chillon in 1845, and found the poet's name inscribed on the wall of the prisoner's cell. 'All the time I thought of the pale man who came there one day, walked up and down, wrote his name on the stone, and left.'[8] The two young men who form the centre of interest in Flaubert's first version of his classic, *Sentimental Education* (completed in the year of his visit to Chillon, but unpublished till 1912), refer frequently enough to Byron, but the poet's real contribution to the novel is the voice of the quizzical and worldly narrator of *Don Juan*. Each human being is different, Flaubert's narrator suggests, but 'It is a very different matter with sheep':

> when you see them grazing on a hillside, or being driven along the high road, huddled together and bleating, you assume that they have but a single thought, whether the grass is sweet; but one love, the ram who is bearing down upon them; but one fear, the dog snapping at their heels; but one worry, the red-faced man with the big knife, who is waiting to slaughter their lambs. But, with human beings, how can you tell what is going on inside all those skulls, under all those hats. Who knows where this huge, sad-eyed herd is making for?[9]

'Stendhal' (pen-name of Henri Beyle, 1783–1842) met Byron briefly in Milan in 1816, and dined out on the experience for the rest of his life, providing increasingly unreliable accounts of the English poet as time went on. But the ingenuous heroes of *Scarlet and Black* (1830) and *The Charterhouse of Parma* (1839) are recognizably akin to Byron's Juan: impetuous but also sensitive, and as likely to be seduced by women as to seduce them.

'Perhaps it's simply because Germany has had Goethe, and England Shakespeare and Byron,' the French poet Charles Baudelaire (1821–67) wrote, 'that [Victor] Hugo was legitimately owed to France' – which certainly put Byron in esteemed company. Baudelaire also commented on the 'systematically Byronic tone' of his own poem 'Le Voyage' from the epoch-marking *Flowers of Evil* (1857), and was clearly influenced by what he saw as Byron's satanism in the 'Révolte' section of that collection. It was Alfred de Vigny who coined the expression '*poète maudit*' (cursed poet) in 1832, but Baudelaire made the notion his own, and allied it with his notion of the Byronic dandy as a disengaged observer of modern existence.

Byron was also a significant influence on two colossal German poets. In his later life Goethe (1749–1832) became obsessed with Byron, whom he called 'the greatest genius of our century' – though he also said that 'Byron is only great as a poet; as soon as he reflects, he is a child.'[10] Certainly, Byron was the original for Euphorion, the extravagantly symbolic product of a union between the Mediterranean (Helen of Troy) and Northern Europe (Faust), mourned by the Chorus in the thirteenth scene of *Faust*, Part Two (published after Byron's death): 'Blessed with gifts, with noble name, / Soon, alas, self-lost and falling / In the bloom of youth and fame!'[11] Byron was enormously flattered by the attentions of a writer he called 'the first of living masters' (*CPW* VI. 15). Heinrich Heine was a poet on a completely different model to Goethe, and revealed an entirely different aspect of German culture: ironic, disillusioned, and obsessively lyrical. Many of his shorter poems combine passion with a Byronic strain of irony, but his witty and subversive travel-poem, *Deutschland: A Winter's Tale* (1844), is, as T. J. Reed points out, 'first cousin to the Byron of *Don Juan* or the Pushkin of *Eugene Onegin*'.[12]

We do not usually associate the realist plays of the Norwegian Henrik Ibsen (1828–1906) with Byronism in any shape or form. But the two poetic dramas that preceded Ibsen's turn to realism, *Brand* (1866) and *Peer Gynt* (1867), are less clear-cut. Though it was of *Peer Gynt* that Ibsen said, 'that was my *Manfred*. Who knows if a belated Byronist hasn't persisted in me?',[13] modern readers would be more likely to see *Brand* as Ibsen's equivalent of *Manfred*, especially in its opening scenes, where the isolated and existential hero wandering in the mountains repeatedly rejects the comforts and compromises of everyday life.

A prophet is rarely welcomed in his own land, and Byron's literary reputation in Britain was an object of greater ambivalence than it proved to be on the Continent. 'The Reverend the Moral and the fastidious may say what they please about Lord Byron's fame and damn it as they list', the poet John Clare (1793–1864) wrote after Byron's death, '[but] he has gained the path of its eternity without them and lives above the blight of their mildewing censure to do him damage.'[14] Later in life Clare wrote both a 'Child Harold' and a 'Don Juan' of his own. When he heard the news of the poet's demise, the future laureate, Alfred, Lord Tennyson (1809–92), walked out into the Lincolnshire countryside and wrote 'Byron is Dead' on a rock. But Victorian poets blew hot and cold on Byron, and even Matthew Arnold (1822–88) – whose selection of purple passages from the poet published in 1881 was an important attempt to save him for a late-Victorian readership – was ambivalent. In his poem 'Haworth Churchyard', Arnold compared Emily Brontë to Byron, 'The world-famed Son of Fire'. In 'Memorial Verses' he was more circumspect: 'He taught us little', he wrote, 'but our soul / Had *felt* him like the thunder's roll.' In his philosophical fantasy *Sartor Resartus* (1834) Thomas Carlyle (1795–1881) famously advised his reader to 'Close thy *Byron*; open thy *Goethe*', but John Ruskin (1819–1900) commented positively on Byron as a realist throughout his career, from *Modern Painters* (1856) to *Fiction, Fair and Foul* (1881) and (especially) his autobiography *Praeterita* (1889).[15]

Charles Dickens (1812–70) and William Makepeace Thackeray (1811–63) pretended to find Byron merely amusing – perhaps because they shared the poet's sense of *arriviste* social insecurity. Thackeray attacked Byron bitterly in *Notes of a Journey from Cornhill to Grand Cairo* (1846) and his *Book of Snobs* (1848), but Dickens found it difficult to wash the poet away so easily. Eugene Wrayburn, the caddish, egocentric young barrister from *Our Mutual Friend* (1865) is recognizably Byronic, as is the glamorous and selfish James Steerforth from *David Copperfield* (1850). And Byron helped power two of the greatest English novels of the century: *Wuthering Heights* and *Jane Eyre* (both 1847), by Emily Brontë (1818–48) and Charlotte Brontë (1816–55), respectively. Both of the novels' heroes are indebted to the Eastern Tales that all four Brontë siblings read feverishly in their youth, and recycled in their juvenilia (the 'Gondal' and 'Angria' stories – in many instalments). Like the Giaour, Heathcliff is revisited by his dead lover, and Rochester has the habit of galloping around the Yorkshire countryside after dark. Even George Eliot (1819–80), as un-Byronic an author as could be imagined, ponders the question of his appeal in *Felix Holt: The Radical* (1866). The eponymous hero, a high-minded Chartist, scorns Byron as a 'misanthropic debauchee, whose notion of a hero was that he should disorder his stomach and despise mankind'. But the heroine's other potential suitor is Harold Transome, recently returned from the East with an adoptive child. Young Harold's mother, he tells Esther Lyon, 'had been a slave – was bought, in fact'. 'Hitherto', the narrator goes on, 'Esther's acquaintance with Oriental love was derived chiefly from Byronic poems, and this had not sufficed to adjust her mind to a new story where the Giaour concerned was giving her his arm.'[16] Whereas Thomas Hardy (1840–1928) made no particular creative use of Byron in either his fiction or his poetry, he was vexed when the Dean of Westminster prohibited Byron a place in Poets' Corner on the centenary of his death in 1924, and wrote a bitter satirical poem, 'A Refusal', to register his protest.

Politics and philosophy

Once Byron had died in Greece he entered the DNA of European popular nationalism. Three political leaders of the nineteenth century expressed that gene – sometimes without being aware they were doing so – and theirs is perhaps the most unexpected legacy Byron left to the world.

'Leader' is not always the right word to use of the Pole, Adam Mickiewicz (1798–1855), the Italian, Giuseppe Mazzini (1805–72), and the Jew, Theodor Herzl (1860–1904). All of them sought to fill that role, as Byron did in Greece. But, like him, their practical influence on events was less important than their role as lightning rods for the awakening self-consciousness of the peoples they served. 'The initiative of the European movement at the present day belongs',

Mazzini wrote, 'to those peoples whose task it is to constitute their nationality', and not those who already possessed such a thing. 'The only idea I believed to have the power to resuscitate the Peoples', he went on, was 'the Idea of Nationality.'[17] Byron's not being a Greek, and his capacity to stand above the squabbling groups claiming to be the authentic guardians of Hellas, was precisely the factor that allowed him to become a national hero. 'I did not come to join a faction', he wrote, 'but a nation' (*LJ* XI. 32) – and he encouraged the Greeks to think of themselves in precisely those terms.

In a similar fashion, Mickiewicz ('the Byron of his country',[18] as the French critic Charles Sainte-Beuve called him) was in fact born a Russian citizen in Lithuania. At 26 he was exiled to Russia, which he left in 1829 before settling in Paris; he would never see his native land again. As a political leader his career was disastrous, coming to a climax in 1848, when he persuaded a dozen or so Poles living in Rome to form a detachment alongside the Italians fighting for liberty against the Austrians in Lombardy. This platoon 'marched' by train and carriage across Italy, picking up uniforms made for them by the English wife of an expatriate Polish painter working in Florence, before they ran out of steam and finance in Milan. Ultimately, however – and without Mickiewicz himself, who had returned to Paris – the Polish 'legion' did indeed fire some shots on Austrian troops near Lake Garda, two months before an armistice was signed.

It was as a poet, not as a politician, that Mickiewicz inspired the Polish nation. At one end of the spectrum of his work there is *Konrad Wallenrod* (1828), a melodramatic tale of assumed identity in which a mysterious Lithuanian takes charge of the German Teutonic Knights – sworn enemies of Lithuania – and confounds their purpose as a double agent. (Konrad is as Byronic as his name suggests: 'foremost he to scale / Beleaguered walls; his ship the first to sail / Grappling the pagan galleys'; but also 'With an indifferent ear he turned from praise, / On lovely faces bent a distant gaze, / From charming discourse drew himself apart', and so forth.)[19] At the other end of the spectrum there is the bucolic, nostalgic, and digressive masterpiece, *Pan Tadeusz* (1834), Mickiewicz's equivalent to *Don Juan*, set in 1812, when his people dreamed of the freedom that Napoleon might bring with him on his way to conquer Russia. 'For people of my generation', the poet Zygmunt Krasiński (1812–59) wrote of Mickiewicz,

> he was honey and milk and bile and spiritual blood. We all stem from him. He had swept us away on a wave of inspiration and cast us into the world. He was one of the pillars supporting a vault made not of stone, but of so many living and bloody hearts – a gigantic pillar he was, although itself cracked … The greatest *wieszcz* [bard, prophet] not only of the nation, but of all Slavic tribes.[20]

And this despite Mickiewicz's turning his back on Polish Catholicism to pursue various forms of sub-Christian mysticism.

Giuseppe Mazzini was no *wieszcz*, though he was a lifelong enthusiast for Byron. What he shared with Mickiewicz (and with Byron himself, twice banished as the poet was – from the Mediterranean when in England, and from England when in the Mediterranean) was the experience of exile. Like Mickiewicz, he was driven from his homeland in his mid-twenties, and never saw it again. He lived the rest of his life on the run in France and Switzerland before finally settling in England – indeed, his native Genoa was almost the only region of Italy he knew. He was a more conventional ideologue than Mickiewicz: a believer in the 'doctrine of progress' and the 'religion of the future', with their corresponding faiths and certainties. 'My nature was strongly subjective, and master of itself', he wrote[21] – which one could never say of the Polish poet. So his autobiography is a record of fact rather than feeling. But the labyrinth of exile is perceptible in the despair Mazzini experienced when his early plans collapsed and he fled to safety in England in 1837. There he spoke of 'the tempest of Doubt, which I believe all who devote their lives to a great enterprise, yet have not dried and withered up their soul … beneath some barren formula, but have retained a loving heart, are doomed – once at least – to battle through'.[22]

Theodor Herzl's store of self-belief was too large for him to suffer tempests of doubt, at least for long. But the father of modern Zionism was more tormented than either of the two men discussed so far. Every Jew of Herzl's time was born into exile, but he was exiled even from Jewishness. (Indeed, some of his best friends, intellectually speaking, early in his career, were moderate anti-Semites: like them he felt the best thing the Jews could do would be to stop drawing attention to themselves as Jews, and assimilate as quickly as possible.) With an impeccably secular and bourgeois background in Budapest and Vienna, Herzl's early life rotated entirely around social cachet, which he planned to achieve by writing brilliant social comedies for the theatres of central Europe. Much to his surprise this failed to happen, though he built a successful career as a journalist. Then, out of the blue, he wrote a play as bad as any of its predecessors, but this time on a Jewish theme: one that presented the ghetto as a state of mind rather than a physical location. It followed that the idea of assimilation was a fantasy, and that, like the Italians and the Poles, the Jews needed (to borrow Mazzini's expression) 'to found a nation, to create a people'. For this they needed a homeland, and in 1895 there crystallized within Herzl 'the dynamic synergy of manifest pathology, flawed perceptions, and supreme gifts that transformed the thirty-five-year-old journalist into a messianic leader'.[23] His pamphlet, *The Jewish State* (1896), made it clear, to himself at least, that two elements in Jewish history were ineradicable: anti-Semitism and the desire of the Jewish people to return to Palestine. Almost every practical step he took thereafter was futile: he wooed the German Kaiser, the Russian Tsar, the Turkish Sultan, and the governments of Britain and France, faithfully believing that the movers and shakers he exhausted himself in courting would recognize the inevitability of his project and make it come to pass – which they had no intention of doing.

Herzl knew almost nothing of Jewish life or history – especially in Eastern Europe, which he never visited. When mobbed by common Jewish people in London's East End he was horrified and embarrassed. He seems to have regarded the Jewish faith as hardly more than a regrettable superstition, and never observed its practices. But none of this mattered, any more than Byron's marginal preference for the Turks over the Greeks mattered in the campaign he engaged in. Though Herzl could never see it in these terms, his contribution was simple: to persuade the Jewish people that it *was* a people, whose leaders could negotiate with the leaders of every other nation of the world. 'Believe me,' he wrote in his diary, 'policy for an entire people … can only be made with lofty imponderables.'[24]

Herzl marks an extreme case of the Byronic nationalist. But all three politicians discussed here carried with them Byron's passionate commitment to the freedom of a people in certain respects hardly their own, accompanied by a rationalist reserve and distance from ethnic sentiment (itself accompanied by a clear understanding of the power of 'lofty imponderables'), alloyed with a theatrical sense of themselves half-reluctantly caught up in forces they had helped to unleash.

Herzl was not the only great nineteenth-century Jewish politician whom Byron infected. The other was one of Britain's greatest and least likely prime ministers, Benjamin Disraeli (1804–81). Disraeli's father had known Byron in his years of fame, the son's Grand Tour was a carbon copy of Childe Harold's, and many of Disraeli's novels – from *The Young Duke* (1831) and *Contarini Fleming* (1832) to *Venetia: The Poet's Daughter* (1837) – are saturated with Byronism. Disraeli even met and took into his employ Byron's Italian man-servant, Tita Falciere. But he was also the senior member of 'Young England', a short-lived political movement of the early 1840s, a leading ideological purpose of which was a rehabilitation of the principle of aristocracy in a country that was being broken into 'two nations' of rich and poor by the onset of mature capitalism. Rich and poor there had always been, but Young England criticized capitalism from the right, seeing it as an economic innovation that destroyed traditional social relations and left nothing in their place. For Young England, Byron was a representative type of the good aristocrat: as liberal as he was patrician, with a clearer sense of the interests of the people than any mill-owner or plutocrat, and capable of forging an organic link between the monarch and the people. 'Viewed in its widest context,' Disraeli's biographer argues, 'Young England … was the reaction of a defeated class to a sense of its own defeat – a sort of nostalgic escape from the disagreeable present to the agreeable but imaginary past.'[25] That is a half-truth; the British aristocracy was by no means a 'defeated class' in the early 1840s, though in retrospect it is possible to read the signs of its long-term decline. But certainly Byron was a quixotic choice to represent what Disraeli called 'the high spirit of a free aristocracy'.[26]

The pampered minions of Eton and Oxbridge who associated with Disraeli were tiny objects compared to the historical phenomenon they reacted to. It is typical of Byron that his appeal should have been as strong among the working people of Britain as it was among the two-nation Conservatives who sought to improve their condition. And it was *Don Juan* that working people read. At the great Chartist demonstration held at Newcastle on 27 June 1838, several banners carried quotations from Byron's epic poem – *DJ* XI. 671–2, for example:

REVOLUTION
I have seen some nations, like o'er-loaded asses,
Kick off their burdens, – meaning the high classes.[27]

By 1838, Byron's poetry had entered what historian William St Clair calls 'the radical canon' of the nineteenth-century working class. Because *Don Juan* was considered beyond the protection of copyright due to its scandalous nature, and because in any event half the copyright lay with John Murray and half with Byron's heirs, it was a pirate publisher's dream. In 1824, the official edition of the poem cost fifty-seven shillings; by 1825, it was available for six shillings and sixpence; by the 1870s, the poem could be bought for sixpence: 1 per cent of its original asking price.[28] 'If we estimate, say, 200,000 copies of *Don Juan*, official and pirated before 1840,' St Clair concludes,

> multipliers imply a readership of part at least of the poem in a range which might be was wide as half a million to a million and a half. … The conclusion is inescapable – *Don Juan* was read by more people in its first twenty years than any previous work of English literature.[29]

Nor was it only fire-and-brimstone radicalism that such readers got from Byron. He also offered something broader and more humane, as 'Mark Rutherford' (William Hale White, 1831–1914) testified in his novel, *The Revolution in Tanner's Lane* (1887). The hero, a Manchester clerk, 'found in the *Corsair*', Rutherford wrote, exactly what answered to his own inmost self, down to its very depths. The lofty style, the scorn of what is mean and base, the courage … that dares and evermore dares in the very last extremity, the love of the illimitable, of freedom, and the cadences like the fall of waves on a sea-shore were attractive to him beyond measure.[30]

Byron's poems, the Chartist Thomas Cooper said, 'seemed to create almost a new sense within me'.[31] This is a case of a moral awakening as well as a political one.

As the chapter on Byron in Bertrand Russell's *History of Western Philosophy* suggests, Byron's contribution to that progress was more along the lines of what we would call 'thought' than philosophy as such. The Byronic hero was an expression of individualistic pessimism, tending towards satanic rebelliousness at the state of the world. 'In general', Russell remarked, 'Byron's ethical theory, as opposed to his practice, remains strictly conventional'; but 'sometimes … Byron approaches more nearly to Nietzsche's point of view'[32] – that is, to a position of religious and moral antinomianism.

Certainly, Friedrich Nietzsche (1844–1900) is the only canonical philosopher who acknowledged the influence of the poet – and it was *Manfred* in particular, with its rejection of everything external to the individual, which inspired him. (Nietzsche was also an amateur musician, and composed a 'Manfred-Meditation' in 1872.) 'I must be closely related to Byron's *Manfred*', he wrote in his intellectual autobiography, *Ecce Homo* ('Behold the Man'; 1898); 'I have found all these abysses in myself … I do not have a single word, just a glare, for anyone who dares to pronounce the word "Faust" in the presence of Manfred. Germans are *incapable* of any concept of greatness.'[33] More significantly, Nietzsche (albeit as a schoolboy) called Byron's magus a '*geisterbeherrschender Übermensch*' ('spirit-mastering superhuman')[34] – and the *Übermensch* is a central, though controversial, element in Nietzsche's thought. For some, it has fascist overtones; for others, it constitutes Nietzsche's call for a healthy and salutary form of moral self-attainment, beyond the realm of the all too human, beyond good and evil, and beyond conventional humanism.

'Man is a rope, fastened between animal and Superman', Nietzsche wrote in the 'Prologue' to *Thus Spoke Zarathustra* (1885), 'a rope over an abyss.' What Byron would have made of such a view is anybody's guess, but certainly he and his writings are on that rope.

Notes

Preface

1 Andrew Rutherford (ed.), *Byron: The Critical Heritage* (London: Routledge and Kegan Paul, 1970), 39.
2 Ernest J. Lovell (ed.), *His Very Self and Voice: Collected Conversations of Lord Byron* (New York: Macmillan, 1954), 31.
3 Leslie A. Marchand, *Byron: A Biography* (London: John Murray, 1957), 676.
4 Lovell, *His Very Self and Voice*, 470.
5 Ibid., 317.
6 See Rutherford, *Byron: The Critical Heritage*, 455.
7 T. S. Eliot, *The Sacred Wood: Essays on Poetry and Criticism* (London: Methuen, 1960), 54. There is a feline study of Byron in Eliot's *On Poetry and Poets* (London: Faber and Faber, 1957).
8 W. P. Ker, 'Byron', in *Collected Essays*, ed. Charles Whibley, 2 vols. (London: Macmillan, 1923), I. 210.
9 R. G. Collingwood, *An Autobiography* (Oxford University Press, 1978), 31.

Chapter 1   Life

1 Frederick L. Jones (ed.), *The Letters of Percy Bysshe Shelley*, 2 vols. (Oxford University Press, 1964), II. 57.
2 Thomas Moore, *Letters and Journals of Lord Byron, with Notices of His Life*, 2 vols. (London: John Murray, 1830), I. 347.
3 Doris Langley Moore, *Lord Byron: Accounts Rendered* (London: John Murray, 1974), 193.
4 Jones, *Letters of Percy Bysshe Shelley*, II. 423.
5 Charles Richard Sanders (ed.), *The Collected Letters of Thomas and Jane Welsh Carlyle*, vol. 3 (Durham, NC: Duke University Press, 1978), 70.

Chapter 2   Context

1 Jonathan Parry, *The Rise and Fall of Liberal Government in Victorian Britain* (New Haven, CT: Yale University Press, 1993), 30.

2 Ian R. Christie, *Stress and Stability in Late Eighteenth-Century Britain: Reflections on the British Avoidance of Revolution* (Oxford University Press, 1984), 92.

3 Parry, *Rise and Fall of Liberal Government*, 28, 30.

4 Eric J. Evans, *Political Parties in Britain 1783–1867* (London: Routledge, 2003), 3.

5 Lawrence Stone and Jeanne C. Fawtier Stone, *An Open Elite? England 1540–1880* (Oxford University Press, 2001), 14.

6 Boyd Hilton, *A Mad, Bad, and Dangerous People? England 1783–1846* (Oxford University Press, 2006), 424.

7 Peter Laslett, *The World We Have Lost*, 2nd edn (London: Methuen, 1971), 202.

8 John Beckett, *Byron and Newstead: The Aristocrat and the Abbey* (Newark: University of Delaware Press, 2001), 16.

9 John Cannon, *Aristocratic Century: The Peerage of Eighteenth-Century England* (Cambridge University Press, 1984), 113, 115.

10 Ibid., 117, 110.

11 Norman Gash, quoted in John Plowright, *Regency England: The Age of Lord Liverpool* (London: Routledge, 1996), 60.

12 Hilton, *A Mad, Bad, and Dangerous People?*, 286.

13 Evans, *Political Parties in Britain 1783–1867*, 22.

14 Hilton, *A Mad, Bad, and Dangerous People?*, 209.

15 Christie, *Stress and Stability in Late Eighteenth-Century Britain*, 156.

16 Paul Schroeder, *The Transformation of European Politics 1763–1848* (Oxford University Press, 1994), 413.

17 Clive Emsley, *British Society and the French Wars 1793–1815* (London: Macmillan, 1979), 48.

18 J. R. Dinwiddy, *From Luddism to the First Reform Bill: Reform in England 1810–1832* (Oxford: Basil Blackwell, 1986), 19–20.

19 Andrew Nicholson (ed.), *The Letters of Lord Byron to John Murray* (Liverpool University Press, 2007), 301.

20 Ernest J. Lovell (ed.), *His Very Self and Voice: Collected Conversations of Lord Byron* (New York: Macmillan, 1954), 518, 568.

21 Charles J. Esdaile, *The French Wars 1792–1815* (London: Routledge, 2001), xv.

22 William Hazlitt, *Collected Works*, ed. P. P. Howe, 21 vols. (London: J. M. Dent, 1934), VI. 74.

23 Emsley, *British Society and the French Wars*, 133.

24 Esdaile, *The French Wars*, 85.

25 Schroeder, *The Transformation of European Politics*, 52.

26 Tim Blanning, *The Pursuit of Glory: Europe 1648–1815* (London: Penguin, 2008), 611–14.

27 Hazlitt, *Collected Works*, VII. 73.

28 Hilton, *A Mad, Bad, and Dangerous People?*, 297.

29 See Clive Emsley (ed.), *The Longman Companion to Napoleonic Europe* (London: Longman, 1993), 134–7.

30 Emsley, *British Society and the French Wars*, 119.

31 Schroeder, *The Transformation of European Politics*, 230.
32 Blanning, *The Pursuit of Glory*, 673.
33 Esdaile, *The French Wars*, 83.
34 Schroeder, *The Transformation of European Politics*, 576,
35 Ibid., 579, 580.
36 A. D. Harvey, *English Literature and the Great War with France* (London: Nold Johnson, 1981), 2.
37 Earl Grosvenor's and other parliamentarians' speeches are quoted according to date from Hansard, the official record of the Houses of Parliament, available on the Internet through http://hansard.millbanksystems.com.
38 Deirdre Le Faye (ed.), *Jane Austen's Letters*, 3rd edn (Oxford University Press, 1995), 191.
39 Harvey, *English Literature and the Great War with France*, 12.
40 Betty Bennett (ed.), *British War Poetry in the Age of Romanticism: 1793–1815* (New York: Garland, 1976), 1.
41 Quoted in Hilton, *A Mad, Bad, and Dangerous People?*, 311.
42 L. H. Houtchens and C. W. Houtchens (eds.), *Leigh Hunt's Literary Criticism* (New York: Columbia University Press, 1956), 129.
43 Isaiah Berlin, *The Roots of Romanticism* (London: Pimlico, 2000), 1.
44 Ibid., 21–2.
45 Ibid., 42.
46 Ibid., 14.
47 Andrew Graham-Dixon, *A History of British Art* (London: BBC, 1996), 128.
48 Dror Wahrman, *The Making of the Modern Self: Identity and Culture in Eighteenth-Century England* (New Haven, CT: Yale University Press, 2004), xiii.
49 Ibid., xi, 168.
50 Ibid., xiii, 18.
51 Ibid., 128.
52 Linda Colley, *Britons: Forging the Nation, 1707–1837*, rev. edn (New Haven, CT: Yale University Press, 2005), 145.
53 Ibid., 209.
54 Hilton, *A Mad, Bad and Dangerous People?*, 151.
55 London Missionary Society, *Four Sermons Preached … at the Second General Meeting of the Missionary Society* (London, 1796), 61.
56 Gordon Rattray Taylor, *The Angel Makers: A Study in the Psychological Origins of Historical Change, 1750–1850*, rev. edn (New York: Dutton, 1974), 21, 55.
57 Nicholson, *Letters of John Murray to Lord Byron*, 310.
58 See Andrew Rutherford (ed.), *Byron: The Critical Heritage* (London: Routledge and Kegan Paul, 1970), 265–7.

Chapter 3   The letters and journals

1 William Hazlitt, *Complete Works*, ed. P. P. Howe, 21 vols. (London: J. M. Dent, 1934), XII. 17.

2 Andrew Rutherford (ed.), *Byron: The Critical Heritage* (London: Routledge and Kegan Paul, 1970), 296.

3 G. Wilson Knight, *Byron's Dramatic Prose* (Nottingham University, 1954), 15, and John Ruskin, *Works*, ed. E. T. Cook and Alexander Wedderburn, 39 vols. (London: George Allen, 1903–12), XXXV. 145.

4 Michael Ratcliffe, 'Byron: Minus the Asterisk', *The Times*, 4 Oct. 1973.

5 Peter Porter, 'In the Fact', *New Statesman* 94 (2 Sept. 1977), 309.

6 Rutherford, *Byron: The Critical Heritage*, 316.

7 George Brandes, *Main Currents in Nineteenth-Century Literature*, 6 vols. (New York: Macmillan, 1905), IV. 276.

8 James Hamilton Browne, 'Voyage from Leghorn to Cephalonia with Lord Byron', *Blackwood's Edinburgh Magazine* 35 (Jan. 1834), 57.

9 Donald H. Reiman and Neil Fraistat (eds.), *Shelley's Poetry and Prose*, 2nd edn (New York: Norton, 2002), 120.

10 Thomas Moore, *Letters and Journals of Lord Byron: With Notices of his Life*, 2 vols. (London: John Murray, 1830), I. 393.

11 Ibid., I. 355–6.

12 Ibid., I. 79.

13 John D. Jump, 'Byron's Prose', in John D. Jump (ed.), *Byron: A Symposium* (London: Macmillan, 1975), 17.

14 Harriet Beecher Stowe, *Lady Byron Vindicated: A History of the Byron Controversy from its Beginnings in 1816 to the Present Time* (Boston, MA: Fields, Osgood, 1870), 20.

Chapter 4   The poet as pilgrim

1 Alexander Dyce, *Recollections of the Table-Talk of Samuel Rogers* (London: H. A. Rogers, 1887), 232.

2 Bernard Blackstone, *Byron: A Survey* (London: Longman, 1975), 90, and Caroline Franklin, *Byron* (London: Routledge, 2007), 5.

3 Catherine Addison, 'Little Boxes: The Effects of Stanzas on Poetic Narrative', *Style* 37.2 (2003), 124–5.

4 Ibid., 130.

5 Ibid., 140.

6 Bernard Beatty, *Byron's Don Juan* (London: Croom Helm, 1985), 143.

7 John Ruskin, *Works*, ed. E. T. Cook and Alexander Wedderburn, 39 vols. (London: George Allen, 1903–12), XXXV. 141.

8 William Hazlitt, *Collected Works*, ed. P. P. Howe, 21 vols. (London: J. M. Dent, 1934), VI. 179–80.

9 Blackstone, *Byron: A Survey*, 215.

Chapter 5   The orient and the outcast

1 William Hazlitt, *Collected Works*, ed. P. P. Howe, 21 vols. (London: J. M. Dent, 1934), V. 153.

2 Daniel P. Watkins, *Social Relations in Byron's Eastern Tales* (Cranbury, NJ: Associated University Presses, 1987), 138.

3 Bernard Blackstone, *Byron: A Survey* (London: Longman, 1975), 97.

4 William St Clair, *The Reading Nation in the Romantic Period* (Cambridge University Press, 2004), 586–7 (Byron), 579 (Austen), 649 (Shelley).

5 Ibid., 170.

6 Ibid., 181.

7 Andrew Nicholson (ed.), *The Letters of John Murray to Lord Byron* (Liverpool University Press, 2007), 257.

8 James Kennedy, *Conversations on Religion with Lord Byron and Others* (Philadelphia, PA: Carey and Lea, 1833), 174.

9 St Clair, *The Reading Nation in the Romantic Period*, 398.

10 Francis Jeffrey, in Andrew Rutherford (ed.), *Byron: The Critical Heritage* (London: Routledge and Kegan Paul, 1970), 60.

11 John Ruskin, *Works*, ed. E. T. Cook and Alexander Wedderburn, 39 vols. (London: George Allen, 1903–12), XVII. 32.

12 See Edward Said, *Orientalism* (London: Routledge and Kegan Paul, 1978), though Said spends little time on imaginative writers in general or Byron in particular. See also Mohammed Sharafuddin, *Islam and Romantic Orientalism: Literary Encounters with the Orient* (London: Tauris, 1996).

13 Bernard Beatty, *Byron's Don Juan* (London: Croom Helm, 1985), 56.

14 Bernard Beatty, 'Inheriting Humors, Legating Humor: The Will of Manfred', in Cheryl A. Wilson (ed.), *Byron: Heritage and Legacy* (London: Palgrave Macmillan, 2008), 145.

Chapter 6   Four philosophical tales

1 Bernard Beatty, 'Introduction', in Bernard Beatty, Tony Howe, and Charles E. Robinson (eds.), *Liberty and Poetic Licence: New Essays on Byron* (Liverpool University Press, 2008), 1.

2 Drummond Bone, 'The Rhetoric of Freedom', in Alan Bold (ed.), *Byron: Wrath and Rhyme* (London: Vision Press, 1983), 168.

3 Mark Storey, *Byron and the Eye of Appetite* (London: Macmillan, 1986), 63.

4 Jerome J. McGann, *Fiery Dust: Byron's Poetic Development* (University of Chicago Press, 1968), 167.

5 Andrew Rutherford (ed.), *Byron: The Critical Heritage* (London: Routledge and Kegan Paul, 1970), 122.

6 Bernard Beatty, *Byron: Don Juan and Other Poems; A Critical Study* (Harmondsworth: Penguin, 1987), 46.

7 David Nichol Smith and Edward L. McAdam (eds.), *The Poems of Samuel Johnson*, 2nd edn (Oxford University Press, 1974), 134–5.

8 Storey, *Byron and the Eye of Appetite*, 73.

9 Nigel Leask, *British Romantic Writers and the East: Anxieties of Empire* (Cambridge University Press, 1992), 64.

10 Peter Graham, *Lord Byron* (New York: Twayne, 1998), 103.

Chapter 7   Histories and mysteries

1 Ernest J. Lovell (ed.), *His Very Self and Voice: Collected Conversations of Lord Byron* (New York: Macmillan, 1954), 277.

2 Friedrich Schlegel, *Lectures on the History of Literature, Ancient and Modern*, trans. John Gibson Lockhart (London: Henry Bohn, 1859), 282–3.

3 R. A. Foakes (ed.), *Coleridge on Shakespeare: The Text of the Lectures of 1811–12* (London: Routledge and Kegan Paul, 1971), 100.

4 Herbert Lindenberger, *Historical Drama: The Relation of Literature and Reality* (University of Chicago Press, 1975), 104.

5 Bernard Blackstone, *Byron: A Survey* (London: Longman, 1975), 242.

6 David Hume, *Enquiries Concerning the Human Understanding and Concerning the Principles of Morals*, ed. L. A. Selby-Bigge, 2nd edn (Oxford University Press, 1902), 83.

7 Paul Ricoeur, *History and Truth*, trans. Charles A. Kelbley (Evanston, IL: Northwestern University Press, 1965), 28.

8 Robert Ryan, 'Byron's *Cain*: The Ironies of Belief', *Wordsworth Circle* 21 (1990), 44.

9 Jerome J. McGann, *Fiery Dust: Byron's Poetic Development* (University of Chicago Press, 1968), 245.

10 John Ruskin, *Works*, ed. E. T. Cook and Alexander Wedderburn, 39 vols. (London: George Allen, 1903–12), XXXIV. 328.

11 Anne Barton, '*Don Juan* Transformed', in Andrew Rutherford (ed.), *Byron: Augustan and Romantic* (London: Macmillan, 1990), 211.

Chapter 8   *Don Juan*

1 Andrew Rutherford, *Byron: The Critical Heritage* (London: Routledge and Kegan Paul, 1970), 164, 197, 260.

2 Peter Vassallo, *Byron: The Italian Literary Influence* (London: Macmillan, 1984), 48.

3 William Hazlitt, *Collected Works*, ed. P. P. Howe, 21 vols. (London: J. M. Dent, 1934), V. 44.

4 Catherine Addison, 'Little Boxes: The Effects of the Stanza on Poetic Narrative', *Style*, 37.2 (2003), 130–1.

5 Peter Graham, 'Nothing So Difficult', in Alice Levine and Robert N. Keane (eds.), *Rereading Byron: Essays Selected from Hofstra University's Byron Bicentennial Conference* (New York: Garland, 1993), 55.

6 Bernard Blackstone, *Byron: A Survey* (London: Longman, 1975), 278.

7 Elizabeth French Boyd, *Byron's* Don Juan: *A Critical Study* (New York: Humanities Press, 1959), 69.

8 Rutherford, *Byron: The Critical Heritage*, 258.

9 W. H. Auden (ed.), *George Gordon, Lord Byron: Selected Poetry and Prose* (New York: Signet, 1966), p. xi.

10 Bernard Beatty, *Byron's* Don Juan (London: Croom Helm, 1985), 82.

11 John Gaskin (ed.), *The Epicurean Philosophers* (London: Dent, 1995), 5.

12 Marcus Aurelius, *Meditations*, trans. Maxwell Stanniforth (Harmondsworth: Penguin, 1964), 56, 58.

13 Caroline Franklin, *Byron's Heroines* (Oxford University Press, 1992), 99.

14 S. L. Goldberg, *Joyce* (Edinburgh: Oliver and Boyd, 1962), 73.

15 George Santayana, *Three Philosophical Poets: Lucretius, Dante, Goethe* (Cambridge, Mass.: Harvard University Press, 1947), 31.

16 Ibid., 33.

17 Ibid., 53.

18 Jerome McGann, *The Beauty of Inflections: Literary Investigations in Historical Method and Theory* (Oxford University Press, 1985), 287–8.

19 Ibid., 280.

20 Ibid., 287.

21 Ibid., 277–86.

Chapter 9   Afterword

1 Andrew Rutherford (ed.), *Byron: The Critical Heritage* (London: Routledge and Kegan Paul, 1970), 340.

2 C. R. Leslie, *Memoirs of the Life of John Constable* (Oxford: Phaidon, 1951), 123.

3 Andrew Wilton, *Painting and Poetry: Turner's* Verse Book *and His Work of 1804–1812* (London: Tate Gallery, 1990).

4 David Blayney Brown, *Turner and Byron* (London: Tate Gallery, 1992), 63.

5 Hubert Wellington (ed.), *The Journal of Eugène Delacroix*, trans. Lucy Norton (Oxford: Phaidon, 1951), 39.

6 Hector Berlioz, *Memoirs*, trans. David Cairns (New York: Norton, 1975), 166.

7 Michael Ferber (ed.), *European Romantic Poetry* (New York: Pearson Longman 2005), 119, 151, 185, 195, 252, 386, 440.

8 Francis Steegmuller (ed. and trans.), *The Letters of Gustave Flaubert, 1830–1857* (London: Faber and Faber, 1981), 32.

9 Gustave Flaubert, *The First Sentimental Education*, trans. Douglas Garman (Berkeley: University of California Press, 1972), 49–50.

10 Johann Peter Eckermann, *Conversations with Goethe* (London: J. M. Dent, 1930), 211, 82.

11 Johann Wolfgang Goethe, *Faust: Part Two*, trans. David Luke (Oxford University Press, 1994), 169.

12 Heinrich Heine, *Deutschland: A Winter's Tale*, trans. T. J. Reed (London: Angel Books, 1997), 15.

13 Michael Meyer, *Henrik Ibsen*, vol. II, *The Farewell to Poetry* (London: Rupert Hart-Davis, 1971), 75.

14 Eric Robinson (ed.), *John Clare's Autobiographical Writings* (Oxford University Press, 1983), 147.

15 The views of Arnold, Carlyle, Ruskin, and other Victorians are conveniently collected in Rutherford, *Byron: The Critical Heritage*.

16 George Eliot, *Felix Holt, The Radical*, ed. Fred C. Thomson (Oxford University Press, 1980), 62, 353.

17 Joseph Mazzini, *Life and Writings*, 6 vols. (London: Smith, Elder, 1890), I. 192; II. 5.

18 Roman Koropeckyj, *Adam Mickiewicz: The Life of a Romantic* (Ithaca, NY: Cornell University Press, 2008), 247.

19 Adam Mickiewicz, *Konrad Wallenrod and Other Writings*, trans. Jewell Parish, *et al.* (Berkeley: University of California Press, 1925), 11, 12.

20 Koropeckyj, *Adam Mickiewicz*, 460.

21 Mazzini, *Life and Writings*, II. 3.

22 Ibid., II. 161.

23 Ernst Pawel, *The Labyrinth of Exile: A Life of Theodore Herzl* (London: Collins Harvill, 1990), 214.

24 Ibid., 224.

25 Robert Blake, *Disraeli* (London: Eyre and Spottiswoode, 1966), 171.

26 Ibid., 208.

27 Philip Collins, *Thomas Cooper, The Chartist: Byron and the 'Poets of the Poor'* (University of Nottingham, 1969), 19.

28 William St Clair, *The Reading Nation in the Romantic Period* (Cambridge University Press, 2004), 329–30.

29 Ibid., 333.

30 Ibid., 408.

31 Collins, *Thomas Cooper, The Chartist*, 5.

32 Bertrand Russell, *The History of Western Philosophy* (London: Allen and Unwin, 1954), 777.

33 Friedrich Nietzsche, *The Anti-Christ, Ecce Homo, Twilight of the Idols, and Other Writings*, ed. Aaron Ridley and Judith Norman, trans. Judith Norman (Cambridge University Press, 2005), 91.

34 Friedrich Nietzsche, *Gesammelte Werke*, 23 vols. (Munich: Musarion, 1920–9), I. 38.

Further reading

Life

Leslie Marchand's three-volume *Byron: A Biography* (London: John Murray, 1957) remains authoritative. There is a one-volume redaction, *Byron: A Portrait* (London: John Murray, 1971). Phyllis Grosskurth, *Byron: The Flawed Angel* (London: Hodder and Stoughton, 1997), Benita Eisler, *Byron: Child of Passion, Fool of Fame* (London: Hamish Hamilton, 1999), and Fiona MacCarthy, *Byron: Life and Legend* (London: Faber and Faber, 2002) are generally reliable alternatives, if treated with a grain of salt. Caroline Franklin's *Byron: A Literary Life* (London: Macmillan, 2000) concentrates on his professional career.

Three other studies are particularly recommended: Iris Origo's *The Last Attachment* (London: John Murray and Jonathan Cape, 1949), on Byron's love affair with Teresa Guiccioli; and two books by Doris Langley Moore: *The Late Lord Byron: Posthumous Dramas* (London: John Murray, 1961), on his aftermath, and *Lord Byron: Accounts Rendered* (London: John Murray, 1974), on his finances.

Byron's conversations are collected in three books, all edited by Ernest J. Lovell, Jr.: *His Very Self and Voice: Collected Conversations of Lord Byron* (New York: Macmillan, 1954), *Medwin's Conversations of Lord Byron* (Princeton University Press, 1966), and *Lady Blessington's Conversations of Lord Byron* (Princeton University Press, 1969).

Context

On politics and aristocracy, see John Beckett, *Byron and Newstead: The Aristocrat and the Abbey* (Newark: University of Delaware Press, 2001), John Cannon, *Aristocratic Century: The Peerage of Eighteenth-Century England* (Cambridge University Press, 1984), and John Plowright, *Regency England: The Age of Lord Liverpool* (London: Routledge, 1996). On Napoleonic Europe, see Clive Emsley, *British Society and the French Wars 1793–1815* (London: Macmillan, 1979), Charles J. Esdaile, *The French Wars 1792–1815* (London: Routledge, 2001), and D. G. Wright, *Napoleon and Europe* (London: Longman, 1984). On The Romantic movement, see Isaiah Berlin, *The Roots of Romanticism* (London: Chatto and Windus, 1999), Tim Blanning, *The Romantic Revolution* (London: Orion Books,

2010), and Marilyn Gaull, *English Romanticism: The Human Context* (New York: Norton, 1988). These are three very different, but complementary, approaches.

Works

Texts

The *Collected Poetical Works*, ed. Jerome J. McGann, 7 vols. (Oxford University Press, 1980–93), *Byron's Letters and Journals*, ed. Leslie A. Marchand, 12 vols. (London: John Murray, 1973–82), and *Complete Miscellaneous Prose*, ed. Andrew Nicholson (Oxford University Press, 1991) are the standard modern editions. (Marchand's *Lord Byron: Selected Letters and Journals* (London: John Murray, 1982) is a good way into the complete edition.) Two older one-volume editions of the poems remain useable: *The Poetical Works*, ed. Frederick Page (Oxford University Press, 1904; rev. edn 1970) and *The Poetical Works of Lord Byron*, ed. Ernest Hartley Coleridge (London: John Murray, 1905). Modern selections include *Lord Byron: The Major Works* (Oxford University Press, 2000) and *Selected Poetry* (Oxford University Press, 1997), both edited by Jerome J. McGann, and *Selected Poems*, ed. Susan J. Wolfson and Peter J. Manning (Harmondsworth: Penguin, 1996). *Byron's Poetry and Prose*, ed. Alice Levine (New York: Norton, 2009), contains poems, letters, and journals, and critical comment. *Don Juan*, ed. T. G. Steffan, E. Steffan, and W. W. Pratt (Harmondsworth: Penguin, 1982) is an adequate substitute for the McGann edition. *The Manuscripts of the Younger Romantics: Byron*, ed. Alice Levine, *et al.*, 12 vols. (New York: Garland, 1985–98) reproduces Byron's original drafts, sometimes with transcription and commentary.

Criticism

A good place to start is Andrew Nicholson's chapter on Byron in Michael O'Neill (ed.), *Literature of the Romantic Period: A Bibliographical Guide* (Oxford University Press, 1998), which gives excellent guidance on specialist studies and monographs. Andrew Rutherford (ed.), *Byron: The Critical Heritage* (London: Routledge and Kegan Paul, 1970) collects nineteenth-century opinion. See also Oscar José Santucho, *George Gordon, Lord Byron: A Comprehensive Bibliography of Secondary Materials in English, 1807–1974* (Metuchen, NJ: Scarecrow Press, 1977), supplemented by Clement Tyson Goode, *George Gordon, Lord Byron: A Comprehensive Annotated Research Bibliography of Secondary Materials in English, 1973–1994* (Lanham, MD: Scarecrow Press, 1997).

Some collections of essays are particularly useful for readers starting out on Byron: Drummond Bone (ed.), *The Cambridge Companion to Byron* (Cambridge University Press, 2004), Robert F. Gleckner, *Critical Essays on Lord Byron* (New York: G. K. Hall, 1991), John Jump (ed.), *Byron: A Symposium* (London: Macmillan,

1975), and two collections edited by Jane Stabler: the *Longman Critical Reader: Byron* (London: Longman, 1998), and *Palgrave Advances in Byron Studies* (London: Palgrave Macmillan 2007). Readers who consult any of these will quickly get up to date with recent developments in the field.

More specialized collections include Bernard Beatty and Vincent Newey (eds.), *Byron and the Limits of Fiction* (Liverpool University Press, 1988), Bernard Beatty, Tony Howe, and Charles E. Robinson (eds.), *Liberty and Poetic Licence: New Essays on Byron* (Liverpool University Press, 2008), Alice Levine and Robert N. Keane (eds.), *ReReading Byron* (New York: Garland, 1993), Andrew Rutherford (ed.), *Byron: Augustan and Romantic* (London: Macmillan, 1990), and Cheryl A. Wilson (ed.), *Byron: Heritage and Legacy* (London: Palgrave Macmillan, 2008).

For general surveys, see Bernard Blackstone, *Byron: A Survey* (London: Longman, 1975), Jerome J. McGann, *Fiery Dust: Byron's Poetic Development* (University of Chicago Press, 1968), and Mark Storey, *Byron and the Eye of Appetite* (London: Macmillan, 1986).

On *Don Juan*, see Anne Barton, *Byron:* Don Juan (Cambridge University Press, 1992), and two studies by Bernard Beatty: *Byron's* Don Juan (London: Croom Helm, 1985), and *Byron:* Don Juan *and Other Poems* (Harmondsworth: Penguin, 1987). *Byron's Don Juan*, ed. Truman Guy Steffan, 2nd edn (Austin: University of Texas Press, 1970), vol. I, *The Making of a Masterpiece*, is informative.

Two academic journals specialize in Byron: the *Byron Journal* and the *Keats–Shelley Journal*, which also prints an annual bibliography of publications relating to the poet.

Index

Cambridge Introductions to …

AUTHORS

TOPICS